Re-takes

Re-takes

Postcoloniality and Foreign Film Languages

John Mowitt

University of Minnesota Press
Minneapolis • London

A portion of chapter 2 was originally published as "The Hollywood Sound Tract" in *Subtitles: On the Foreignness of Film*, edited by Atom Egoyan and Ian Balfour (Cambridge, MA: The MIT Press and Alphabet City Media, 2004). A portion of chapter 3 originally appeared as "Sembene Ousmane's *Xala*: Postcoloniality and Foreign Film Languages," *Camera Obscura* 31 (1993).

Published by the University of Minnesota Press
111 Third Avenue South, Suite 290
Minneapolis, MN 55401-2520
http://www.upress.umn.edu

Library of Congress Cataloging-in-Publication Data

Mowitt, John, 1952-
  Re-takes : postcoloniality and foreign film languages / John Mowitt.
    p. cm.
  Includes bibliographical references and index.
  ISBN 0-8166-2890-4 (hc : alk. paper) — ISBN 0-8166-2891-2 (pb : alk. paper)
  1. Motion pictures—Developing countries. 2. Aliens in motion pictures. I. Title.
  PN1993.5.D44M68 2005
  791.43´091724—dc22

                                                    2004027415

Printed in the United States of America on acid-free paper

The University of Minnesota is an equal-opportunity educator and employer.

12 11 10 09 08 07 06 05   10 9 8 7 6 5 4 3 2 1

For A. M., whence came the sound and the light

Contents

Credits

Although customary, the gesture of acknowledging assistance while assuming final responsibility for its outcome is rather hollow. Like the infant, it is radically premature: it comes well before its consequences have any content. By the time one comes upon the sort of errors, whether of judgment or of fact, that authors attempt to shield their collaborators from, it is too late. All are implicated. Better then to embrace error and, in sharing it, forge the only community worth having, the one where accidents must happen.

In stressing the ideological effects of the apparatus's suppression of what has been dubbed film work (modeled, obviously, on *Traumarbeit*), too little attention has been paid to the work of the spectator in this process. What Roland Barthes neglected to tell us in "Upon Leaving the Movie Theater" was whether he stayed for the credits, that endless scroll of, typically, names underscored with synergistic strains of tunes destined to stick in our heads. To rewind from the end and thus contribute, on the spectator's side, to the critique of the ideological effects of the basic cinematic apparatus, I will start from the credits.

This project has been under way for some time. Although originally conceived on the basis of recurrent course offerings at the University of Minnesota, it has become something else entirely. Many people helped that "something else" happen, and they deserve more recognition than can be recorded here.

First and foremost I thank the research assistants who helped gather the primary archival materials—documents, films, videos, and so on—on which the project is built. Through financial support from the Graduate School at the University of Minnesota (specifically through two "grants-in-aid of research") I was able to secure the indispensable help of Polly Carl and Negar Mottahedeh. Both helped me to get my intellectual bearings, and Negar in particular helped me keep faith in the concept of enunciation. Additionally, a McKnight Summer Research Grant enabled me both to get some undisturbed writing done and, in the context of the research fellows seminar, to get a wonderful first reading of the "rushes." Scholar of the College support allowed me to secure the invaluable help of Gretchen Gasterland-Gustafsson (and occasionally Lily, her newborn). Without her, and the technical assistance of Dieter Bohn, the text would have been devoid of visual evidence.

Other archivists who deserve special recognition are the women at the Margaret Herrick Library in Beverly Hills. Specifically, I want to thank Linda Mehr, Barbara Hall, and Libby Wertin for their indulgent patience both in answering my questions and in assembling an astonishing array of relevant materials for my review. I especially thank the Academy of Motion Pictures Arts and Sciences for giving me permission to cite from its archival material, especially Hall's oral history with Robert M. W. Vogel.

Similarly, I want to thank Mohammed Kamara and Hamid Naficy for inviting me to attend the first Houston Pan-Cultural Film Festival and, in Hamid's case, for facilitating my contact with Ousmane Sembene. This is an absolute debt.

Many people and organizations deserve deep thanks for having given me the occasion to present bits and pieces of this project. Specifically, I acknowledge Debra Castillo, for inviting me to present my work on her panel on bilingualism and literature in Latin America at the annual convention of the Modern Language Association; Frieda Ekotto and the Department of Romance Languages at the University of Michigan, for inviting me to participate in its African Cinema Conference; Barbara Engh and the Department of Fine Arts and Cultural Studies at the University of Leeds, for inviting me to give the Centre CATH seminars; Keya Ganguly (now a colleague here at Minnesota) and the English department of Carnegie Mellon University, for inviting me to its postcolonial theory seminar; Jonathan Kahana and Bruce Robbins (both then in the English department at Rutgers), for inviting me to address a graduate seminar on film theory; and Leigh Payne and Tina Chen, for inviting me to participate in the "Legacies of Authoritarianism" conference at the University of Wisconsin–Madison. The exchanges that took place in each of these settings helped me, as they always do, to hear what my writing was trying to tell me.

I also would like to acknowledge the enormous impact my remarkable colleagues both here and elsewhere had on this text. Specifically, "props" are owed to Fernando Arenas, Réda Bensmaïa, Tim Brennan, Cesare Casarino, Tom Conley, Jigna Desai, Barbara Harlow, Qadri Ismail, Amy Kaminsky, Liz Kotz, Silvia López, Horacio Machín, Lary May, Tom Pepper, Paula Rabinowitz, Rita Raley, Jani Scandura, Ajay Skaria, Charlie Sugnet, and Haidee Wasson. Apart from specific and direct help in the form of "feedback," I thank these folks for sustaining a dialogue in which the gentle but startling touch of "afterwardness" (as Jean Laplanche urges us to translate *Nachträglichkeit*) remains vital, indeed crucial to intellectual life.

This project began in the classroom. It would therefore be remiss of me not to thank all of my fabulous students (even the quiet ones), but especially José Artilles, Sara Buchanan, Dawn Rae Davis, Reshmi Dutt, Ana Maria Gomez, Jennifer Horne, Astrid Klieveland, Premesh Lalu, Monika Mehta, Marissa Moorman, Adam Sitze, Angela Smith, Karen Steigman, and Lynne Turner. Ana Maria, Adam, and Astrid (the A-list) are owed special thanks for helping to screen, think, and write, often together.

So long in coming, this project has profited from several editors at the University of Minnesota Press. I expressly and warmly acknowledge Janaki Bakhle, who convinced me to bring the text to Minnesota; Micah Kleit, for indulging my passion for Mattelart; Jennifer Moore, for believing down my neck; and, especially, Richard Morrison, for figuring out how to get it all done. Along similar lines I thank Ian Balfour and Atom Egoyan at *Alphabet City* and Sharon Willis at *Camera Obscura* for publishing parts of this text in its earlier incarnations. These too are absolute debts.

As I refer to Jeanine, Rosalind, and Rachel (and now Bette), the "girls." Always "the girls." The daily failure to repay this debt is the daily life of the academic intellectual. I am no exception. They are.

Introduction

The muted "spoonerism" of my title ("foreign film languages" versus "foreign language films") is not one, to my knowledge, ever uttered by the good Reverend William Spooner. Having ministered during the emergence and subsequent international development of the cinema he, at least in principle, could have. Indeed, one of his best known "spoonerisms," "Please sew the ladies to their sheets," not only effortlessly applies to the cinema, but it is worthy of Sam Goldwyn, whose "Anyone seeing a psychiatrist should have his head examined" set the very standard of the studio malapropism. That Freud, who theorized the enabling conditions of such "slips," such *Versprechen*, never made much of his influential contemporary is perhaps more genuinely surprising. Surely Spooner and Freud are among the very few who have actually had parapraxes named after them ("Goldwynisms" never circulated much outside Hollywood). Perhaps therein lies the cause of Freud's reticence. Perhaps. However, what is important here is not the anxious matter of influence. More pressing is the relation between the terms of my titular spoonerism and the moment of its intervention.

First and foremost this text belongs to the moment of disciplinary self-reflection that is currently gripping the field of cinema studies. Beginning in 1996 with the publication of Bordwell and Carroll's *Post-Theory: Reconstructing Film Studies*, and continuing on during the new century with Gledhill and Williams's *Reinventing Film Studies*, Tinkcom and Villarejo's *Keyframes*, Grieveson and Wasson's forthcoming *Inventing Film Studies*, and even, in a certain sense, Cherchi Usai's *The Death of Cinema*, we have witnessed a steady stream, indeed a virtual flood, of disciplinary self-scrutiny. Although significant differences (differences of purpose, differences of perspective, and so on) separate these studies from one another, it is clear that they are all responding to a crisis (or, as Benjamin or Schmitt might have said, a state of exception) in the field, a crisis in how the disciples of cinema studies have come to construe the object of their collective exertions: the cinema. Indeed, in 2003 perhaps the premier professional organization of cinema scholars in the United States, the Society for Cinema Studies, renamed itself the Society for Cinema and Media Studies (a point observed in the press coverage of the annual conference in Minneapolis), doubtless as an expression of this emergent situation.

For my purposes it is helpful to approach this crisis by thinking about it in terms of a double displacement. On the one hand, it seems clear—if we concede that cinema studies, regardless of its relative distance from film production, is largely if not exclusively an academic affair—that cinema studies is being reconfigured by a resurgence of interest in media studies, a resurgence provoked, according to many, by the historical advent of the so-called new media. On the other hand, within those academic precincts most involved with cinema studies— largely the humanities (including journalism and communications)—a new problematic has appeared on the horizon, that of globalization. Although the point is seldom elaborated explicitly, globalization putatively challenges the relevance of postcoloniality by offering to better name the world historical situation that has arisen at the so-called end of history, that is, in the wake of both colonialism and, as the official story has it, empire. Precisely because it purports to coincide with the real itself, globalization outmaneuvers postcoloniality by rendering it passé. To the extent that the practical deconstruction of Eurocentrism we associate with multiculturalism has taken hold within cinema studies (the active enthusiasm for things international, independent, and foreign is a sign that it has), it has done so by making the postcolonial problematic matter there. It is for this reason that the emergence of globalization (whether as concept or as event) comprises a second displacement menacing cinema studies.

An obvious conclusion would seem to follow. If the double displacement is constituted as I propose, then the movement from cinema to media is a symptom of globalization. Further, if the movement from cinema to media is precisely what has sown doubt among disciples about the object of cinema studies, then the disciplinary self-reflection defining the moment of this intervention is itself a symptom of globalization. The urgent question thus becomes: does the problematic of globalization provide one with the concepts through which to think this situation? Answering this question, even if provisionally, will help clarify what is at stake in the disciplinary crisis evoked here.

Appealing to a text to which I will return, Bordwell and Carroll's *Post-Theory*, one can efficiently illuminate a relevant issue. In the introduction the authors make it clear that, with the reputed decline of Theory in the late 1980s and throughout the 1990s, film studies (as they prefer) has been forced to rethink its foundations. This, they suggest, must be done with an eye toward everything from curricula and pedagogy to institutional location and professional affiliation. In other words, as film studies disciples reflect on their intellectual and professional identities they will be confronted with the fact that the old dispensation is incapable of providing them an orientation with regard to these decisive issues. More than a crisis of belief, this is a crisis of action: What are film educators supposed to do in the classroom? How are they to conduct their own research? From whose ranks are future disciples and masters to be culled? As one would expect from a disciplinary crisis, everything bearing on a discipline's institutional identity here is up for grabs.

As though this weren't grave enough there is also—regardless of one's priorities—the matter of belief, or more particularly of the concepts one deploys in making sense of a given situation. Consider, in this light, the concept of the symptom. As invoked above, it works not only to link globalization and the moment, the circumstance, of this study, but in accord with the spatiality endemic to the concept, the symptom places globalization beneath both cinema studies and this analysis of it. Precisely where this "beneath" is changes dramatically depending on the discourse from which one's concept of the symptom is derived (the semiotic, the clinical, the therapeutic, and so on), but the causal corollary of this depth remains consistent. That which supports something else is said to cause it. Now, if we ask ourselves the question, how do we know that the event of globalization is under way? and include in our response active reference to the distinctly global reach of films, television and radio broadcasts, internet exchanges, virtual transactions of intellectual property in general, in short, precisely those things made intelligible within (among other places) cinema studies, then are we sure that globalization is "beneath" its effects? Perhaps globalization *is* these effects, in which case the otherwise reliable concept of the symptom is not terribly useful for the task of disciplinary self-reflection after all. Freud, Lacan, Althusser, and Žižek (to name only the most obvious figures) have all puzzled over the concept of the symptom and have done so with far more rigor than befits an introduction; but the point is that the crisis gripping cinema studies cannot be restricted to the ends of disciplinary self-reflection. It must also be understood to apply to the very means of such reflection. Put formulaically, the crisis to which this text is addressed and to which it belongs is one in which the who, the what, and the how of cinema studies are all in dispute.

But what then of the question posed above: does the problematic of globalization provide one with the concepts through which to think this situation? Everything hinges on what is understood by "provide" here. In this study the accents will fall on the conceptual conflict animating the displacement of postcoloniality by globalization. In other words, this study proposes that the pressure placed on the postcolonial problematic by globalization provides one with the means by which to intervene within cinema studies, but (and it's a big but) only if this very pressure is harnessed to sharpen or otherwise intensify the concept of postcoloniality. I take this to index the state of affairs Michel Foucault had in mind when, in a late interview, he stressed the importance for his own work of the concept of "problematization."[1]

Of course, one needs to proceed prudently. There is little to be gained by responding to pressure fraught with self-defeating difficulties. Thus, it is important to take stock here of what might be called some of the contradictions of globalization. For the sake of expediency—after all, the literature on globalization is expanding at the rate of the process itself—I will appeal here to the work of Bill Readings and Armand Mattelart, work that is both theoretically rich and multiply pertinent, for Readings is concerned with the enabling conditions of academic thought (although not cinema studies per se), and Mattelart thinks academically (though not merely so) about the relation between globalization and the cinema.

In *The University in Ruins*, Readings explains the shift from the modern university of culture to the postmodern university of excellence by arguing that globalization has stripped the nation-state of its political authority vis-à-vis the economy. This is a by now familiar argument and the first Gulf War would be a recent case in point. Because the university maintained its legitimacy by providing the nation-state both with a national cultural tradition and the informed citizens willing to invest in such a tradition, when globalization displaces the nation-state, the university loses the basis of its legitimacy. Learning is replaced by consuming, teaching by training—a baleful development I assume many educators are familiar with. But here's the rub: at the same time that Readings wants to insist on globalization's sublation of the nation-state, he wants to treat Americanization as a synonym for globalization. Does this mean, and surely it is implied, that America, the U.S.A., is not a nation-state? For students of the cinema this resonates in an all-too-familiar way with Hollywood's long-standing refusal to acknowledge its blatantly national character. For Left critics of globalization this draws immediate attention to Readings's reluctance to think through the relation, both structural and historical, between the United States, postmodern capital, and empire. Globalization cannot both mark the end of the nation-state and be synonymous with Americanization.

Armand Mattelart has been fretting about globalization for some time. Because the relevant issue is stated very clearly in *Mapping World*

Communication, these comments will center on its closing chapters. Concerned with the politics of cultural globalization, and reluctant to Americanize it directly, Mattelart proposes that a dialectic animates the very structure of globalization. At one level, globalization—which for him is as much about the introduction of international electronic banking as it is about the holding of worldwide rights for the distribution of cultural commodities—involves the transnational corporatization of the Earth. At another level, but in the same instant, globalization involves the reinvigoration of national culture, precisely as a mode of resistance to transnational corporatization. This, however, produces not one rub, but two. Although Mattelart's discussion is framed in political terms, it is clear he is very uneasy with the fact that a reinvigoration of national culture might always devolve into a recidivistic nationalism, where, tragically, the "grave digger" of globalization would become busily occupied with filling the mass graves of those sacrificed to the national ethnic conflicts with which we are already too familiar. By the same token, giving up on the logic of a global antagonism of national cultures represents a form of political resignation that Mattelart cannot abide. In other words, the precise terms and content of the dialectic of globalization threaten to neutralize its political utility. Globalization cannot both stimulate a progressive cultural nationalism and guard against nationalist violence. The neoliberal "transitions" under way throughout Latin America (and elsewhere) must surely be on his mind.

The point of these brutal summaries is a cautionary one. While it is surely important not to fall prey to similar contradictions, even more urgent is the task of reconfiguring the problematic from which they derive. In other words, out of the problematization of postcoloniality a way of rethinking the relation between Americanization and the concept of national culture ought to be made to emerge, especially in the cinematic field. This means discovering not the distinctively national character of American culture (a task no doubt best left to Ken Burns), but rather the means by which Americanization produces an alibi for those inclined to deny its national character. Globalization as Americanization allows, in effect, Americans to misrecognize the distinctly un-American character of their national culture. As one often hears: American films are popular abroad because people "everywhere" can and do identify with American values. Pressed to delineate what makes such shared values distinctly American, partisans invariably appeal to the transcultural and transhistorical values of western humanism (in short, democracy), suggesting, obviously, not only that democracy has come but that America and democracy are one and the same. Given that this defers yet again the question of what constitutes the distinctively American character of the values in question, the critical theorist is confronted with the task of illuminating how the sheer power to enunciate a properly global spectacle becomes the distinctively American character of the values people everywhere are said to identify with. No doubt this is what is meant when America is characterized—as others often do—as arrogant. Faced with such an accusation, it behooves one not to assume the ready posture of belligerence ("bring it on!") but to pose anew the problem of how American culture (especially the products of the culture industry) manages both to exploit and deny its un-American character. A concept this text will argue is useful here is that of enunciation. It may or may not be useful enough.

To proceed then with a prudent re-articulation of postcoloniality and cinema studies, appropriate subrubrics are called for. I propose two such tried and true subrubrics—politics and poetics—and it is to their justification I turn.

Precisely because globalization is typically linked to Americanization it necessarily associates the post-Eurocentric totality (in other words, the multicultural ontology of one planet/many worlds) implicitly, though sometimes explicitly, evoked in postcolonial criticism with a political, indeed a geopolitical, question that such criticism often finds difficult to pose. If, as Enrique Dussel (1998) has argued, Eurocentrism emerged within the context of Europe's cultural and economic displacement of Asia—a displacement conditioned by the conquest of the New World—then what geopolitical arrangement might lie beyond Eurocentrism? Is the properly postcolonial world the world of what Michael

Hardt and Antonio Negri call "empire," and if not, why not? Or, to broach the matter from a different angle, if postcoloniality adequately designates the endlessness of something called history, the differently shared condition of globality as such, then how are we to rethink the political in light of this? Although a responsible engagement with Gayatri Spivak's *Critique of Postcolonial Reason* lies beyond the scope of an introduction, it is appropriate here to stress that her "Kantian"-inspired examination of the enabling conditions of postcolonial reason repeatedly stresses the political failings of postcolonial critiques that misrecognize the violence that conditions their elaboration. Equally telling, of course, is Terry Eagleton's bristling defense of precisely the concept of the political probed in Spivak's searching meditation.

To a certain extent this way of questioning the politics of the postcolonial is familiar. It is important not to lose sight of its distinctly institutional dimension. Although Readings does not broach the matter (in other words, he does not locate the critique of excellence in the university of excellence) Pierre Bourdieu and Loïc Wacquant, in their contention that "multiculturalism" is not the definitive outdistancing of Eurocentrism but rather the conceptual artillery barrage preparing the various nationalisms (both cultural and political) for the final solution of globalization, provide one with the means for doing so. That is, by illustrating that the very field of American cultural studies is an institutional manifestation of globalization and therefore of little or no value to the critics of globalization, they provoke us to think carefully about the emergence of postcolonial studies. Are its cortical concerns—migration, hybridity, memory, borders, epistemological violence, othering, and so on—all garbled emanations of global speak? Here the political question posed to postcoloniality is not about its positions or about its location but about the relations between its positions and their locations, in short, what Said astutely called "contiguities." True, like Readings, Bourdieu and Wacquant do not situate themselves, or France for that matter, within the terms of their analysis, but this is no argument against thinking through the politics of postcolonial studies from within the concerns they identify. They certainly clarify the need for a better answer to Kwame Anthony Appiah's famous question: "Is the Post- in Postmodernism the Post- in Postcolonial?"

Thus far the re-articulation or problematization of the postcolonial has been elaborated in strictly politico-institutional terms. It has remained silent on the matter of the many challenges to the postcolonial that would be difficult to index to the question of globalization (I am thinking here of the long history of the term's repudiation, a history archly invoked by Eagleton in his review of Spivak). Perhaps turning to the concept of poetics will prove a productive way to, if not break, then modulate this silence.

When Jameson wrote his now infamous, and much maligned, "Third World Literature in the Era of Multinational Capitalism," he might have spared himself considerable grief had he concentrated on the practice of postcolonial literary criticism rather than on the concept of Third World literature. For regardless of whether a generic boundary can be maintained between literatures deemed psychological and those deemed sociological in orientation, it is clear that allegorical readings (whether national or not) can and are given to a great many of the texts that have attracted the attention of postcolonial critics. There are important exceptions to be sure, and not all allegorical readings heed the apparently indispensable dictum, *nomen est omen*, but a considerable portion of what passes for postcolonial literary criticism is largely thematic criticism, and Jameson was certainly right to draw attention to the important way tracing the themes of the nation and the individual might productively illuminate texts from quite different cultural and political contexts. Even in seminars with titles such as "The Postcolonial Novel," attention to the potentially complex ways that postcoloniality and what the young Georg Lukács designated as the generic embodiment of "transcendental homelessness" (*Abdachlösigkeit*, "loss of shelter") is not consistently on the agenda. This is nowhere more true than in the re-emergent domain of media studies, where avid readers of Benedict Anderson's provocative discussion of the novel's role in nation building might certainly be expected to raise questions about the aesthetic specificity of film or television, but hesitate to do so. Instead, we tend to see thematic, indeed often unabashedly allegorical, treatments of the products of various national media. One might even speculate that, had Jameson addressed himself to Sembene's film rather than his novel, he might be said to have founded yet another critical discursivity, this time in postcolonial media studies. Regardless, at some point one will have to repeat the question posed by Lukács to Benjamin, namely, what precisely is the allegorization of culture an allegory of?

The point worth hanging on to in what is otherwise something of an unfair caricature is that the articulation of a postcolonial poetics remains unnecessarily muted. Regardless of whether one believes that, if postcolonial theory and criticism have taught us anything, they have taught us that there can be no single poetics of something called post-colonial culture, a variation of the task remains: how are we to think the structural, formal, and semiotic particularities of something we might be willing to call postcolonial cultural production and reception? By having framed these remarks in terms of a problematization of the post-colonial effected by its encounter with globalization, no doubt the ex-pectation has been generated that globalization bears in some important way on the articulation of a postcolonial poetics. Indeed it does.

Whether one turns back to Marshall McLuhan's tempered effu-sions about the "global village"—surely a decisive early avatar of global-ization—or consults the discussion of globalization that transpires in Néstor García Canclini's more recent *Consumers and Citizens,* the con-nection between the global and local (however complicated topograph-ically) is understood as largely forged through popular culture. Casting his lot with Jameson's underground party of utopia, McLuhan argues that media networks, precisely to the extent that they erase the signifying bar between the medium and the message, promise to restore community at the planetary level, reversing trends advocated by various corporate and political nationalisms. Some forty years later García Canclini, although preoccupied with the more narrowly political question of global citi-zenship, sees globalization like Mattelart does, as having revitalized dis-tinctly cultural nationalisms. Though less wide-eyed than McLuhan, García Canclini is reluctant to hear in this development the death knell of utopianism, suggesting instead that if the paradigm shift that brought an end to the Gutenburg galaxy was indeed sponsored by Sony, then perhaps the national forms of resistance that have risen up to oppose the shift are themselves significantly utopian if not yet fully radical. Condensing, as such views do, some of the key theoretical positions that define the debate over globalization, they remind us not only that globalization has a history but that it is a distinctly cultural history, one reduced to economic developments (especially comparatively recent ones, for example, the international implementation of risk distribution models that effectively "globalized" the U.S. stock market during the 1980s) at considerable cost.

In the following passages from *Consumers and Citizens* one finds García Canclini wrestling with matters that will help bring this introduction to a close. He writes,

> In debates prompted by the GATT negotiations, European motion picture associations defended their jobs, but they also put forth the argument that film is not exclusively a commodity. It is also a powerful instrument for the expression and self-affirmation of one's language (*idioma*) and culture, and their dissemination beyond one's borders. They made reference to the contradiction whereby the United States demands the free circulation of its communications in foreign countries, while article 301 of its own commercial law permits restrictions on cultural products from abroad. (98)

Later, the topic of language returns as he is delineating what he calls the "Americanization of spectatorship." He writes, with reference to a decidedly national cinema,

> Mexican cinema's role in shaping a mass audiovisual culture and a symbolic language to express social process lost its effectiveness because of a combination of factors. The most important were the reduction of state support; the closing off of the Cuban market with the revolution and the contraction of South American markets due to economic difficulties; the rapid expansion of television as a new agent of entertainment

and conditioner of the social imaginary; competition from U.S. cinema, which, revamped thematically and formally and strengthened by large investments and greater effectivity in distribution, gained control of international markets. (112)

Important here is the reiterated stress put on the link between cultural expression and language, a link as vital to a certain kind of resistant, anticapitalist nationalism as to the specificity of the case in question, namely, the cinema. The point obviously is not to downplay or ignore the pervasive violence of commodification, but to establish the symbolic, perhaps even linguistic, articulation of culture as commodification's first victim and prime target. Not only does this place the question of poetics on the political agenda, it also provides a point of reference for thinking this agenda differently.

While García Canclini in his chapter on spectatorship does enumerate four important aspects of "global" cinematic specificity, he, like so many before him in the Latin American tradition of cultural criticism, prefers to let the concept of language flourish but primarily as an evocative, even fraught, figure. This, I would argue, obliges him to fall significantly short of articulating a postcolonial poetics for the cinema. To re-invoke my book's Spoonerist title, letting language stand merely as a literal figure makes it difficult if not impossible to grasp what might be at stake in a "foreign film language," not, as we shall see, a foreign language film, but a language of the cinema that is at once organized by its systemic transferability (as a cultural technology) and its more nationally, even locally, inflected narrative dialects. If, as this formulation implies, the cinema is at once *langage* and *parole*, then the concept of language through which it can be thought lies outside the literal/figural box.

As has been intimated, it is here that the film theoretical concept of enunciation becomes indispensable. First applied to the cinema in the 1970s, this originally linguistic concept came to designate the active presence in films of the sources of their messages. Because it was almost immediately reframed in psychoanalytical terms—referring then to the specifically repressed presence of the apparatus in the experience of the spectator—its utility for industrial analysis went unremarked. The source of a film's messages was definitely not its mode of production. In reasserting the relevance of enunciation I am explicitly trying to fuse its linguistic and psychoanalytical past to the task of thinking about the transnational history of the cinema, a history in which production is as much about product as empire. Because enunciation insists on the so-called formal systems active in film texts, it allows one to think the complexity, indeed the heterogeneity, of this history without—and this is vital—reducing the film to its themes. In effect, enunciation provides a means by which to mend the gap between text and industry. Surely, as Umberto Eco reported, the Chinese were right to protest Antonioni's representation of China, but have those of us involved in theorizing the cinema allowed our work to be gripped by the lesson embedded in this protest? Have we in other words got past the reductive insight that the regime was unhappy with Antonioni's fascination with the revolution's "uneven developments"? I am not sure. Although this study will not revisit this famous flap explicitly (and, to my mind, its depths remain to be plumbed), it will energetically advocate not on behalf of depriving language of its "mere" figurality, but on behalf of taking the figure of language, especially film language, seriously. More particularly, this study will be concerned to use the concept of film language, or more precisely what I will call "bilingual enunciation," to further the articulation of a poetics for postcolonial cinemas.[2] Framed within the concerns of postcolonial studies, enunciation thus makes it possible to read the different film languages active within postcolonial films, that is, films produced (although not necessarily received) in geopolitical sites now defined by the ambivalent cultural legacies of colonialism and imperialism. It is this ambivalence that, in complicating the geopolitics of this legacy, implicates Western cinema studies in the postcolonial, not because the United States is a former European colony in denial but because the West has been separated from its reputed identity by the struggle (at once "here" and "there") over the readings of its history.

But how does this help us address the contradictions of globalization? How does this help us think about the relation between Americanization and the un-American character of American culture? Further, how do responses to such questions help us to rearticulate the conceptual specificity of postcoloniality? Because this study is an extended, though uneven, reply to the various issues raised here, I will move to outline the ensuing chapters by broaching a few issues vital to that reply.

If we say that, at one level, Americanization operates by fusing national values with what in cinema studies are called "production values" (indeed the former literally disappear into the latter), then it becomes important to recognize and analyze the film language that constitutes the grammar of such production values. In addition to what this teaches us about Hollywood film language, there is the matter of what this tells us about the typically poor U.S. reception of postcolonial films, that is, films enunciated through radically plural film languages. Instead of settling here for a tolerant embrace of "foreign" themes or "other stories" (the feckless solution of multiculturalism), we need to turn the concept of bilingual enunciation back upon American cinema itself. In doing so two questions suggest themselves: first, how does "the foreign" arise in relation to the historical elaboration of Hollywood's grammar; and second, how does this affect our relation to "the foreign" within? Where, in other words, do un-American styles of enunciation appear beneath the erasures and edits constituting the production values of American cinema? This study, which approaches the question of foreign film languages comparatively, proposes that answering such questions not only saves postcoloniality from itself, but it may also clarify how a distinctly cultural resistance to globalization need not lapse into what Frantz Fanon once called the "pitfall" of the national.

What then of the concept of postcoloniality? Is there really anything left unsaid here? Perhaps. In his essay on Spivak, Aijaz Ahmad reminds us that "postcolonialism," which had currency among the social sciences during the anticolonial struggles of the mid-twentieth century, is to be sharply distinguished from "literary postcoloniality," or what is referred to here simply as postcoloniality. While I do not agree with the way he frames this distinction (it is meant to bolster his invidious construal of the absolute difference between politics and theory), he is certainly right to stress its importance. Spivak, who receives only slightly better treatment from Ahmad than from Eagleton (the former's discussion predates *A Critique of Postcolonial Reason*), obviously concurs, devoting much of *A Critique* to, as I put it, saving postcoloniality from itself (the allusion to her signature phrase, "white women saving brown women from brown men," I hope is clear). Surely her characterization (1999, xi) of the books that hers might be shelved with is meant to engage the opening conceit of Ahmad's essay. But how then are we to think about this difference? Rather than reduce the matter to a distinction between a state (the aftermath of colonialism) and a concept (the term by which qualities of this state might be provided with a logic), it may be worth revisiting Appiah's meditation on the "post." What does the "post" do to or with colonialism?

Without summarizing its intricate argument recall that Appiah's essay is, among other things, a critique of postmodernism; indeed, this is why the "post" of postcolonialism is *not* the "post" of postmodernism. In this his piece is disturbingly resonant with Edward Rothstein's post-9/11 editorial, "Attacks on U.S. Challenge Post-Modern True Believers," which likewise repudiates the excesses of postmodern relativism. Although her explicit target is Fredric Jameson, Spivak in the "Culture" chapter of *A Critique* usefully answers Appiah by driving a wedge between postmodernism and poststructuralism, inviting us to ask: Is the "post" of postcoloniality the same as the "post" of poststructuralism? Well, yes and no. Yes, in that, as others have argued, what is designated in the "post" of postcoloniality is a displacement, a movement through which identity has become and remains impossible, or as I prefer, un-livable. If postcolonialism designates the state, typically though by no means exclusively national, that arises in the wake of colonialism, then postcoloniality designates the unlivable coherence of that state, indeed of the very concept of a state poisoned, as it were, for all affected parties by the colonial encounter itself. Even when "identity" is not the explicit term on the table, for example, when the stake of postcolonial struggle is "sovereignty" (Hawai'i being a case in point), the same strictures apply: although imagined to be that which renders the lack of sovereignty livable, postcolonial sovereignty will remain unlivable. Who or what will decide which exception?

By the same token, the "post" in poststructuralism is *not* the "post" of postcoloniality because poststructuralism—with the crucial exception of certain voices within a French feminism which was not one[3]—never articulated the link between an investment in the structural impossibility of identity and the specifically colonial limit of what many of its partisans were content to call the West. Putting aside, for the moment, the bluntness with which such a formulation cuts through the incoherent identity of poststructuralism, it is important to recognize here not that it was ahistorical, but that it had difficulty weaning itself from a philosophically driven investment in structural causality.[4] The power structuring the subject's relation to language problematized the political without consistently putting into question the politics, indeed the geopolitics (after all, poststructuralism arrived from the United States marked "return to sender"), of this insight.

This, at any rate, is how I would formulate what is at stake in the critique of identity politics that surfaces from time to time in Spivak's analysis. Not only is this politics consistent with a liberalism content to sacrifice emancipation to recognition, but it is utterly unwilling to think through the anxiety that attends its organizing concept, that of identity itself. This perhaps is a more "genealogical" way to think about Eagleton's reading of Rule One in the secret postcolonial handbook: "Begin by rejecting the whole notion of post-colonialism." In other words, rather than being a rule, this analytical protocol is an articulation of the critique of identity—even in reading practices completely unaware of the fact—active within the very concept of postcoloniality. Which means that postcoloniality cannot inhere in some state or states, and that it arises in the reading practices that struggle and fail to represent these states. A similar point might be made about postcolonial nationalism, namely, that its perceived inadequacies are not only not unique to so-called postcolonial states, but that, when the sun finally sets, the nation too is but another avatar of an unlivable identity, of a community divided by its social imaginary. Indeed, the disciplinary crisis with which this chapter opens is caught up in the very reading practices that have problematized the object of the cinema, as an earlier formulation about its necessary encounter with the postcolonial implied.

I realize, of course, that such a view threatens to subordinate post-structuralism fully to postcoloniality, and while this would be a difficult argument to sustain, it nevertheless has a certain appeal. After all, it is a far more compelling thought experiment than the more familiar one, that is, the one in which the postcolonial condition is reduced to a largely theoretical extrapolation of the categories and concerns of post-structuralism. Jacques Derrida was doubtlessly onto something when, in "Structure, Sign, and Play in the Discourse of the Human Sciences," he noted that the enabling negation of Lévi-Strauss's concept of structure was written into ethnography's failure to think the violence and the limit of the West. I by no means wish to suggest, of course, that every un livable identity is a postcolonial identity, but I do want to argue that the reading practices currently engaged in across the globe, wherein identity is produced and articulated as unlivable, exhibit the quality of what I am calling postcoloniality. Almost certainly this is why both politics and poetics have appeal as the specific stakes of a problematization of postcoloniality.

The perhaps extravagant emphasis given here to the relation between politics and poetics deserves a final comment. A risk run by a certain Left critique of globalization (I am thinking here of the brilliantly provocative work of Masao Miyoshi) is the return of "economism," that is, the notion that not only will Althusser's "last instance" (the moment of ultimate structural determination) *always* come, but that it, and the formulation would annoy him, *has always already come*. On this reading, "globalization" carries the profoundly contradictory charge of being simultaneously the nightmare of capital *and* the new dawn of the totality, a concept often deemed indispensable to any legitimate form of cultural critique properly inspired by Marxism. Ideally, this ambivalence is dialectical, that is, transitional or preparatory, but crucial here is the question: transitory to what? The past or the future? If, as is clear in Miyoshi's dismissal of contending totalities (for example, Lévi-Strauss's concept of "the exchange of women"), the point is to establish that the only concept of totality worthy of the term is an economic one, then Marxism has fallen back not only behind Baudrillard in *The Mirror of Production*, but also behind the rich discussion of "totalization" to be found in Merleau-Ponty and especially Sartre, both crucial even if troubled voices, on the Left. Under such circumstances culture is indexed immediately to the economic, and instead of it serving as the locus for an alternative articulation of totality, it simply becomes that which the economic has yet to assimilate, precisely the state of affairs García Canclini was decrying when criticizing the impact of GATT on film as an instrument for the "expression and self-affirmation of one's language and culture" (98). To affirm, even dialectically, globalization as the motor of a new economic totalization must then require the dismissal or subordination of contending totalities (even if flawed in their own ways), because one thereby secures an alibi for his or her own Faustian pact. This, I would contend, is good neither for politics nor poetics, and it drains the remaining and perhaps justly beleaguered critical energy out of the concept of postcoloniality. Surely materialism (whether cultural or not) is richer than economism, and while the struggle to reformulate the concept of determination continues, there is little if anything to be gained from foreclosing upon the intricate dialogue between the humanities and the social sciences that has opened over the past forty years.

In the chapters that follow, aspects of the vexing matters raised here are agitated with differing degrees of concentration and intensity. Following through on the proposition that film theoretical concepts belong to the contemporary history of media culture, the first chapter addresses itself to the concept of "enunciation," the claim being that, though controversial, this concept is vital to the project of articulating a politicized poetics of postcolonial cinemas. While conceding that narrowly linguistic construals of enunciation are flawed, they do not exhaust the concept. It is here that the earlier evocation of "bilingual enunciation" finds its theoretical footing and does so through a perhaps startling advocacy of Guattari's—not Deleuze's—theory of the cinema. The chapter concludes with an airing of differences that have arisen in the controversy surrounding enunciation. Drawing on Christian Metz's posthumous *L'Enonciation impersonnelle, ou le cite du film* (itself deeply influenced by Francesco Casetti's *Inside the Gaze*), I side against the positions elaborated on behalf of "narration" (as opposed to enunciation) by David Bordwell and Noël Carroll.

Further elaborating the strategy of implicating U.S. media culture (at once scholarly and industrial) in the emergence and delimitation of postcolonial cinemas, chapter 2 concerns itself directly with the Western construction of the link between foreignness and language within the cinema. Two avenues of inquiry are pursued. First, through a detailed institutional analysis of the development of the category "foreign language film" within the Academy of Motion Picture Arts and Sciences (AMPAS), the professional discourse organizing U.S. reception of the national cinemas of other countries (indeed many of those now deemed "postcolonial") is both delineated and analyzed. Second, in light of the important link drawn within the AMPAS between "foreignness" and speech (at times "dialogue" but at other times "the soundtrack" in its entirety), I examine the filmic speech of Native Americans, feral children (specifically Tarzan), and aliens for signs of how foreignness is inflected in the flicker between film language and film speech. Discovering here a marked and linguistically charged phenomenon, namely, the suspension of the copula, the chapter concludes with a dual reflection on how "foreign language films" are delimited so as to render film language "foreign" to the cinema and how the copula can be brought to bear on the concept of enunciation, indeed, bilingual enunciation.

The two chapters that conclude the study are sustained discussions of the work of two filmmakers, Ousmane Sembene of Senegal and Jorge Sanjinés of Bolivia. As such the chapters obviously embody a more practical, perhaps even culinary turn wherein the proverbial pudding is sampled for proof. The considerations involved in the identification and selection of Sembene and Sanjinés are these. First, they share a certain political vision of the cinema. Both have aligned themselves throughout their careers not only with the political opposition in their respective countries, but they have described their work, often at great length and with considerable eloquence, as Marxist. While this quells suspicion about whether one is "forcing" the political issue, it also provides the work of comparison with something like a toehold. These are varieties of banana, not oranges and bananas.

Second, both Sembene and Sanjinés appeal continually and systematically to the figure of language when elaborating the poetics of their cinematic projects. Indeed both filmmakers have either spoken or written extensively about the importance not just of language but of the politics of language; that is, the fact that in their respective countries the confrontation between majority and minority languages lies at the very heart of national cultural life. As part of that life the cinema cannot circumvent the cultural politics of language. At the risk of making the lame allusion to García Márquez a little too obvious, again, they are varieties of the same fruit.

Third, and last, it struck me as equally important that each filmmaker lived a distinctive incarnation of the postcolonial. For Sembene, whose experience coincides with the theoretical preoccupations of the academic field, making film in Senegal is very much about the thankless task, as Audre Lorde famously put it, of trying to dismantle the master's house using the master's tools. Sembene's famous term for this is *mégotage*, where the French slang for cigarette butt is edited to *montage*, giving us the Baudelairean image of the addict filmmaker fishing for film stock amid smoldering ruins. For Sanjinés, and no doubt some would argue for Latin America as a whole (at least as concerns the analytical relevance of postcolonial theory and criticism), the encounter with the postcolonial is decisively mediated by that with imperialism, particularly of the North American or Yankee variety. Though no friend of *el indigenismo*, Sanjinés rightly insists to both the Left and the Right at home and abroad that Bolivia has yet to come to terms with the Indian. For the first nation peoples of Latin America, the postcolonial question has hardly been posed, much less resolved. With the acquisition of independence and later with the onset of what Gunder Frank and others called dependency, the critique of northern imperialism has effectively preempted the postcolonial question, and this despite the fact that one of its keywords, "hybridity," both literally and associatively (one thinks here of *el mestizo* or *el antropófago*) is, as it were, native to the region. In other words, the examination of these filmmakers seemed fruitful also because, in addition to the ways in which they represented varieties of bananas, comparing them was also like comparing oranges and bananas. Less whimsically of course this means that the elaboration of a post-colonial poetics of the cinema—even as a hypothesis—must at some level confront the fact that different struggles are indeed different fights and that the enunciative strategies that arise within these struggles may well be incommensurable.

The last chapter concludes with a brief coda. Its aim is to reiterate the point that its concerns are located more "here" than "there." While a certain theoretical circumspection as concerns "others" has been justly criticized as being little more than an acquiescent fetishism, the opposite of fetishism is not without its, well, shortcomings. Since the affirmation of sameness is no clear hedge against new age ethnocentrism, and since, as Said warned in "Traveling Theory," the vigilance necessary to avoid reading difference on one's own terms is difficult to come by, much less sustain, agitating in the so-called belly of the beast may have a great deal to be said for it, particularly if, and why not assume there is some agreement about this, colonialism, imperialism, globalization, and so on begin today where westerners call home. They may also end there, but not if the only real critical work of consequence can be done from the outside. Besides, where exactly is the outside? Thus, the coda returns to matters raised in "Take One" of the opening chapter, matters bearing in different ways on the task of articulating a concept of the cinema that makes it immediately relevant to the practical deconstruction of Eurocentrism, but that also confronts cinema studies with the double displacement of its object.

CHAPTER 1

The Return of Enunciation

Take One

Like cultures, disciplines invent traditions. These serve to ground and thus stabilize significant features of the disciplinary objects that orient work within and among disciplines. Though much controversy attends the dating of the traditions thought to be relevant to the emergence of the concept of postcoloniality within the discipline of English literary studies and across the disciplinary divide between the humanities and the social sciences (for example, do we or do we not include here Marx and Lenin on imperialism, Hegel on the master/slave dialectic, and so on?), something like a consensus has formed around the notion that culture is crucial to the logic of the concept of postcoloniality. One might even argue that the "cultural turn" driving more and more work in the social sciences these days owes much to the emergence of the problematic of postcoloniality. And while this might lead one to conclude that the concept of culture has thus been clarified—one thinks here of Raymond Williams's Herculean struggle with it in *Keywords*—it has not. At least not decisively so. It has, however, made it considerably easier to recognize the centrality of the culture industry to any cultural study that seeks to take culture seriously. The cinema, that ungainly institutional montage of science, art, and commerce, might well figure as the leading edge of the culture industry, and for this reason any attempt, however inconclusive, to elaborate a postcolonial poetics of the cinema must at some point near its beginning say something about how it approaches the concept of the cinema. This chapter begins by doing precisely that.

To proceed while keeping the concept of postcoloniality in focus, even if momentarily offscreen, it makes sense to revisit—in a more sustained way—the topic of Eurocentrism. In particular, how has its critique been taken up within the precincts of First World film theory? Although abrupt, this cut away to theory is entirely defensible. With the development of paraprofessional film schools (that is, schools in which film consumers are not simply being trained to produce films, but are also being educated in the history and theory of their production), theory can no longer be eliminated from the final cut of any film. Moreover, since theory tends to be the place where the cinema becomes most self-conscious (and here I am affirming the importance of Gilles Deleuze's proposal that the cinema has produced the conditions of its own theorization), it is precisely the place to turn when attempting to track how various concepts converge in the elaboration of this self-consciousness. This implies that, Edmund Husserl's millennial call to "return to the things themselves" notwithstanding, one is always already in the thick of things.

As intimated in the introduction, the critique of Eurocentrism has now installed itself at the very core of film theory. The question is how? and perhaps even why? To reply in a manner that keeps the as yet unthematized concept of enunciation at least in play requires that a prior relationship be theorized, namely, that between the critique of Eurocentrism and multiculturalism, a relationship that is at the core of much debate within the humanities and the social sciences as well as within U.S. society at large. At the risk of adding to the ever growing list of scholars who, in articulating their reservations about the multicultural initiative, have cast a perhaps fatal suspicion upon the entire enterprise, I will declare myself as a partisan aligned with that portion of the Left committed to a practice of cultural critique that, in refusing the compromise of "inclusivity," calls for a transformation of the sociohistorical conditions wherein Eurocentrism has sustained itself now, if we accept Dussel's calculations, for the past five hundred years. Since

risk, or gambling more generally, is the addictive motor of late capitalism, it cannot yet be avoided, so let me simply suggest that failing to
"take back" the critique of Eurocentrism from the dominant, and often
corporate, multiculturalists constitutes a greater risk than does casting suspicion—indeed one often indistinguishable from the rantings of
Buchanan, Schlesinger, and Coulter—on the extant practical deconstruction of Eurocentrism known as multiculturalism. But beyond the new
receptivity to things non-Western, why, precisely, does the cinema, or
film theory more particularly, belong to this debate?

Consider the now somewhat tired—it has been hurtling past us on
bumpers for decades—slogan: Think globally, act locally. Is this message
not equally, perhaps even more true in inverted form? Globalization, for
reasons already delineated, has emerged as an obsession of educators and
policy makers alike precisely because it names without disclosing the fact
of North American, or perhaps Western, planetary hegemony. Pursued
in the context of Slavoj Žižek's provocative relocation of ideological
mystification in action rather than thought (1989), this insight might
lead one to conclude that, contrary to counterintuition and all appearances, "we" (those who, if not directly profit, certainly benefit from the
perpetual survival of capitalism) in fact, act globally. Not, of course, in
the sense that we or our surrogates *are* everywhere, but in the sense
that the logic of commodification dictates the terms and conditions of
planetary interaction and exchange, in short, of communication. This
is important because we need not accept the local as a political consola-
tion prize—and, as Mattelart reminds us, a problematical one at that—
if the critique of globalization begins by acknowledging the fact of commodification. By the same token, why surrender thought to the global as
though it were only accessible to us through the conceptual portal of the
universal? This is precisely one of the effects of the discourse of globalization, and it would appear to be this that Spivak is seeking to avoid in
her recent (2003) reclamation of "the planetary." Like Kant's infinity, the
global exists primarily as a concept of reason (albeit a stunted one). If,
however, we began thinking with greater discernment about the local
and, in particular, about the way our global actions manifest themselves

there in all their deadening obviousness, perhaps we would be in a better position to concentrate on the politically crucial task of generating the means by which the global and local/thought and action become "response-able" to one another. Obviously, the point is not to stop thinking globally (or to stop acting locally), but rather to let both thought and action absorb the consequences of "our" capacity to act globally. Global village idiocy is not worth the political risks it demands.

An obvious question is, by what historical means did this state of affairs come to pass? A comprehensive answer to this rather basic question might actually constitute "the greatest story ever told," and suffice it to say my ambitions here are decidedly less epic in proportion. Nevertheless, if I pose the question at all it is because in some sense I think it is indeed a necessary one. To frame a response it is essential—especially if my earlier query about the pertinence of the cinema here is not forgotten—that one broach the topic and problematic of communication, a problematic whose defining questions and answers are all composed of words like space, time, sign, media, difference, power, and so on. I will approach it first through the history of theory.

In 1975 a schism developed within the editorial board of *Screen*, at the time arguably the most important Anglophone journal circulating and producing film theoretical scholarship. In the very issue (Summer 1975) that contained a translation from Christian Metz's *The Imaginary Signifier* appeared an editorial statement denouncing the introduction of psychoanalytical theory into cinema studies. The editorial specifically stated that such theory threatened to undermine the educational commitment of the journal. This was followed (Winter 1975) with a statement on psychoanalysis and film that, in addition to reserving special scorn for Stephen Heath's "Film and System: Terms of Analysis" (a detailed reading of Welles's *Touch of Evil*), repeated the charge that such work was incompatible with the credo of the Society of Education in Film and Television, the publisher of the journal. A year after the first salvo, in the summer of 1976, an editorial appeared announcing the resignation of four editors and their replacement by the likes of Annette Kuhn, Steven Neale, and Richard Dyer, among others. Typically, this controversy is seen as having centered on the tension between Marx and Freud, or between theory and history, which in significant ways it certainly was. However, another of its features also bears emphasis; even as the partisans of psychoanalysis (or, again, theory) successfully defended themselves against the charge of de-politicization (see the "Reply" in *Screen* 17, no. 3), their avoidance of the disciplinary questions at stake resolved the dispute in a way that has deepened a divide in film theory, or perhaps cinema studies more generally, between a literary problematic ("textual analysis") and a sociological or even historical problematic. In contemporary film theoretical debates, "identity politics" has emerged as the most recent incarnation of the suture rejoining these disciplinary paradigms, but still more needs to be done (or perhaps "redone," if one reads carefully *Muriel* by Claude Bailblé, Michel Marie, and Marie-Claire Ropars) to bring the work of people like Mattelart or Robert McChesney together with the likes of, say, Raymond Bellour or Maureen Turim, in other words, scholars more typically regarded as concerned with the poetics of the cinema. This is not because holistic medicine is good for all that ails us, but because—to cite Jean-Louis Baudry—the ideological effects of the basic cinematic apparatus cannot adequately be described in the absence of an encounter between these conflicting paradigms.

This warrants emphasis because one of the aims of this study is to contribute to, without necessarily endorsing, the efforts of those like Robert Stam, Ella Shohat, Marcia Landy, Roy Armes, and others to effect the paradigmatic encounter sketched above. As the introduction made clear, this is one means by which I will seek to intervene within the crisis of cinema studies in the United States. More importantly though, I digress on the now largely forgotten *Screen* debate in order to situate the topic of communication (whether with a public, or in Marx's sense of the movement of commodities, people, information, and capital) within cinema studies, not to reveal a subtext, but rather to suggest how the concept of communication provides us with a way to link the cinema in its technical and cultural specificity to the distinctly ideological problem of "acting globally." Thus one begins to clarify in what sense film and Eurocentrism implicate one another. At the risk of being accused of indulging in "Grand Theory" for saying so, it will be one of the persistent aims of this study to support the by no means novel proposition that cinema studies cannot now (if it ever could) avoid the problem of what Edward Said has called "cultural imperialism."

Needless to say, the earlier invocation of Mattelart was deliberate. In both *Mapping World Communication* and *The Invention of Communication*, a decisive historical argument is advanced about the structural relations among war, rapid transit (specifically the development of international railway links), and mass communications; an argument perversely confirmed in the now failing corporate merger of Time Warner and America Online with which the last century ended.[1] As will become evident, this establishes an important framework for the more apocalyptic arguments of Paul Virilio, who proposes that the displacement of "seeing" by "flying" is crucial to the very historical emergence of the cinema.

Recognized as a masterful, even compulsive synthesizer, Mattelart and his work defy easy paraphrase. However, the basic premises of his argument in *Mapping* can be summarized. Most fundamentally, of course, he is working out the details of the claim perhaps first advanced in *The Manifesto of the Communist Party:*

> Modern industry has established the world market, for which the discovery of America paved the way. This market has given an immense development to commerce, to navigation, to communication by land. This development has, in its turn, reacted on the extension of industry; and in proportion as industry, commerce, navigation, railways extended, in the same proportion the bourgeoisie developed, increased its capital, and pushed into the background every class handed down from the Middle Ages. . . . The bourgeoisie, by the rapid improvement of all instruments of production, by the immensely facilitated means of communication, draws all, even the most barbarian, nations into civilization. The cheap prices of its commodities are the heavy artillery (*schwere Artillerie*) with which it batters down all Chinese walls, with which it forces the barbarians' intensely obstinate hatred of foreigners to capitulate. It compels all nations, on pain of extinction, to adopt the bourgeois mode of production; it

compels them to introduce what it calls civilization into its midst, i.e., to become bourgeois themselves. In one word, it creates a world after its own image (*eigenen Bilde*). (Marx 1974, 71)

Mattelart extracts from this Eurocentric biblical parody the themes of communication, warfare (the "artillery" of commodification), and the internationalization of bourgeois culture (the discursive articulations of its self-image, *Bildung*) and traces how the communication of information (notably through the telegraph and then the penny press)—which followed and facilitated international rail travel—not only accompanied, but also conditioned the development of capitalist modernity.[2] His point, and it's a good one, is to remind those of us too young to remember that capitalist modernity imposed itself by force and that information as a distinctly cultural commodity, that is, as a good circulated through the exchange of signs, is indissociable from this force. Through the concept of information he integrates mass culture in general and the cinema in particular within the framework of his discussion, borrowing from Virilio (and in a less explicit way from the Friedrich Kittler of *Gramophone, Film, Typewriter*) the *dromocratic* insight that, once speed becomes the dominant concern of those preoccupied with the transmission of information, a social desire for the state of affairs epitomized in William Randolph Hearst's infamous quip, "You furnish the pictures, I'll provide the war," is produced. This demonstration of the pertinence of what in *The German Ideology* is called "the second materialist premise of history" (the notion that the satisfaction of needs produces new ones) is usefully deployed to read, however briefly, the well-known scene from *Citizen Kane* where Hearst's misadventures in the Caribbean are satirized. Of course, Mattelart is quite justified in treating this scene as an emblematic moment of self-reflection on the part of the cinematic medium. Far too often it is treated as yet more evidence of Welles's endearing chutzpah. However, precisely for this reason it is crucial to think the satiric force of the scene all the way through, that is, to its framing within the narrative of the film, where this challenge to the cinema's veracity is literally advanced by a film purporting to reveal the truth about its subject (Charles Foster Kane), a truth pointedly marked as absent from the frame within the frame. Here, his reluctance to "read" the film closely compromises the force of his insight.

For the time being let's set aside the implication of this last remark and concentrate on what may well be the essential, namely, the fact that Mattelart is urging us to situate cinema studies within a context comprehended through a concept of communication that renders "industrial," or for that matter, "national" approaches to cinema history as necessary as they are insufficient. The challenge he extends invites us to construct the disciplinary object of cinema studies in a manner that both recognizes the profound structural link between the cinema and so-called global capitalism, regardless of how one addresses the blend of art and industry within the filmic medium (the details of which are the distinctive concerns of a poetics), and also acknowledges that scholarship is information and as such is fully dependent upon the world system of communication. Perhaps because the construction of disciplinary objects is my issue, not his, Mattelart leaves much to be said about how the production, storage, and dissemination of knowledge about the cinema might be conceptually organized so as to take at least some responsibility for its geopolitical locations. In other words, if the cinema as a communication medium is part of the historical establishment of the contemporary world system, and if the cinema includes the theory stimulated by it, then the reservations one might have about the consolidation and reproduction of this system ought, by dint of the rigors of reflexivity, find expression not simply in one's values, but in one's acts, whether physical or psychical. This study finds itself implicated in this call.

The objection that the existence of the cinema in the former Soviet Union, Cuba, or the People's Republic of China contradicts the claim that it harbors a fundamental relation with capitalism, strikes me as rather feckless. Not only does its implicit conflation of a state apparatus with an economic mode of production trivialize what Marx and Engels understood by capitalism (has anyone convincingly shown that "commodities" were no longer being produced and consumed in the former Soviet Union?), but it ignores the fact that the genealogical field of the cinema—think here of the enormously important scholarship being produced today on audiences, genre, narrative, spectacle, mass culture, communication technologies, visuality, et cetera, et cetera—came into existence when capitalism was culturally consolidating its economic and political triumph over its class antagonists. That emergent socialist states fostered the development of national cinemas is evidence of the banal, but often underappreciated fact—and here I acknowledge that the necessary contingency that links capital and the cinema poses other political and aesthetic problems that demand, and will receive, attention—that socialism has long been understood to be the sublation of capitalism and might thus be better comprehended in terms of what Mattelart, Arjun Appadurai, and Néstor García Canclini (among others) have called the dynamic of "alternative modernities."[3] But the fact that one finds cinemas in national territories administered by states characterizing themselves as noncapitalist, in no way breaks or otherwise stresses the link insisted upon in Mattelart's analysis. Cinemas such as these might well constitute what Raymond Williams (1977) might be tempted to call "residual" cultural practices.

The deeper and more important question addresses itself to the consequences, the significance of the link between the cinema as a mode of communication and capitalism as a cultural, economic, and socio-political world system. Such a question has many, perhaps even innumerable, implications. Setting aside for now the, let's call it "methodological," problem of whether this question can even be posed much less answered, however partially, without recourse to "Grand Theory," I return to the problem of the critique of Eurocentrism with which this chapter began.

For some, Mattelart's recasting of the cinema as information, and therefore a phenomenon to be subsumed under the heading of communication, no doubt seems odd. In what sense is a film like a telegram? From the standpoint of substance the comparison seems forced indeed. However, Mattelart's perspective is actually more functional—his own unequivocal repudiation of American functionalism of the post-War period notwithstanding—in that he treats the film as a message, that is, as a complexly organized signal transmitted across a network whose function is to connect and render interdependent at least two separate sites. He is, of course, very clear about the fact that this interdependence affects the two sites differently, scoring his functionalist account with a critical groove that, like Virilio's, stresses the bellicose character of the history behind the establishment of the information network. This is important, and it is not always emphasized in accounts of the international economics of, in particular, North American cinema, accounts that tend to concentrate on the problem of market saturation and its consequences for indigenous production without always emphasizing that receivers cannot but interpret such effects as part of the message whether intended or not. Within the West, of course, Sergei Eisenstein was among the first not simply to articulate this insight, but to develop a cinematic response to it.[4] Now, if we concede that the statement made by a particular film commodity is key to its status as a message—even if the details of that statement are subject to debate—then the fact that its receivers include their (largely subordinate) relation to the network presupposed by its transmission within the message renders the link between capitalism (as the organizing logic of the network) and cinema a significant one indeed. For not only does it bleed into every dimension of the projected film, but this link also subjects receivers (and here I mean to invoke both "audiences" and "terminals") to the experience of communication organized by the global reproduction of Western economic and cultural hegemony. Mattelart captures this situation evocatively in his observation that the telegraph produced both the model of and the incitement for the standardization of track gauge that made international and transcontinental rail commerce possible. As we know, "standardization" (*Vereinheitlichung*) is a hallmark of the Frankfurt School analysis of the culture industry, and even those who otherwise deplore its "pessimism," especially scholars of the technological and economic aspects of cinematic development, recognize that, as with the market itself, competition persistently tends toward monopoly, that is, the imposition of a standard, or, in a somewhat more frank term, a brand.

In Shohat's and Stam's tour de force, *Unthinking Eurocentrism*, the general contours of Mattelart's perspective on the cinema are bent specifically to the task of articulating its role in both the promulgation and contestation of Eurocentrism. As indicated earlier, theirs is a reflection on the limits of multiculturalism with which I feel certain sympathies even if, at the end of the day, I am not persuaded that the "polycentrism" they herald delivers on its promises. However, what is elaborated persuasively—especially in "The Imperial Imaginary" chapter—is a trenchant argument about the cinema's role in disseminating the West's view of its others around the globe. Obviously, this supplements Mattelart's discussion at a crucial point, namely, at the moment precisely where specification of the communicated message is required. Through a rich and wide-ranging discussion of the Western (as genre), Shohat and Stam demonstrate that cinematic narrative, through the distribution of characterological positions and resultant plot motivation—almost regardless of the ideological stance taken within any given film—constructs stories in which westerners find confirmed the visions of alterity their identities depend upon. Within this vision others menace, they assimilate, they even provoke interventions that save them from themselves (yet another avatar of "white men saving brown women from brown men"). Coupled with an ethnographic destiny derived from the scientific side of the cinema (Shohat and Stam characterize the latter as "schizophrenically" both art and science, a term we will encounter again in Tzvetan Todorov's discussion of bilingualism), this narrative construction of a "constitutive outside" implicates the cinema—precisely as the contingent montage of a technological apparatus and the social practice of storytelling—in the development of Eurocentrism.

In an important, and to my mind underdeveloped, elaboration, they bring together and detail two gazes: the cinematic and the imperial. That this is important is best established not by reiterating the terms of their analysis (the proposal that both gazes reveal the self's dependence on the image of the other is a bit predictable), but by underscoring the metanarrative, or enunciative, character of the concept of the gaze. In other words, sensitive to the need to resist reducing the cinema to the generic forms organizing its delivery of narrative, Shohat and Stam foreground (indeed, this is one of their key terms) the cinema's capacity to position spectators receptive to its messages. The analytic value of this insight outweighs the complications that arise in what many scholars, including the critics of Eurocentrism, regard as the putting at risk of spectatorial agency implied by it. It does so because the problematization of agency—the emergence of agency as a source of intellectual and political anxiety—presupposes an account of the relation between the cinema and the subject, indeed, one that might actually illuminate the place and status of agency in the cultural articulations of modern subjection. However, because Shohat and Stam are keen to bring their discussion to bear on Benedict Anderson's influential account of the link between print capitalism and the "imagined community" of the nation, they blunt the impact of their evocation of the gaze by misconstruing the problem posed by "literacy" in the cinematic field. Wisely, of course, they insist that the notion of "simultaneity along time" (Anderson's characterization of the temporality of community within a distinctively national space) is more effectively realized in media such as radio and the cinema than in the novel or the newspaper. In particular, they stress that typographic literacy dramatically limits the communal inclusivity that the newspaper might be able to generate, thus clarifying that only a certain class of citizens (those literate in the printed language) would constitute the national imagined community. Against this they contend, "unlike the novel, the cinema is not premised on literacy" (103). Frankly, I welcome this supplement of Anderson's analysis, whose value has been both over- and underestimated (nowhere more so than in Ranajit Guha's review of the first edition of *Imagined Communities*); however, Shohat's and Stam's whole discussion of Gillo Pontecorvo's justly influential *The Battle of Algiers* belies this account of "literacy." Specifically, the elements they highlight to establish how the film does not succumb to the romance of self-representation (that is, overcoming the tyranny of stereotypes by allowing the other to speak in his or her own voice)—perspective, address, focalization, and so on—all point to a capacity to "read" the film against the literacy demands imposed upon its audiences by what Shohat and Stam call "Hollywood language" (193). In other words, contrary to their earlier assertion, there *is* a form of literacy—in North America one hears much these days of something called, without precision, "visual literacy"—at work in the cinema, and even though it must be sharply distinguished from "alphabetization," only at one's peril is it factored out of a reflection on the cinema that seeks to comprehend the political consequences of its status within the world system of communication. In fact, insofar as the cinema participates in the contestation of Eurocentrism, it does so precisely to the extent that it "talks back" in and to Hollywood language. What I have called the "un-American" status of this language is otherwise inaccessible.[5]

To return, then, from the vantage point provided by *Unthinking Eurocentrism* to the significance of the link drawn by Mattelart between capitalism and the cinema. The obvious point is that, if the scholarly analysis of something presumes familiarity with its conditions of emergence, its structure, and its function, then an analysis of the cinema wishing to be taken as scholarly is obliged to acknowledge, if not confront, precisely these aspects of its history. This will not necessarily be a pretty picture, particularly when one considers that the standardization of production values (among countless other subtleties) imposed around the world by Western cinemas may be every bit as odious as the narrateme of the "white man's burden," which is now widely decried if not actually retired. The somewhat less obvious point is that, even when North American scholars struggle to take stock of the geopolitical history of Hollywood language, the link between capitalism and the cinema fosters a certain disciplinary and professional distortion that reduces "language" (and therefore literacy) to the nihilistic slasher we thought we subdued, once and for all, when it was announced in the 1990s that the quintessentially French moment of Grand Theory was over. Put less extravagantly, one of the consequences of Mattelart's take on cinema as information is that cinema studies—as a mode of information production—must actively resist lapsing into a homeostatic, or what Paul Lazarsfeld might have called "administrative," pattern. Otherwise, the discipline will cohere around an object that reflects back the misunderstanding its disciples share concerning their relation to the global flow of information, a situation where participation or, if you prefer, complicity is either factored out as an inconsequential variable or simply denied. The argument that the remainder of this chapter will defend is that the concept of enunciation is crucial to an intervention within cinema studies in North America, for without it, "our" study of the cinema not only becomes administrative and to that extent mistaken, but the vital role cinema studies might play in the multicultural repudiation of Eurocentrism is pointlessly compromised.

Take Two

In what sense then are cinema studies and the multicultural initiative bound up with one another? Though one should never underestimate the explanatory power of so-called coincidence (in this case, the fact that hiring in postsecondary education is exploiting the potential convergence between scholars working in media studies and scholars working on non-Western or "minority" cultures), another, perhaps more theoretical, line of analysis also suggests itself. One of the hallmarks of the fraught encounter between modernism and mass culture is the contention that the latter, in "democratizing" the production and reception of culture, neutralizes the practice of evaluation, making it difficult, if not impossible, to discern quality from within the phantasmagoria of plenty. This view has partisans on all sides of the political spectrum, allowing theo-conservatives to charge others with being elitist, and radicals to hold the masses and their advocates in thinly veiled contempt. This *differend*, as Jean-François Lyotard would have called it, might thus be said to constitute a necessary contingency of modernity. Those who have fought to legitimate the academic study of mass culture—and the emergence of departments of cinema studies in the U.S. academy during the late 1970s and early 1980s constitute the "spoils" of such fights—are all too familiar with this state of affairs. Indeed, the persistent suspicion that study (that is, scholarly treatment) of mass culture severs one's relation with it, thereby requiring a supplemental, often pedagogical, legitimation of the need to study it is a sign that this business remains unfinished. The same might be said of the effort to "aestheticize" mass culture (nowhere more present than in cinema studies), but what is crucial here is the notion—implicit in both perspectives—that, in extending the range of what counts as the object of legitimate scholarly inquiry, the very possibility of judgment is undermined. The terrible beauty of enchantment is never far behind.

Of course, it is precisely this theme that dominates much of the debate over multiculturalism in this country, a debate—as Avery Gordon and Christopher Newfield have reminded us—that is often as parochial (particularly from an international perspective) as it is passionate. Though always willing to repeat the mistakes of the past, North America (and I am explicitly including here the "Heritage Movement" in Canada) has nevertheless managed to sustain, now for more than a decade, a multicultural initiative that has both juridical and educational manifestations. This is not to say that the question of judgment or cultural evaluation has not been posed. Indeed it has, and at times by groups whose characteristic cultural disenfranchisement might otherwise secure their allegiance to multiculturalism. In addition, the popularization of "globalization" has produced a frame of intelligibility—if you will, a national discourse—within which affirmations of difference and specificity have been rendered regressive, and this in spite of the fact that globalization has almost everywhere meant reprivatization at the local level, privatization that has only intensified the tendency toward cultural disenfranchisement on the part of women, racial and ethnic minorities, and "foreigners." This "late" irony notwithstanding, the debate over multiculturalism cleaves to the problem of evaluation even as it rotates the polarities at stake within it. No doubt, this is due to the fact that the world system of communication mapped by Mattelart is recognized as having played a role—perhaps even the lead role—in producing the hierarchy of values appealed to in the labor of cultural evaluation. In other words, if cinema studies and the multicultural initiative share a decisive relation, this is because their shared present is currently convulsed by a gaping history, one strangely open to those who wish to intervene within it. Thus, in constructing the object of cinema studies, one's task is not only to grasp its informational character, as proposed earlier, but also to situate cinema studies in the institutional and (inter)disciplinary moment it repeats. This means confronting the multicultural initiative, not in order to relieve oneself of the task of thinking about it further, but precisely in order to subject it to an etiology critique, that is, to reflect upon its ends, particularly as these have developed in response to a characterization of what this initiative is designed to overcome. That would be, in the educational setting, Eurocentrism. To proceed here by "circling the wagons" (the western cliché is deliberate) around the discipline, risks both cutting cinema studies off from its institutional setting and surrendering it to an industrial matrix that, through various professional schools, sustains it.

The *parti pris* of my own relation to multiculturalism, though declared, has not yet been defended. Such a defense however would be of little value if it did not illustrate what implications it held for the task of constructing the cinematic object. Thus, I turn directly to the analytic concept of enunciation. Its role in the critique of multiculturalism will become clear in what follows.

Enunciation came to matter for cinema studies through its film theory subsidiary. It was a split concept from the very outset, embodying as it did the concerns of both linguistics and psychoanalysis. To the extent that this encounter and the "critique of the subject" it fostered are hallmarks of what has come to be known as poststructuralism, enunciation has played a fundamental role in the latter's emergence and has, through the exertions of Homi Bhabha, Gilles Deleuze, and Félix Guattari, gone on to become an important element in both post-Marxism and postcolonialism. Because film theorists typically overlook this later development in particular it will receive special emphasis here.

From the standpoint of linguistics, at least in the western European context, enunciation received its most influential theorization at the hands of Emile Benveniste. Perhaps his most tightly focused and sustained discussion transpires in the 1959 essay "The Correlations of Tense in the French Verb" where, in order to follow through on his call to reexamine the structure of the French verb, he proposes a distinction between two "planes of utterance" (*énonciation*): the plane of *histoire* (at once history and story) and the plane of *discours*, or discourse when used, as is now common, to designate the entire field of linguistic and trans-linguistic performance.[6] Of course, the word *énonciation* had long been in circulation, but the epistemological and ultimately methodological value that arose from its pairing with *énoncé* derives from—especially for film theory—the specifications brought to it by Benveniste. Significantly, Benveniste neither defines enunciation (from here on out I will simply replace Meek's [his translator's] "utterance" with "enunciation") nor does he directly mobilize the pairing with "statement" (*énoncé*). Instead, he details the implications of this pairing in his discussion of history/story and discourse. Noting that a verb-tense redundancy between the imperfect and the "simple" past can apparently be correlated to a distinction between speech and writing, Benveniste goes on to propose that this distinction be reconceived in relation to a distinction active on the plane of enunciation. On one side we have history/story that is enunciation that, in eschewing even the hint of autobiographical derivation, addresses itself to us as though it comes from nowhere. Its "disinterested"—we could also say "objective"—character derives from its refusal to "make use of the formal apparatus of discourse" (206) or, more precisely, from its effectiveness in not disclosing its use of this apparatus. Though Benveniste's most immediate polemical target here appears to be the smug positivism of postwar French historiography (one senses here a striking re-investment in the Romanticism of Jules Michelet), it is clear that the link to history/story verges on the arbitrary. The key, in fact, is whether or not a statement, produced in any disciplinary genre, foregrounds the signs of its enunciation. Obviously, discourse names that plane of enunciation in which such foregrounding occurs. Benveniste writes,

> Discourse must be understood in its widest sense: every enunciation assuming a speaker and a hearer, and in the speaker, the intention of influencing the other in some way. It is primarily every variety of oral

discourse of every nature and every level, from trivial conversation to the most elaborate oration. But it is also the mass of writing that reproduces oral discourse or that borrows its manner of expression and its purposes: correspondence, memoirs, plays, didactic works, in short all the genres in which someone addresses himself to someone, proclaims himself as the speaker, and organizes what he says in the category of person. (209)

He goes on to make the obvious point, namely, that any given speaker persistently shifts between these two planes (and it is this shifting to which preterite selection is to be coordinated), but what emerges here as concerns the concept of enunciation is that this last designates the source, the "formal apparatus," controlling the production of statements, not their form, but their locus of derivation. Statements that are properly historical derive their force from their silence about their source. Statements that are then properly discursive render that source conspicuous.

Though there is much to say here about the relevance of this discussion to the early work of Michel Foucault—especially once we recognize that the formal apparatus of enunciation foregrounds itself through the deictical markers (personal, possessive, and demonstrative pronouns, shifters, and so on) of a statement—this is not the portal through which enunciation gained access to film theory. This took place through Christian Metz's appropriation of the work of Jacques Lacan, for whom Roman Jakobson (not Benveniste) was always the more important linguist.[7] Lacan's various pronouncements on the topic of enunciation are strewn throughout the pages of his seminars from the 1950s and 1960s and demand more exegetical attention than the present circumstances will allow. Nevertheless, a clearly crucial discussion takes place in Seminar 11, where Lacan brilliantly deploys the enunciation/statement pairing to illuminate, if not resolve, the so-called liar's paradox. Among other things, this discussion clarifies in what sense enunciation entered film theory as a split concept, that is, as a disciplinary amalgamation of linguistic and psychoanalytic concerns. Framed within a general discussion of transference, the pairing is used to graph the statement

"I am lying" so as to establish how its falsity is true, how, in fact it gestures toward the locus of truth in analysis. Following, at least implicitly, Bertrand Russell's lead, Lacan proposes that we recognize the statement's dual status: it is both a statement and a metastatement. To do this we need to split the first person singular pronoun between the statement and its enunciation so that, while the subject of the statement may be lying, the subject of the enunciation truly must produce this "false" statement. Relevant though this is to the problem of the analysand who seeks the prolongation of suffering through treatment, Lacan is eager to draw the Cartesian problem of radical doubt into the discussion. He does so to show that the rational kernel of the *cogito* is structured like the liar's paradox, a structure that seven years earlier had prompted him to rewrite Descartes's famous assertion thus: "I think where I am not, therefore I am where I do not think."

These formulations invite the following observations. First, Lacan folds Benveniste's insistence upon the link between the subject and discourse back onto the planes of enunciation thereby recasting a diachrony (Benveniste's recognition that in the course of an exchange "speakers" shifted back and forth between history/story and discourse) as a synchrony, but a synchrony then predicated upon a division now located within the speaking subject (indeed, Lacan is, during this period, also given to using formulations such as "the subject of the statement" or "the subject of the enunciation"). And second, Benveniste's "formal apparatus of discourse," in accord with the division introduced within the subject, comes to be lodged within a key source of the subject's speech, namely, the unconscious, a move that complicates while reiterating Benveniste's claim that through discourse the speaker intends to "influence the other in some way." The so-called intellectual history at stake here, fascinating though it may be, need not detain us.[8] Suffice it to say when Metz, on the pages of his path-breaking *The Imaginary Signifier* avails himself of the enunciation/statement pairing, it is in the wake of precisely these developments.

Though *The Imaginary Signifier* virtually opens with the invocation of this pairing, it is not until the brief chapter "Story/Discourse:

A Note on Two Voyeurisms" that it is taken up systematically. As the title makes plain, Benveniste sets the terms of this discussion. In many respects this brief discussion is meant to do little more than tease out the implications of the concept of the imaginary signifier for a theory of cinematic identification. However, because this is also where Metz is revisiting Benveniste, identification is immediately split along the division structuring the pairing of enunciation and statement. This yields primary and secondary identification and the titular two voyeurisms. As with the history/story and discourse pairing—where, it will be recalled, discourse rendered enunciation conspicuous in the statement while history/story occluded it—primary identification is understood to involve the spectator's investment in the agency of the camera, the "formal apparatus" of the filmic statements, while secondary identification, predictably, designates the spectator's investment in the history/story. In accord with the tenets of a widely diffused Brechtean aesthetic, identification with the statements made in and by the history/story presupposed identification with the formal apparatus, an identification that was, as Lacan had proposed, necessarily unconscious. The different voyeurisms mirror primary and secondary identification, with discursive voyeurism organizing itself around a disavowed, but nevertheless exciting, experience of watching the film *as though* it were aware of one's presence, and "historical" voyeurism organizing itself around the more typical, though no less exciting fantasy of the peeper, the one who watches undetected. If, as Metz argues, spectatorship transpires within a fetishistic field, that is, within a context where we all know that the spectacle is imaginary but stare as though it were real, then primary identification and the repression of enunciation it sets in motion acquires a distinct analytical value for those seeking to comprehend the efficacy and functioning of cinematic histories/stories. In the 1970s Metz was content to break off at this point, leaving us with a concept of enunciation that supplied it with a dynamism, specifically, an account that, in using enunciation to refer to the formal apparatus of the filmic statements, also implied that these statements mattered to spectators precisely to the extent that they colluded in the fetishistic pact.

Metz returned to these concerns in his last, posthumously published text, *L'Enonciation impersonelle, ou le site du film*. Though much of this text devolves into what might uncharitably be characterized as a *Guide Bleu* of filmic enunciation (the taxonomy and exemplifications become quite tedious), it opens with a provocative and subtle reflection on the question of enunciation in light of then recent works by Gianfranco Bettetini and Francesco Cassetti. As if to confirm the decisively split character of the concept, Metz proceeds directly to challenge both the linguistic and the psychoanalytic sides of enunciation. The following citation makes it clear however that the former is confronted more directly than the latter.

> For what is enunciation, basically? It is not necessarily, or always, "I—
> HERE—NOW". It is, more generally speaking, the ability some utter-
> ances (*énoncés*) have to fold up in some places, to appear here and there
> in relief, to lose (*se desquamer*) this thin layer (*pellicule*) of themselves
> that carries a few engraved indications *of another nature* (or of another
> level), regarding the production not the product, or rather, involved in the
> product by the other end. Enunciation is the semiological act by which
> some parts of a text talk to us about this text as an act. However, resorting
> to the complicated and quasi-inimitable mechanism of the deixis is not a
> necessity. (In Buckland, 146)

In the absence of further reading, of course, one might justly conclude that psychoanalysis has become irrelevant to Metz's account of enunciation (indeed, David Bordwell, among others, has claimed as much). However, the formulations here bearing on "production" and the "semiological act" circle directly back to the already mentioned opening of *The Imaginary Signifier*, suggesting that this account will be settled, as would be fitting, gesturally. Without elaborating the point in great detail, it is worth observing that, as Metz recasts enunciation as a folding back upon itself of a text, his own gesture produces such a fold in the single text then fabricated out of *The Imaginary Signifier* and *L'Enonciation impersonnelle*. What might be the "formal apparatus" at work here? No doubt a long story. More immediately, however, what surfaces in the citation is the repudiation of the linguistic account of enunciation, modeled by Benveniste, around the deixis. Although here Metz appears to be grumbling about the cumbersomeness of the deictical model, what he is truly exercised by is its implicitly anthropomorphic character. Lest this be taken as a late veer back toward humanism (as though Metz objected to the attribution of agential qualities to a machine), an explanatory—though speculative—digression is warranted.

Metz was certainly not alone in working on the concept of enunciation during the 1970s. His friend and colleague Raymond Bellour also left a distinctive mark on this enterprise. In particular, through a series of studies on the films of Alfred Hitchcock, Bellour developed the notion of what he—again following linguistic practice—called the "enunciator." Through it he sought to gauge the effects of Hitchcock's signature cameo appearances, arguing that these representations of the source of the filmic statements within those very statements both marked Hitchcock's films as radically reflexive (thereby pointedly complicating a certain notion of the cinematic avant-garde) and provided analysts (if not spectators) with significant information about the rhythm of the plot. This is important first because Bellour, in reiterating Benveniste's contention that enunciation necessarily manifested itself through statements (whence the relevance of "foregrounding"), was clarifying the need to comprehend the structured interactions between statements and enunciation (about which more later) rather than driving some sort of quasi-ontological wedge between them. And second, through the shift from enunciation to enunciator, Bellour was at once re-inscribing Lacan's inclination to join statement and enunciation in the subject, while deftly recrafting the auteurist tradition that had its origins in France.

Taken together these points suggest that it is precisely against the tendency they chart, that is, a tendency toward thinking about enunciation as a metaphor for the director and his or her crew, that Metz's critique of anthropomorphism is directed. However, even in the passage cited, Metz characterizes the text as talking about itself, suggesting, I would argue, that there may be more to this dispute than meets the eye.

Specifically, because Metz's critique of the deictical model turns directly to the reflexive notion of the film's semiological act, it would appear that he concedes the point about the necessary inscription of enunciation within statements, while at the same time—and here I think his tenacity is important—insisting that we not pull the rabbit of the subject out of the hat of *self*-referentiality. Instead, he is proposing that we treat the deixis as a subset within a larger, as he says, more general, class of enunciative phenomena, a class that, in at least appearing to borrow a grammatical model of reflexivity, avoids the anthropomorphism of the deixis, not by abandoning linguistics, but by revisiting and revising its categories. In this, he and Marin find common ground.

Now, if we splice together the discussion of history/story and discourse with the later discussion of reflexivity, what results is an account of enunciation that begins by treating all films as discourse, that is, products that derive from sources that are rendered differently perceptible within the statements conveyed by them. No doubt this is what accounts for Metz's decision to devote the rest of his text to charting the different forms through which reflexivity operates to wrinkle the discursive surface of films. But what if anything remains to be said about the split—at once disciplinary and, if we are to believe Lacan, structural—within the concept of enunciation? Does reflexivity simply recast it as the bend or crease that conditions the folding back upon itself of the text? Moreover, what implications might answers to these questions have for thinking about what Benveniste called "the formal apparatus of discourse"? Surely a more general account of enunciation, of the sort Metz proposes, carries with it the call for a more general account of the apparatus, indeed, one responsive to a perception of the cinema as a mode of information, that is, as a component of the communication networks that constitute the current world system.

No doubt the most important recent contributions to the dialogue between psychoanalysis and the cinema have come from the so-called Slovenian school and the "Giant of Ljubljana," Slavoj Žižek. Though his thinking has wandered far from the formulations that appear in the early *Looking Awry*, these retain their pertinence in the present context because of the explicit way they take up the legacy of the split in enunciation.

Given that the explicit aim of *Looking Awry* is to introduce readers to the thought of Lacan through reflection upon popular culture, it comes as no surprise when, in the concluding chapter, Žižek dusts off and redeploys Lacan's distinction between the subject of the statement and the subject of the enunciation. Though characterized as having a properly linguistic provenance, the distinction is said to find its "perfect use" in elaborating the topographical relation between the ego and the superego when brought to bear on the question of morality. Because Žižek is keen on delineating the "ethics" of fantasy, this formulation is introduced without further comment. However, within the context of the chapter "Democracy and Its Discontents," the formulation acquires associations that are mine to tease out. Specifically, Žižek uses the concept of enunciation to describe the agency of the superego, arguing that the ego's capitulation to the superego's demand that it renounce enjoyment and adhere to the moral law is paired with, in fact is driven by, the suspicion that the superego is hoarding the enjoyment it denies to the ego. The subject of the statement becomes the law-abiding ego, and the superego becomes the subject of the enunciation. In both Žižek and Lacan, enunciation is thus associated with a modality of agency that is not, as it were, subject to the ego's exertions. However, by linking enunciation and the superego—a psychic instance consistently regarded as a psycho-social formation by Freud (in *The Ego and the Id*, to which Žižek refers us, one can read, "social feelings rest upon identifications with other people, on the basis of having the same ego ideal" [2001, 20:39])—Žižek throws his weight behind those who give a social meaning to the agency that eludes egoic machinations. In doing so he invites us to conceive of the split within enunciation, the split between the ego and the superego, along the lines of a social division, drawn not between the subject and society, but *within* the subject insofar as it is a social being. Indeed, as the final chapter unfolds, first democracy and then the nation are strained through the analysis of enjoyment, an analysis that, in establishing the "perfect use" of the statement/enunciation pairing, would appear to render indissociable enunciation and the varying formations of collectivity that bound and border the subject. Julia Kristeva, in both *Strangers to Ourselves* and *Nations without Nationalism*, has elaborated these issues in complementary and deeply suggestive ways, but the contributions here of Homi Bhabha are in fact the most immediately illuminating. This is largely because his formulations help sustain the effort to think of the split of enunciation not simply in social terms, but in terms that matter to film theory especially as it has struggled with the task of reflecting upon the relation between the cinema and the post-colonial condition.

To be sure, enunciation is a concept that circulates readily in Bhabha's prose, thus making any attempt to provide a comprehensive account of its work difficult, if not simply doomed. However, in his polemic "The Commitment to Theory" (written in reaction to the Edinburgh Third Cinema conference of 1986), enunciation is used to realize rather particular effects, indeed ones that are at once pertinent and parsable. Much of the second part of his essay, where the discussion of enunciation transpires, is given over to nailing down his signature distinction between cultural diversity and cultural difference. This matters because, in order to complicate the heritage of theory and thereby refute the charge that in being Eurocentric it is irrelevant to considerations of Third Cinema, Bhabha must supplement the cliché that theory is a form of practice with a demonstration that, despite appearances, theory does not belong to Europe. Presumably because the "patient gray work of genealogy" does not appeal to him, he makes his case by articulating a theory of cultural difference that renders Europe a stranger to itself, in effect, unlivable. Significantly, Bhabha deploys the Lacanian account of enunciation to realize this aim. After glossing "cultural diversity" as an object of knowledge and "cultural difference" as the process articulating the intelligibility of such an object, he spells out the following details.

> The concept of cultural difference focuses on the problem of the ambivalence of cultural authority: the attempt to dominate in the *name* of a cultural supremacy which is itself produced in the moment of differentiation.

And it is this very authority of culture as a knowledge of referential truth which is at issue in the concept and moment of *enunciation*. The enunciative process introduces a split in the performative present of cultural identification; a split between the traditional culturalist demand for a model, a tradition, a community, a stable system of reference and the necessary negation of the certitude in the articulation of new cultural demands, meanings, strategies in the political present, as a practice of domination, or resistance. (35)

Later, in order to drive home the structural implications of this argument, he adds,

The linguistic difference that informs any cultural performance is dramatized in the common semiotic account of the disjuncture between the subject of a proposition (*énoncé*) and the subject of enunciation, which is not represented in the statement but which is the acknowledgement of its discursive embeddedness and address, its cultural positionality, its reference to a present time and a specific space. The pact of interpretation is never simply an act of communication between the I and the You designated in the statement. The production of meaning requires that these two places be mobilized in the passage through a Third Space, which represents both the general conditions of language and the specific implications of the utterance in a performative and institutional strategy of which it cannot "in itself" be conscious. . . . The splitting of the subject of enunciation destroys the logics of synchronicity and evolution which traditionally authorize the subject of cultural knowledge. . . . In other words, the disruptive temporality of enunciation displaces the narrative of the Western nation which Benedict Anderson so perceptively describes as being written in homogeneous, serial, time. (36–37)

Of the many themes introduced here, those that subtend the link drawn between enunciation and what is called the Third Space solicit sustained comment. For not only are these the themes through which Bhabha seeks to conceptually outmaneuver the Third Cinema partisans, but they are also the ones that, in circling back to Anderson's discussion of the nation, keep us, as it were, on task. At first glance, Bhabha—especially in reiterating the linguistic and psychoanalytical heritage of enunciation—appears simply to be restaging the distinction between statements and enunciation, thus avoiding altogether the split within enunciation. However, it is clear that, in using formulations such as "the splitting of the subject of enunciation," more is at stake. What emerges, if one reads with a certain patience, is something like the following proposition: precisely because statements about cultural identity (whether one's own or another's) are produced within the general process of cultural differentiation (inter- and intracultural exchange), the subject of enunciation is not simply split off from his or her statements but is split between and among the multiple cultures that condition the act of enunciation. In short, no culture is simply identical to itself, and the ambivalence that results cuts through and divides the process of cultural identification. If this process is, at a certain level, synonymous with enunciation, it is because producing linguistic statements is like producing culture, except that the "speaker" is a conflicted collectivity inevitably beset by other like and unlike bodies, bodies similarly traversed by the overarching social divisions of class, race, gender, and sexuality. Thus, for Bhabha, like Žižek, all cultural values—the marks of distinction put in play through the work of cultural differentiation—are smeared by the conflicts waged through and around their production. The authority of Eurocentrism, from such a perspective, derives from its partisan's suppressed activation of a conflicted relation—a cultural difference—whose projection onto a host of disadvantaged parties is in the last instance sustained by force of arms. I think it important that enunciation be invoked here to designate the conflicted "source" of cultural statements or, to preserve the more ambitious formulation, the statement of culture. For what results is a nuancing of the concept of "the split" when conceived in relation to enunciation. Instead of thinking of enunciation as divided by a clean cut from top to bottom, Bhabha's discussion invites us to think about it as divided both by its relation to statements and by the multiple conflicts it registers once understood to belong to the production of cultural statements/the statement of culture. The split of enunciation is a split, split.

While perhaps not immediately apparent, these issues bear directly on the concept of a Third Space. Granted, given that Bhabha's reflection on this term ranges well beyond the limits of either this citation or this essay, my elaboration cannot but be partial. However, several of the important conceptual features of Third Space can be teased out. To begin with, it is surely no accident that Bhabha introduces the concept in the context of the discussion of the deixis, the personal pronouns *I* and *you*. As if to express his solidarity with those dissatisfied with a deictical reduction of enunciation (Metz, for example), Bhabha insists that the production of meaning happens in "another scene," indeed, one where the utterance is implicated both in language as such and in a performative and practico-institutional context. This prompts him to appeal to the concept of a Third Space, as a way to name the site toward which the pronominal places are routed in order for meaning to be produced. Strictly speaking, it is unclear whether this space is produced at the point of convergence between the place of the sender and the place of the receiver, or whether these places, insofar as they can be distinguished, presuppose the prior production of a Third Space, but the link to enunciation is pronounced in any case. It is so through the principle of the performative derivation of the utterance. By moving to subordinate the deictical relation to a process that subtends it, and retaining in his characterization of this process the split between language and cultural context, it becomes clear that the enunciation—precisely to the extent that it is multiply split, or conflicted—belongs to what Bhabha is calling Third Space, that is, a space divided by two places, the language enabling their communication and the cultural contexts that differentiate those places. By further invoking the Lacanian concept of the unconscious "in itself," he makes it difficult, if not impossible, to conclude that enunciation is not what is meant when the "production of meaning" is invoked.

In addition, it is not without interest that Bhabha implicitly superimposed the unconscious (at an earlier point in my discussion, the Lacanian subject whose truth requires that she or he lie) on a concept so obviously freighted with allusions to the geopolitical category of the Third World. Ashis Nandy (1995), while underreading the fact that Moses was an Egyptian, has perhaps had the last word on the tendency expressed here, but the immediate context of Bhabha's comments, the Edinburgh festival, invites us to underscore his equally pertinent allusion to Third Cinema. Certainly, as numerous commentators have observed, there is no easy equation between the Third World and Third Cinema. Indeed, some would no doubt argue that harking back to the Third World risks a certain political obsolescence. This notwithstanding, Bhabha's formulations do invite one to speculate that enunciation may well be the crucial concept through which to situate the cinema within the spatial divisions that organize what Mattelart understands by the uneven world system of communication. In other words, if we accept that nations are culturally as well as politically unstable and therefore troubled constructs, then so are national cinemas. Indeed, the cinema as a distinctly international institution is fundamentally involved in producing this instability. If national cinemas, precisely to the extent that they vie for cultural authority on the international scene, are subject to the interminable process of cultural differentiation, then they are dependent upon a Third Space that mediates and divides the encounter between senders and receivers of filmic messages and about which they are to varying degrees unconscious. Because Bhabha is primarily concerned to protect the theoretical enterprise as such, he does not linger over the implicit task of specifying how filmic enunciation might be conceptualized in relation to Third Space, nor does he really come to terms with the cultural political conflicts his own discussion at once reflects and theorizes. This does not, to my mind, vitiate the decisiveness of his contribution. It only clarifies the need to supplement his account of enunciation with one that recognizes the complexities he has delimited while refusing to abandon the political challenges they pose.

In point of fact, what is called for here is recourse to the psychoanalytic concept of anaclisis, or "leaning on." To clarify why, it is worth restating the questions that prompted recourse to both Žižek and

Bhabha, namely, what further must be specified about the split—at once disciplinary and, if we are to believe Lacan, structural—within a more general concept of enunciation, and what implications might this work of specification have for thinking about what Benveniste called "the formal apparatus of discourse"? So far, the split in enunciation has been read in conjunction with the themes of democracy, nationalism, and cultural difference, all means by which to think about how the production of statements is divided and redivided. The task of rethinking the "formal apparatus of enunciation," especially as it bears on the cinema as a communications technology, remains. Thus, if I open this summary by invoking the concept of "leaning on," it is to draw attention to the procedural necessity of propping Žižek and Bhabha up against each other, while adding to this configuration Félix Guattari, whose concept of "the collective assemblage of enunciation" (*l' agencement collectif d' énonciation*) pressures especially Bhabha's account of the cinema in ways that illuminate the concept of the "formal apparatus." By the same token, Guattari's discussion, devoted as it is to the invention of concepts, profits enormously from the pressures exerted upon it by the postcolonial preoccupations of Bhabha. Lastly, because Metz (and, for that matter, Bettetini and Cassetti) figure prominently in Guattari's discussion of enunciation and the cinema, a move that might otherwise be chalked up to a typical Western obsession with tripods/trinities, will in fact find its motivation and warrant in the so-called matter at hand.

In spite of the intimate working relation between Deleuze and Guattari, the latter's writings on film have been largely forgotten in the wake of Deleuze's two-volume study published in the mid-1980s. For my purposes, it is important that this work has deep roots (rhizomes?) in Guattari's abiding interest in non-Peircean semiotics where one finds his most probing discussions of enunciation, discussions whose conclusions are transposed, though incompletely, to his work on the cinema.[9] To be sure, enunciation (whether collective or not) figures persistently in Guattari's writings, but his 1974 essay "Towards a Micro-politics of Desire" contains formulations whose terms engage immediately the issues being agitated here. In squaring off against Lacan he writes:

The strata of the formalization of the content thus produces a subjectivity that is essentially detached from the real, empty and transparent, a subjectivity of pure signifying that corresponds to Lacan's formula: a signifier represents it for another signifier. This subjectivity has to be accounted for under two headings—the subject of the statement and the subject of the enunciation. By the effect of a reductive echolalia, the subject of the statement has become the report of the subject of enunciation. In accord with a bi-univocal model, every enunciation must lose its polyvocity and revert to the subject of the statement. Such is the program of linguistic Oedipalization. Linguists can then say that the subject of enunciation is only what remains of the process of enunciation in that of the statement. Our perspective is the reverse: what interests us is recovering the polyvocity of enunciation across statements subjected to the strata of signifying semiotics. What we seek to retain are the indices, the residual traces, the transverse flights/escapes of a collective assemblage of enunciation that constitutes, in any case, the real productive instance of all semiotic machinery. (92–93, translation modified and completed)

Here, under the heading of enunciative polyvocity, Guattari rewrites the split within enunciation and does so by relieving it of both its linguistic and its psychoanalytic heritage. At stake appear to be two things: first, the very concept of multiplicity at work within the concept of the split between statements and their enunciation, and second, the link between enunciation and subjectivity, specifically, individuated subjectivity. With regard to the first, Guattari argues that, due to a drive toward formalization within the field, the psychoanalytical subject is divided from itself only insofar as this division does not compromise the sovereignty of the signifier. In effect, it repeats without acknowledgment the division between the signifier and "the real productive instance." And, while this manifestly avoids a confrontation with the Lacanian account of the real, it is clear that the formula "resistance to symbolization" would remain too marked by the work of formalization to satisfy Guattari. This becomes even more apparent when spelling out the issues raised when challenging the link between enunciation and subjectivity. Here the key issue hangs on the opposition drawn between a linguistics content to chart the remains of enunciation in the statement and a perspective committed to recovering the polyvocity of enunciation. Because, however, when he elaborates his perspective Guattari has recourse to "indices" and "traces" (both members of the "remains" paradigm), its distance from the view he opposes threatens to collapse, polyvocity must emerge aligned not only with multiplicity, but with collectivity. This last is crucial because what it clarifies about enunciation is the way it can be made to bear theoretical witness to the collective character of the production of statements. By implication, linguistic or psychoanalytical enunciation—precisely to the extent that they collude in dividing the subject around the split between statements and enunciation—are compromised by a desire (disavowed, to be sure) to *individuate* the production of statements. Clearly, Guattari is dissatisfied with the notion that the production of even patently linguistic statements (the products of speaking or writing) can be accounted for by appealing to what enables an individual speaker to produce such products. Instead, he proposes that the production of such statements (as well as translinguistic ones) can only be adequately described by having recourse to collectivity, specifically, to a collective assemblage of enunciation. In other words, the production of statements presupposes a complex configuration of enabling conditions, a configuration that by virtue of its structure and composition renders all statements "collective" or social at the micropolitical level. As if in anticipation of Bhabha's discussion of cultural difference, Guattari uses collective enunciation not simply as an alternate designation for a "people" (say, speakers of Wolof), but for the linguistic, practical, and institutional formations that agitate them.

Nevertheless, the clarity with which this illuminates what is involved in thinking through the split in enunciation is not yet matched by a characterization of its pertinence for an analysis of the cinema. This must be rectified. "Towards a Micro-politics of Desire" contains only a single passing allusion to the cinema, but it is a suggestive one. It occurs in a footnote where Guattari chides Metz for persisting in aligning his work with those working on the signifier (imaginary or not).

What provokes Guattari however is clearly his recognition that Metz's approach, insisting as it does on the expressive heterogeneity of the cinema, resembles his own. In fact, when in "The Desiring Cinemachines" (from *La révolution moléculaire*) Guattari elaborates his own theory of the cinema, he lets Metz spell out via a long citation precisely in what way the medium frustrates analytical reliance on a semiotics of signification. What is important here is not the ambivalence defining the relation to Metz, but rather the illumination cast by the citation upon the concept of a collective assemblage of enunciation.

First, by drawing attention to the presence within a film of sounds, voices, noises, movements, images, and so on, Guattari invites us to regard this semiotic heterogeneity as a way to rethink or rephrase enunciative polyvocity. Indeed, a few pages after the Metz citation, he invokes by name the concept of the collective assemblage in order to ground the heterogeneity of desires put in play by the cinema. As a result, however, enunciation is framed so as to risk its very connection to the so-called basic cinematographic apparatus. Second, in risking this connection, the polyvocity of enunciation is theorized so as to drive a wedge between the micro- and, for lack of a better term, the macropolitics of desire. Despite the fact that Guattari is plainly committed to an account of the cinema that grasps its character as a mass communications technology— he writes, "Cinema, television and the press have become fundamental instruments in the forming and imposing of a dominant reality and dominant significations" (218)—his treatment of enunciation in the strictly cinematic field concentrates on erasing the contested boundary between the filmic and the cinematic without thereby elaborating the way the cinema, as a means of mass communication, belongs to and articulates with the world system of communications, a system that would appear to constitute a collective assemblage of enunciation, but of a somewhat more massively organized and finely reticulated form. Of course, I understand that Guattari's project is precisely involved in elaborating the political counterweight to systems functioning at this level, but surely there is nothing to be gained in so narrowing the micropolitical that it cannot engage that which escapes or flees it by definition, namely, the macropolitical. To this extent his transposition of the concept of the collective assemblage of enunciation to an analysis of the cinema is incomplete in that there it operates to, as he might say, "transduce" the relays between the cinema and mass communications at the global level. Even if we concede that these relays are corporately administered and increasingly monopolized by, count them, six trans- or multinationals, as irreducible collective assemblages of enunciation they are presumably vulnerable to micropolitical agitation, but only if the production of statements is theorized as traversing the entire political plane. Micropolitics risks its link to the political when it is modeled on microbreweries.

Crucial here is the way Bhabha's discussion of cultural difference, particularly as it inflects his meditation on Third Cinema, foregrounds issues—such as, for example, colonialism and cultural imperialism—that recede into the background of Guattari's treatment of enunciation. It is not that the collective assemblage of enunciation cannot comprehend such phenomena, it is that in tilting so vigorously against linguistics and psychoanalysis much passes, as it were, behind its back. Indeed, one could even argue that Guattari's critique of Lacan rebounds upon him in that his critique overempowers the very object the concept of enunciation is being wrested away from. Be that as it may, it is by no means insignificant that Mattelart himself has been moved to align his perspective with that of Guattari, citing with almost mournful admiration the latter's *Chaosmosis* where, in its opening pages, Guattari—in the name of a reappropriation of technology—insists that a political judgment of "machinic evolution" depends on how this evolution articulates with "collective assemblages of enunciation" (Mattelart 1996, 307–8 and Guattari 1995, 5). I say this not merely to tighten the bibliographic weave of this discussion, but to underscore the fact that as a concept, indeed as a concept to be deployed in media studies however it may come to be construed, the collective assemblage of enunciation retains that degree of analytical resourcefulness indispensable for productively rethinking Benveniste's concept of "the formal apparatus" of enunciation. What it provides is a transdisciplinary (I would also argue, "antidisciplinary") conceptual innovation rich enough to engage (a) the semiotic specificity of the filmic medium, (b) the at once national and cultural in-flections of the basic cinematic apparatus, and (c) the geopolitical char-acter of the world system of communication. To be sure, this concept complicates each of these domains—perhaps nowhere more obviously than with regard to the apparatus, a debate over which has long been mired in the struggle to separate spectatorship from "the" spectator and "his" gaze—but such complication is necessary, especially if one contin-ues to hope that the cinema and its study can be made to matter to the repudiation and overcoming of Eurocentrism.

Needless to say, the concept of enunciation has also been compli-cated by its deployment here as the theoretical means by which to artic-ulate the above three domains. To put the vexed matter succinctly, I think Metz is right in that enunciation can no longer be usefully modeled on the linguistic concept of deixis. However, it is a mistake to proceed too hastily here. Insofar as the deixis embodies, even in linguistic terms, the inscription of enunciative particulars in the statement, it takes on reflexive properties. This is not simply because the statement reiterates its own conditions of production, but because in doing so it acts upon itself by making, as argued earlier, the circumstances of transmission part of the message transmitted. Which is to say what? It is to say quite specifically that the deixis needs to be modeled on reflexivity. Metz too eagerly jettisons deixis in his turn to the reflexive work of self-citation, letting slip the task of elaborating the structural relation between enun-ciation and reflexivity, a task I argue leads one to recognize in the latter the dynamic of splitting that pushes one toward an account of enuncia-tion of the sort being essayed here. Thus, I am proposing that within the logic of enunciation is encompassed a mode of reflexivity that allows filmic statements to act upon themselves by linking them to the con-ditions of their production, understood not in terms of the cinematic apparatus as such, but in terms of the cinema's relation to the geo-political genealogy of its own emergence.[10] When a filmic statement is conveyed through the depiction of a message-conveying device—say, Godard's use of a rolled up art poster in the extended apartment scene between Michel and Patricia in *A bout de souffle*—reflexivity operates here not merely to foreground the cinematic apparatus, but also to make the history of the technical reproducibility of art—a history that joins and separates lithography (the poster) and cinematography (the film)—part of what the statement transmits. Add to this the aggressive sonoric intrusions of the radio in the same scene, and what one has is a mass of statements about the unlivability of heterosexual relations, acted upon and associatively nuanced by multiple enunciative instances, none of which can be neatly bent to the task of signaling, as Metz would have it, the work of the cinema as such. It is not that such work is not signaled, only that the reflexive signal is split both internally and externally and routed through a collective assemblage that situates the cinema in relation to *other* media, all of which form the matrix from which derive the statements it is now in a position to produce.

How, though, does this engage the issues of nationalism, postcoloniality, and cultural difference raised by Žižek and Bhabha? Through language or, more specifically, through what I propose to call "foreign film languages." In saying this I realize that I risk self-contradiction, by once again subordinating enunciation to linguistics. However, my aim is to stretch the concept of language—especially as applied to the cinema—while at the same time retaining from it, through the grammatical instance of reflexivity, the sort of systemic or structural limits that one might appeal to when disagreeing with someone, often a film student, about the sense of the statements being made by a particular film. With regard to the concept of language, I am well aware of the debates regarding its applicability to the cinema that have been raging in various precincts of the Western world since the 1960s. I address them at some length in part two of the following chapter. However, Jurij Lotman's formulation in *Semiotics of Cinema* strikes me as at once elegant and enabling. He writes, "Language is an ordered communicative (serving to transmit information) sign system" (1), which implies that what he calls "cinematic language" is composed of orderings of signs specific, though not necessarily unique, to the medium. Indeed, much of *Semiotics*, when not preoccupied with theorizing the aesthetic as such (a more literal translation of the title would, in fact, be *Cinema Aesthetics*), is devoted to generating something like the lexicography of these signs. Shrewdly, Lotman steers clear of the whirlpool whose menace prompted Roland Barthes to subordinate the sign in general to the doubly articulated structure of the linguistic sign, keeping his account of language open to the semiotic nuances emphasized by Guattari while nevertheless insisting that, at the level of a film, the relations between signifying and asignifying semiotics are ordered. And, truth be told, Guattari himself, after eviscerating linguistics in "The Desiring Cinemachines," finds it within himself, at the essay's close, to contrast the living "language of the cinema" to the dead language of psychoanalysis (1996, 237). Of course, Lotman's insistence on the communicative function of the cinema too quickly subordinates communication to the logic of hermeneutic exchange, but beyond its ill-considered repudiation of what gets lost in transmission lies precisely the perspective that makes Lotman's preoccupations rhyme with those of Mattelart.

Beyond, however, the methodological and theoretical legitimacy of the concept of film language there are other matters that bear emphasis: (a) so-called foreign filmmakers have made, since the 1960s, persistent recourse to the concept of film language, and (b) the centrality of language (whether cinematic or not) to the global genealogy of the cinema, particularly as concerns what John Trumpbour has called the "selling of Hollywood to the world," is beyond doubt.[11] If I stress such matters here, it is with an eye toward shifting the terms of the debate over the legitimacy of the linguistic model. At the end of the day, the matter of whether the cinema is *really* structured like a language misses the point. As the debates within linguistics between the Chomskians and the Pinkerians make clear, the nature of language itself (or at least its origins) is in subtle scholarly dispute. In light of this, to which concept of the reality of language will we appeal in order to argue either for or against the concept of film language? Thus, what would appear to be decisive is the mobilization of concepts whose legitimacy can be debated, but not without implicating the disciplinary constraints that render legitimacy claims intelligible within a given field. Because, as I shall argue in the subsequent chapter, cinema studies in the United States, to the extent that they operate within the discourse professionalized by the AMPAS, has constructed "foreignness" in the filmic domain in such a way that it naturalizes language (that is, it equates language with national tongues), any effort to implicate the constraints of the discipline in the debate over legitimacy is, to some extent, obliged to problematize the concept of language. Moreover, if the encounter between cinema studies in the West and various non-Western national cinemas is one place, perhaps even a crucial place, where the multicultural initiative is finding its footing, then it is vital that this encounter not be missed, either by not taking place or by taking place without displacing the centers of disciplinary reason. Under such circumstances it will be important to struggle to listen to how other filmmakers construct their object and their objectives, a struggle that means working—while listening—to dismantle the listening devices, that is, the disciplinary formations, through which this listening takes place. By the same token, it will be important to become response-able for one's listening, that is to say, answerable to the geopolitical relations presupposed by and reproduced in our capacity to listen, though more often to dictate. The issue here is not primarily a moral one. It is a political one in the sense that what is urgent is the mobilization of concepts that, in going beyond the enhancement of reception, speak to the transformation of relations, indeed, a transformation of what in another context I, following Theodor Adorno, have called "the structure of listening."

My argument is, of course, that the concept of enunciation assumes its importance in this context. Yet, how precisely is it to be linked to language? First, and here I am reiterating something said by Cassetti, enunciation relates to language as the means by which virtual units are converted into a concrete, localizable object or product. This conversion is neither accidental nor disordered. Indeed, if we approach enunciation as quintessentially inscribed in modes of reflexivity, this last can be shown to assume grammarlike properties. Second, the collective assemblage of enunciation, precisely to the extent that it "deterritorial-izes" the cinema, engages, among other things, the linguistic inflection of cultural difference, making it possible to theorize the existence of "foreign film languages" operating within national cinemas to produce statements. Here the split in enunciation can be understood to refer to the way the grammatical properties of reflexivity might differ when, in specific geopolitical contexts, cultural difference is negotiated in and through the clash of languages. Precisely because this negotiation, when conducted through the cinema, registers the genealogy of cultural differentiation—a genealogy that under the conditions of postcoloniality is deeply marked by the violent imposition of the technologies of cultural modernity—a difficult and fraught filmic "bilingualism" erupts within the collective assemblage of enunciation. In the chapters that follow I will attempt, through a comparative gesture, to tease out how such "bilingualism" is differently inflected by the experiences of European colonialism and North American imperialism. To the extent that Eurocentrism has figured decisively in such experiences, confronting it in "our" present may well require us to mobilize concepts that both allow us to recognize our position within the legacies of colonialism and imperialism, while at the same time providing us with the means by which to track the terms of the challenges being addressed to us. To this end, enunciation must be redeemed.

Alternate Takes

As intimated above, the concept of enunciation has its detractors. The most tenacious and intellectually powerful of these have been David Bordwell and his colleague Noël Carroll. Though written some time ago, that is, before Metz's last work and before the English translation of Cassetti, their objections nevertheless deserve a response, if not a reply.[12] Indeed, if their positions are still worth quarreling with, it is not primarily because of their sufficiency as counterarguments. Instead, with Bordwell in particular, one is confronting something of an intellectual ambassador, that is, one regarded by both figures in the industry and the "public" as someone who represents (as both sign and proxy) academic cinema studies.

At the outset it is worth establishing that, on the matter of the inadequacy of a narrowly linguistic account of enunciation (one modeled on what Benveniste called the deixis), all parties are in agreement. Indeed, as we have seen, Metz himself has severed his ties with this approach to enunciation. This skews things somewhat because both Bordwell and Carroll concentrate, in large part, on establishing precisely this point as if it alone settled the matter, whereas, as has been suggested above, partisans of enunciation are not prepared to concede on this ground alone. At issue is the pertinence, indeed the adequacy, of language as a concept through which to approach the cinema, but perhaps even more deeply lies the matter of theory itself within cinema studies.

When delivering his summation at the Centenary of the Cinema conference convened in Madison, Wisconsin, in 1995, Bordwell put those in attendance on notice. In particular, he took the occasion of his keynote to warn against a specter haunting cinema studies, a specter composed of equal parts of "Grand Theory" and incompetence. Though at times conflated, the two were summoned to establish that, faced with a shrinking job market in academia at large, but certainly within the nonprofessional precincts of media studies, it was crucial that only truly qualified applicants be considered for the few available positions. As someone who, by virtue of his position, is expected to train people for academic careers, Bordwell can hardly be faulted for such a concern. However, to determine whether an applicant was truly qualified, he made it sound as though one had only to perform the following litmus test: Does the applicant use the cinema to theorize about something else, or not? Does she approach the cinema from within, that is, on its own terms, or not? Can he do a neoformalist interpretation of a given film, or not? Negative responses were taken to indicate that the applicant was incompetent and therefore unqualified. Moreover, this perspective was mobilized in order to establish that academic units (programs, departments, et cetera) that did not involve themselves in the concerted inculcation of these skills—for example, American Studies departments that teach film, but as part of the study of American culture—should not be trusted to produce qualified applicants for cinema studies jobs. In other words, this was an intervention not simply on behalf of the cinema, but also and perhaps necessarily on behalf of a discipline, suggesting, in ways that threatened to contradict everything being said, that given the evident pertinence of the former to the latter (why give such a speech at such an occasion?) perhaps it *is* urgent that we use the cinema to study something else, namely, its study. Or are they the same? If they are, how is cinema/discipline competently studied? Through the research paradigms of cognitive psychology wedded to a certain neoformalist hermeneutic? Perhaps, but exactly why is not entirely clear, nor can it be made clear without recourse to, alas, theory.

The point of this caricature is not that Bordwell trades in the very theorizing he warns against, but that, when quarrelling over the relevance of enunciation, the status of theory—does the right kind play the right role (the dilemma faced by a studio casting department)—is very much "on the table." Carroll, a philosopher by training, who has weighed in on the theory debate, shares these concerns, although the eccentricity of his structural position (that is, "outside" cinema studies) gives his interventions a perhaps awkward angle. His most sustained treatment of the matter at hand occurs in a section of the "Narration" chapter of *Mystifying Movies*, where what later becomes Grand Theory is cast as the position that holds that narration as such is ideological. Indeed, Carroll's discussion of enunciation is largely framed around the problem and status of ideology critique in film analysis. Reminding us that Bordwell, in *Narration in the Fiction Film*, has exposed the "vagaries, linguistic contortions, and fanciful extrapolations by which contemporary film theorists have attempted to impose Benveniste's categories to film" (152), Carroll goes on to prepare the introduction of his "alternative account" of narration by laying out his own version of Bordwell's objections. After a brief rehearsal of Benveniste's views (undercut later by his admission that he, not being a linguist, may be incapable of judging them), he re-states the notion that the fit between linguistics and the cinema is imperfect. The fit is imperfect because central to the linguistic concept of enunciation is the grammatical concept of person, and clearly the cinema (excluding dialogue and text) lacks such a concept. It is especially defective as concerns the second person. Aside from the concession made above—to the effect that everybody, including Metz, has abandoned a strictly linguistic construal of enunciation—what this point establishes is not simply Carroll's desire to defend realist narrative (after all, why not?), but his commitment to philosophical realism. In other words, his argument is conducted as though the issue involved is whether there *really is* what linguists call enunciation taking place in the projection and screening of a film. Left aside is the grand metaquestion of the conceptual modeling of one's analysis. In other words, what might the concept of enunciation (whether strictly linguistic or not) provoke in the work of film analysis, and is this desirable?

Not insensitive to the matter, Carroll, by superimposing enunciation and ideology critique, suggests that what the former provokes is not in fact desirable, or at least, if film analysts want to raise ideological questions, then they ought to suitably constrain their concept of ideology so that such analyses can be properly conducted by sociologists and other presumed experts in "antecedent beliefs." In effect, as Bordwell was later to argue, ideological analysis is not really what *film* scholars ought to be doing, so why appeal to the "far-fetched" concept of enunciation? For all his clarity, Carroll's view is not terribly compelling even on its own terms. I have trouble understanding how to reconcile the axiom that awareness of the human agency behind every representation is required for our cognitive assimilation of it with the contention that there is nothing like a speaker of the utterance in film. Either we are systematically failing to cognitively assimilate the representations of all films (they are not, after all, *real* speakers, *real* human agents) or, what is more likely the case, we behave *as if* the film and its representations are "spoken."[13] This "as if" (what Metz, following Lacan following Marx, calls the logic of fetishization) introduces some important complications. First, it reminds us that even a real speaker is more than simply a human agent. And second, it stresses the activity of the spectator—not, as Carroll would have it, in her "thought" or her "awareness"—but in her investment (perhaps even libidinal, perhaps even unconscious) in the illusion. Carroll himself has to appeal to this perspective when, in laying out the "erotectics" of narration, he insists upon the "tacit," indeed "subconscious" (173), character of the spectator's role in the film. Like

Carroll, I agree that Vsevolod Pudovkin's perspective on film technique is powerful and extraordinarily useful, but the narrative logic of question and answer (itself a deeply grammatical phenomenon) that Carroll champions in his alternative account of narration is derived by Pudovkin from an explicit analogy with the word (Pudovkin, 23). Aware of this, Carroll attempts to distance himself from Pudovkin's commitment to language, but at the end of the day, there isn't all that much of a difference between the claim that "the film knows that I am watching" (which Carroll ridicules) and the claim that "the film is asking me questions and soliciting hypothetical answers about the plot" (which Carroll endorses). Both are constructions of analysis. Both are ways of making sense of what is taking place in the spectator/screen encounter. One fetishizes the irreducibility of human agency in all intelligible communication, the other fetishizes the enigma of the fetish, the "as if." Because enunciation, in sustaining the later alternative, makes the question of who or what is speaking in the film ("Hollywood International," indeed) belong to cinema studies in a way that narration seems set precisely on not doing, it constitutes an important analytical possibility, one that Bordwell and Carroll have not convinced me to abandon.

CHAPTER 2

Foreignness and Language
in Western Cinema

The concept of "bilingual" cinematic enunciation called for in the previous chapter must now be confronted with the matter of how the relation between language and foreignness has been forged within the cinematic domain. This matter is pressing not because the familiar critique of relativism (that is, "foreign" relative to what?) needs to be made yet again, but because "bilingualism" embodies a mode of foreignness that is far from simply relative. Only from the standpoint of an imperceptible "monolingualism," in other words, from within a film culture where a certain enunciative tendency or stance has become normalized, is "bilingualism" intelligible as foreign. In order to render its unmasking of monolingualism critical, rather than simply innovative, bilingualism's engagement with the construction of foreignness must therefore be thought through. This is the immediate aim of the present chapter.

Several issues need to be examined together. First, there is the matter of how foreign language films have come to be so designated within the West, that is, given the economic and cultural realities of what still seems aptly evoked in McLuhan's phrase "the global village," Hollywood. Second, there is the matter of how foreign languages (notably the speech of "natives," "Indians," and even "aliens") have been represented within Western cinemas. And lastly, there is the matter of how the two preceding issues converge to render language itself "foreign" to the cinema, precisely the state of affairs, I would argue, that has hardened the resolve of the critics of cinematic enunciation. Taken together, these matters illuminate one of the important means by which a certain enunciative monolingualism has become, if not imperceptible, then certainly normalized, thereby casting "bilingualism" into the pit of "foreignness," while providing it with its, albeit attenuated, redemptive power. Surely, "it's all relative" when applied to the designation "foreign" is a premature expostulation. What matters is how appearance, that is, the palpable fact that some things are less relative than others, appears, and this chapter seeks, by practicing a certain kind of institutional history, to illuminate this state of affairs.

The Hollywood Sound Tract

Perusing the "Entries by Country" list of foreign language films entered into competition with the Academy of Motion Pictures Arts and Sciences (AMPAS) one finds notes justifying the designation "ineligible" of the following sort: *Ways of Love*, "it is a composite of the production ability of three different production units who worked in three different countries"; or *A World of Strangers*, "original soundtrack was made in English and no Danish-language version existed"; or *The Harder they Come*, "Calypso (Jamaican) determined to be an English dialect, not a foreign language"; or lastly, *Scenes from a Marriage*, "film released in the Los Angeles area, disqualifying it for Foreign Language Film Award consideration."[1] Of course, many entries were deemed eligible (indeed many were nominated), and it would be a mistake to infer that my interest here is in detecting some conspiracy at work in the disqualification of these particular films (though, truth be told, Perry Henzell's film raises some provocative issues). Instead, what this list calls attention to is the discourse of regulation, the rules that were invoked by the review committee in determining the eligibility of foreign language film entries. Teasing out the genealogy of this regulatory discourse will go some considerable distance toward tracing the official production of the links among film, language, and foreignness.

Though formed in 1927, and originally conceived as an international organization, the AMPAS did not begin officially acknowledging what came to be known as "foreign language films" until Vittorio de Sica's *Shoe Shine* (made in 1946) was brought to its attention in 1948.[2] The space for such acknowledgment was opened within the "Special Awards" category of the Academy Awards rules when, in 1944, subsection I was introduced. It read:

> It being the intention that motion pictures from all countries shall be eligible for consideration for the Awards, the rules shall be construed literally to include such motion pictures, except that they must be shown in Los Angeles within the awards year, must be in English or with English subtitles, and the producers or distributors shall provide prints when necessary for review showing. (AMPAS archive)

When, in 1949, subsection D was introduced to define a then emerging Foreign Language Film Award, subsection I was revised to read:

> Exception to this rule shall be made for the foreign language film award for which pictures need not be in English or have English subtitles and need not to have been shown in the United States. (AMPAS archive)

Subsection D reads:

> Foreign Language Film Award. This award is intended to honor films first made in a language other than English and first released in a commercial theater in the United States during the Award Year. (AMPAS archive)

Obviously, D was developed to ratify the review committee's decision to recognize *Shoe Shine* with a special award, and already one sees an important configuration emerging here, a configuration in which films are characterized as being made "in" certain languages (English serves as the "unmarked" term) and destined for a rather specific form of exhibition (that is, in a commercial theater, in a certain country, during a particular business cycle). However, the process that culminates in the shift whereby foreign language films are recognized under their own rubric as opposed to the "special awards" rubric has a beginning worth reconstructing precisely because of the light it projects onto the significance of the configuration identified above.

In March of 1992, Barbara Hall (an oral historian and archivist at the AMPAS) interviewed Robert Vogel, a man who came to MGM in 1930 to oversee international publicity for the studio, but who joined the AMPAS in 1942 to organize the foreign language film special award and came to serve on the standing review committee for the award once established. Here, from Hall's oral history, is Vogel's account of the process that led to the creation of the category of the foreign language film.

> We had a producer on the lot named Walter Wanger, who happened also to be the Academy president. He came into my office one day and told me that . . . he used the personal pronoun throughout. Whether any or all of this was done with the knowledge of the board, I really don't know, because he talked *I*. He had found out during the war there had developed overseas some very, very fine young directors who had begun to turn out some very, very fine pictures. He named three of them: Clair of France, Kurosawa of Japan, and Rossellini in Italy. And he said, "The day must come, and soon, when these pictures come to be recognized around the world and the Academy will be in the terrible position of appearing provincial if it ignores pictures that are produced outside of Hollywood. So I want to set up a special honorary award for the foreign pictures so that the foreign world will see that we are honoring the great picture-makers of other countries. So I want you to join the Academy . . ." I'm quoting Wanger. "I want you to join the Academy, keep your ears to the ground, look for any pictures that you hear are outstanding, and we'll arrange to get a print for you, long enough for you just to look at. If you hear of any such. And at the end of the year, if you have any picture or pictures to recommend for a foreign special award Oscar, let me know. Will you do that? (Vogel, 298)

Vogel goes on to protest the exclusivity of his proposed authority and Wanger concedes that other studio people (Luigi Luraschi at Paramount and Bill Gordon at RKO) will have to be involved. As with any beginning, this one too is tangled. Did Wanger have the Academy board behind him or not? Had someone "during the war" actually contacted him about the matter later broached to Vogel? Was Vogel revising history for Hall? Nevertheless, what the AMPAS is apparently committed to remembering about the formation of the foreign language film special award is overdetermined in ways that call for extended comment.

Although Walter Wanger is a very interesting character (for example, his intervention as a producer reframed Don Siegel's *The Invasion of the Body Snatchers* so as to rescue the United States from full-tilt paranoia), it is the words that Vogel puts in his mouth that are decisive, beginning, of course, with Vogel's own insistence on Wanger's enunciation. Several points need to be made.

First, as a scholar like Richard Jewel might insist, Wanger/Vogel (a contrivance the preceding observations require) approaches the cinema as an *auteurist*, his deep relation to studio culture notwithstanding. Films are the expressions of their directors (René Clair of France, Akira Kurosawa of Japan, and so on), an assertion that might project some light on Wanger's confidence in Vogel's sovereignty, but that ultimately works to link the foreignness in the cinema to the foreignness of the filmmaker. Language here goes without saying.

Second, perhaps for this very reason, foreign (as an adjective) is put to work grammatically in telling ways. In the passage it modifies "pictures," "world," and "special award Oscar." Pictures are, of course, films (conceived, as has long been the custom, as silent). Thus, a foreign picture is a film made by a foreigner, though grammatically nothing prevents it from denoting a picture coded within conventions of visual literacy unknown to Wanger/Vogel. World, which oscillates between Earth and the quintessential apocalyptic object ("world view"), locates the foreign "outside of Hollywood." Thus, foreign world, as used by Wanger/Vogel, refers in a rather fearlessly Lacanian way to the Other within whose gaze "our" own acts of viewing fall. The vaguely ethical tone of Wanger/Vogel's concern about the United States' appearance of "provincialism" virtually solicits such a reading. The grammatical ambiguity of "foreign pictures" is here restated as a something like a guilty conscience where a world ravaged by war—indeed a war from which the United States emerged as victor—is recast not as an object, but as a subject. It is not just that Wanger/Vogel has come to learn of foreign directors, but that these directors are in a certain sense owed our recognition. The onlooking world expects it. In a final twist, "foreign" is used to modify "special," which is in turn used to modify "award." Here ambiguity is recast, through something like proliferation, as hysteria. On the one hand, "foreign" modifies "special" so as to designate simply a new type of special award category, the honorary award for best "foreign picture." "Foreign special award Oscar" functions as a substantive, and, technically, the adjective is introjected by the noun. On the other hand, syntax—through the syntagma of reiterated modifiers—operates here to introduce foreignness into the special awards category qua category. Thus, the award is not for something foreign, it is something foreign. And, in fact, as the archival material shows, previously nonexistent subsections had to be introduced within the special awards rules in order to address the foreign language film, or "foreign pictures." The matter goes well beyond wary reaction to innovation however, for in a report from Geoffrey Shurlock (a member of the Foreign Language Film Award review board) dated January 1, 1956 to George Seaton, Shurlock recommends *Wages of Fear* and *Samurai*, but goes on to warn of the "political overtones" in the films, recommending that their "anti-Americanism" be edited out (AMPAS archive). Clearly, the foreignness that the "foreign special award Oscar" might introduce within the award category itself is an officially sanctioned anti-Americanism.

Third and lastly, though language, as I have said, goes without saying, its absent presence is manifest throughout the citation, but nowhere more assertively than when Wanger is charging Vogel with the task of scouting for prospects. Note the shifting character of the filmic signifier: "I want you to join the Academy, keep your ears to the ground, look for any pictures you hear are outstanding, and we'll arrange to get a print for you, long enough for you just to look at. If you hear of any such." First, Vogel, through the rigors of a colloquial expression, is counseled to listen for suitable foreign pictures. Then, in the same sentence, he is counseled, this time through the rigors of an idiomatic locution ("look for," as opposed to "look at") to look for foreign pictures that, as the sentence continues, his listening has turned up. In the concluding clause of this sentence, foreign pictures are again reduced to sights, when Wanger promises to arrange things so that Vogel will have prints "just to look at." Then, as if to retrace his own footsteps, Wanger/Vogel concludes by saying, "If you hear of any such."

So what might one conclude? Are foreign pictures things one encounters through the eyes or through the ears? Or both? Regardless, language makes its presence felt here through the way the now familiar distinction between the paradigms of speech and writing underwrite the fickle relation between the eyes and the ears. Remember, in subsection D (cited above) the foreign language film is defined as a film "made in a language other than English." I, of course, am inclined to take such formulations literally, but even if one does not, it is clear that, sticking to the letter of the rule, a foreign picture will exhibit its foreignness not by virtue of what it looks like, but by virtue of what it sounds like. In this sense, the ear is the proper organ for discerning the foreign filmic signifier, and Wanger/Vogel's indecisiveness may precisely have to do with the clash between American speech patterns (whether colloquial or idiomatic) and their subject matter, in this case, films made "in" a language other than English. Which is to say that perhaps, when speaking of foreign pictures, "keeping one's ear to the ground" is not a colloquial expression after all. Or, in the same vein, that "to look for" or "to hear of" are not merely idiomatic. This strongly suggests, beyond the immediate matters at hand, that the long bemoaned "oculocentrism" of film theory may have had a self-defeating role to play in the struggle to pose the problem of what I have been calling "foreign film languages."

But surely I am "overreading" Wanger/Vogel. Surely when he counsels keeping one's "ears to the ground," he just means that one should be attentive to what is now called "buzz." When he promises to arrange screenings "just to look at" prospective nominees, he is simply reassuring his interlocutor that careful, exhaustive study of prospective nominees will not be required. Of course, I must plead guilty here, but just the same, one might argue that it is precisely this sort of unstudied, indeed "spontaneous" discourse that speaks most clearly about the institutional culture from which it derives. Thus, while I am not proposing that Wanger/Vogel is *really* talking about the relation between foreignness and language in the citation, I am proposing that his speech derives from a discourse, a frame of intelligibility, in which more than what he means to say by activating it is at work. Describing this discourse and the relations it has constructed among film, language, and foreignness obviously requires that one be sensitive both to what Wanger/Vogel means but also to what he says and how he says it, let alone what is done in the act of saying it.

There is more than a methodological or theoretical warrant for such claims, and this can be clarified by looking carefully at the history of the "Rules for the Foreign Language Film Award." When, in 1956, the Foreign Language Film Award became recurrent (that is, no longer honorary and therefore subject to the "Special Awards" provisions), the following characterization of the award was written:

1. This award shall be given for the best feature-length motion picture [in 1958 this was specified to mean 3,000 feet] produced by a foreign company with a non-English soundtrack, first release from January 1, 1956 to November 30, 1956 and shown in a commercial theater for the profit of the producer and the exhibitor. The picture need not have been released in the United States and English sub-titles are not required. A story synopsis of the picture written in English must be sent to the Academy when the film is submitted for award consideration.

2. Every country shall be invited to submit its best film and the selection in each country shall be made, wherever possible, by organizations whose aims and purposes compare with those of the Academy of Motion Picture Arts and Sciences. (AMPAS archive)

Also in 1958, one of the more extraordinary features of this characterization of the foreign language film was revised. I am thinking, perhaps predictably, of the formulation "non-English soundtrack," a formulation that, when its brutal conflation of sound and voice is set aside, either evokes, for example, Spanish "barking" ("jau-jau" as opposed to "woof-woof"!?) or an insight into the linguistic organization of sound perception that the very concept of the foreign language film seems determined to interdict. The revised material reads: (between the second and third sentences in 1) "However, if a print is available with titles in English the Academy will be glad to have that print submitted for voting. Prints will not be accepted with a dialogue track other than in the original language." Perhaps uncomfortable with this solution (where the soundtrack simply becomes the dialogue track), a much later revision of the rules (from 1981) restored the decisive status of the soundtrack with the phrase "basically non-English soundtrack," where the adverb compresses concerns that arose in the 1970s over whether dialogue had to be entirely in a language other than English, a matter, as we shall see, of special significance in the postcolonial context.

If I stress such details, it is precisely to underscore the way regulatory discourse within the AMPAS gave voice to precisely the ambiguities that course through the oral history recorded by Hall. In other words, the shifting back and forth between sound and dialogue (even allowing for the constraints of "low budget" production), while not repeating the tension between speech and writing exactly, does nevertheless establish both that foreignness manifests itself sonorically in films and that, contrary to received opinion, language has a rather indefinite relation to dialogue, that is, speech. Perhaps such matters are destined to arise in an "oral" history, but it would appear that Wanger/Vogel is not simply "shooting from the hip" and is instead speaking the difficulties posed for the AMPAS in living up to its internationalist credo. Although surely this is going too far, it may actually be fitting that to learn of distinctly foreign pictures, one has to resort to an "old Indian trick," that is, putting one's ear to the ground.

Needless to say, the unmarked status of English only complicates matters. On the one hand, the AMPAS certainly did not mean to exclude from consideration under the foreign language film rubric films from the "Anglophone" world, say, the UK, Australia, Canada, or the West Indies. On the other hand, however, given the regulatory stipulation that foreign language films had to have been made in languages other than English, films from such countries or regions were excluded *de jure*. This matter was discussed within the AMPAS as early as 1949, and it comes up in Hall's interview with Vogel, who insists that the AMPAS intended to treat Anglophone films as U.S. films, a claim that suggests that the AMPAS was prepared to violate the stricture against multiple submissions routinely (Vogel, 305). Again, though this dilemma openly thematizes the very concept of language (is it, in fact, synonymous with a so-called natural language, or is there something distinctly foreign about "the language" in which, say, *The Piano*, was made?), the conception of language rationalized by a certain enunciative monolingualism, the very monolingualism protecting the unmarked status of English, does not permit the possibilities latent within this dilemma to flourish.

This is precisely what makes the AMPAS's exclusion from consideration of Henzell's *The Harder They Come* so interesting. Officially, as already noted, the film was deemed ineligible because "Calypso" (what might also be called Creole) was determined to be an "English dialect," and thus it was not made in a language other than English. Nevertheless, as Michael Thelwell (the writer approached to "novelize" the film) makes clear, copies of the film that circulated in the United States (indeed the print submitted to the AMPAS review committee) were actually subtitled in English because the "English spoken" sounded foreign enough to surpass the competence of most U.S. audiences (Cham, 178).[3] Because foreign pictures present themselves, as such, to the ear, the AMPAS had both to accept the submission from Jamaica, and to withhold recognition, taking the opportunity represented by the film to tighten the link between language and speech officially. In other words, beyond making the openly linguistic judgment that dialects fall within languages, the review committee also implicitly specified that the "language" referred to in the phrase "foreign language film" was indeed to be modeled on speech, that is, on the vocal sounds to be found on the dialogue track, not the codes of audiovisual literacy organizing the messages of the film.

The implicit character of this more theoretical point derives not from its status as theory, but from the fact that the AMPAS remains conflicted about precisely where it wants to locate foreignness within the cinematic field, and while it is true that any frame of intelligibility (whether institutionally localized or not) stumbles when thematizing its enabling conditions, the problems posed by recognition of the foreign language film are, in a certain sense, unique to the AMPAS.

Further confirmation of the contention that Wanger/Vogel's indecisiveness is due to the conflicted status of foreign language films within the discourse of the AMPAS is to be found in Vogel's response to Hall's query about why recognition of foreign language films ceased being handled under the "special awards" rubric. Here is the exchange:

HALL: In 1956, why did the Academy decide to make the foreign language award an annual award rather than honorary?

VOGEL: Yes, well, I think by that time it was realized that picture-making outside of Hollywood was just as important as picture-making in Hollywood. And that equivalent pictures in quality were being made elsewhere. Didn't want to differentiate between English pictures and non-English pictures, or between Hollywood and the rest of the filmmaking world. (301)

Though Wanger is not invoked directly, his ghost lingers, for in essence Vogel offers here virtually the same explanation offered when he was asked about the development of the special award. Missing, of course, is the guilty tone and the invocation of the war.[4] What is striking though is the equivocal use of "or" in the final sentence fragment. Read as establishing an alternative formulation, the "or" functions again to parallel English and Hollywood, on the one hand, and non-English and "the rest of the filmmaking world," on the other. Because this last would presumably include many of those films Vogel previously sought to equate with Hollywood films (those of the Anglophone world), we again run up against the dilemma of situating foreignness within the cinematic field. Because this dilemma is so obviously endemic to the concept of the foreign language film, it figures prominently in the narrative reconstruction of each developmental episode. It has nothing whatsoever to do with Vogel's limited expository resources or the constraints of an oral exchange.

In fact, there is strong evidence that Vogel recognizes some of the theoretical problems I have been teasing out of his remarks. I offer the two following examples. At one point Hall asks: "Were you looking for films that were just generally excellent artistically or were you interested in films about certain subject matters?" To which Vogel responds: "Oh no. Subject matter never entered into it. I mean, it was never any consideration. . . . After all, we were looking at motion pictures. I don't think the Academy ever looks at subject matter specifically. I don't think it should" (300). The salient phrase is, of course, "after all, we were looking at motion pictures." True, at one level it simply reproduces the tired distinction between form and content, but considered in light of the language problem, what Vogel's response suggests is that he recognizes the degree to which dialogue—as rooted in the subject matter (characters in a particular situation talking about it)—is not as important to the film qua film as would be the craft with which the dialogue is placed within a soundtrack and joined, via the soundtrack, to the image track. True, his view aestheticizes the motion picture, but what such formalism cannot be faulted for is its insistence upon the specific assemblage, the material detail, of any given film. Here Vogel gives voice to the elided concept of language that the AMPAS's construction of the foreign language film depends upon.

Second example, and one whose apparent contradiction of the principle invoked in the first is most intriguing: Responding to Hall's repeated suggestion that the AMPAS has tended—in the name of the foreign language film—to recognize, nominate and award "Western-style" films (that is, films from Western Europe), Vogel proceeds from a defense of the review committee members (they are called "A-1"), to an articulation of the following concession: "The one category of pictures which suffers in my estimation is the Oriental picture, from Japan or China, whose code of living and code of morals are so very different from ours that we can't understand them. A picture having to do with social problems in Japan won't be understood by Yankees [Vogel's affiliation, during the war, with the Office of the Coordinator of Inter-American Affairs may have provided him with the occasion to encounter this epithet]. I don't see how it can win an Oscar" (310). It is difficult not to read this as an insistence upon the importance, indeed the centrality, of subject matter. After all, what would "social problems in Japan" be if not subject matter? But is it not possible to discern in this formulation, through its thick Eurocentric haze, Vogel's recognition that, even if an Anglo-American citizen fluent in Japanese (say, a student in international banking) were to see a film organized in accord with a "code of living" she was unfamiliar with, it is possible, even likely, that such a person would fail to understand the film? In other words, are we sure that, in the first sentence of the cited passage, "them" has "code of living and code of morals" as its antecedent? Or, to reiterate an earlier point, is this an instance of U.S. speech patterns colliding with the foreignness in foreign language films? If so, then perhaps Vogel is not literally contradicting himself. Instead, he is arguing (although that may be too strong a word) that precisely because "Oriental" films are coded differently, that is, expressed in what I am calling a foreign film language, "we" are not likely to understand them, nor is the AMPAS likely to give them any awards.[5] How far into the cultural domain does a "code of life" reach? I would say far enough to shape the way images, sounds, and events get assembled in the medium of film.[6]

I am not here trying to make a case for the subtlety of Vogel's views. Instead, my aim is to suggest how they emerge within a frame of intelligibility shook by the necessity of assimilating something that cannot fail to thematize that frame's, that discourse's, constitutive exclusions. True, the importance of Vogel's "witnessing" derives from the fact that he, rather than a discourse, was given the task of establishing the mechanism whereby foreign language films could be officially recognized by the AMPAS, but just as the language he speaks precedes him, so too does a certain way of thinking about the relation between language and film. When through him his speech and this way of thinking converge on the foreign language film, a certain symptomatic ambiguity results. This is what has been charted above. However, the larger insight at stake here, namely, the significance of the link forged by the AMPAS between film language and foreignness still remains to articulate. To proceed, additional points need to be established: first, the influence of the AMPAS within the United States. In other words, what general status might be claimed for the AMPAS's construction of the link between foreignness and film language, given that other institutions in the Anglophone world (the American Film Institute, the Museum of Modern Art, the British Film Institute, and so on) might also be said to be involved in forging it? Additionally, and this is really the crucial matter, what is the significance of the fact that foreignness becomes the conceptual means by which language is separated from the filmic medium? In ways yet to be determined, these points converge.

Of course, it is one thing to acknowledge that the AMPAS perceived itself as having global significance (witness DeMille's inaugural remarks), and quite another to establish that, whether on its own terms or not, it has indeed had such significance. In Hall's oral history, Vogel relates a relevant anecdote about Kurosawa, whose *Rashomon* (made in 1950) was the first "Oriental" picture to win an Oscar. Hall provokes the anecdote by asking Vogel about why, at the time of their interview, no other Japanese films had won the foreign language film award. Instead of resorting to his "codes of living" argument, Vogel recounts the efforts of Jim Gordon, who worked with the government in Tokyo to set up, as the rules stipulated, an organization with aims comparable to those of AMPAS. Predictably, his efforts culminated in the development of an organization that eventually sought to award Japanese films internally, to in effect develop a Japanese Oscar (the French "César" is probably the most widely recognized example of this phenomenon). Vogel's anecdote then centers on Kurosawa's reaction to the invitation extended to him to accept an "Oscar" from this comparable institution. He says that Kurosawa responded by saying, and the following material is presented as a citation in Hall's text: "Yours is a second-rate Academy. The only Academy that really amounts to a row of beans is the one in Hollywood and I am not going to bother to come to your ceremony"

(301). Vogel then concludes by suggesting that, once slighted in this way, the Japanese film industry refused to promote its own best talent, hence no more Oscars. Why Hall does not remind Vogel of Kinugasa's *Gate of Hell* escapes me, but what is crucial here is that this rich anecdote (what, for example, is "row of beans" a translation of?) speaks volumes about the way the AMPAS represents to itself its, as we say, global reach. Even more important, at least for my purposes, is the fact that, even if Vogel is misquoting (so to speak) Kurosawa, Vogel and the AMPAS are not entirely wrong.

As argued in chapter 1, Hollywood designates a mode of production that has profound, perhaps unseverable, roots in a globalizing capitalism. If, as many have proposed, capitalism is the decisive impetus behind both Western modernity and Western modernism (let us set aside, just to leave room for as yet unthinkable futures, the more general concept of "modernization"), then, to the extent that the cinema belongs to the dialectic of modernism and mass culture, it has played a central role in the cultural globalization of capitalism. "Hollywood" is virtually a metonymy for this process, and it is therefore not simply false to claim that this Los Angeles neighborhood functions—even in the so-called post-studio era—as something of a cinematic center, in the strong sense given to this term by Jacques Derrida in "Structure, Sign, and Play in the Discourse of the Human Sciences." Nevertheless, what distinguishes Vogel, if not from Kurosawa then certainly from the authors of "Toward a Third Cinema," is the tone and rhetoric of proud triumphalism exuded by his characterization. Of course, as always, this "almost nothing" amounts to a great deal.

In Pierre Norman Sands's pioneering study of the AMPAS, he establishes the crucial link between it and Hollywood, the link that allows one to recognize the scope of the AMPAS's influence on global film cultures. Written as a dissertation at the University of Southern California, this study explicitly attempts to answer the question, "why did the founders [of the AMPAS] conceive of the need for a professional society composed of members of the motion picture industry?" The response Sands elaborates is worthy of sustained reflection.

At the risk of parading out another "myth of origins," it is never-theless worth citing the invitation sent to prospective members in the wake of the dinner attended by Fred Niblo (a director), Conrad Nagel (an actor), and Louis Mayer (a producer) where, as legend has it, the concept of the academy was hatched. It read:

> If we producing workers, actors, directors, technicians, cinematographers, and producing executives, who have the future progress of this great universal entertainment at heart, will now join unselfishly into one big concerted movement, we will be able to effectually accomplish those essential things we have hitherto neglected. We can take aggressive action in meeting outside attacks that are unjust. We can promote harmony and solidarity among our membership and among our different branches. We can reconcile our internal differences that may exist or arise. We can adopt such ways and means as are proper to further the welfare and pro-tect the honor and good repute of our profession. We can encourage the improvement and advancement of the arts and sciences of our profession by the interchange of constructive ideas and by awards of merit for dis-tinctive achievements. We can take steps to develop the greater power and influence of the screen. (38–39)

Evident here, as Sands's research shows, are allusions to emerging labor conflicts (the AMPAS has long been regarded as a producers' "union"), the unrelenting public attacks on the industry (the agitation that cul-minated in the Hays Office production code of 1930 actually began in 1922), and the soft-pedaled imperial ambitions of the industry; in short, all the concerns one would expect to find in a cultural industry of the sort so meticulously and thoroughly described by virtually all scholar/historians of the Hollywood mode of production. Perhaps less conspic-uous is the call for "the improvement and advancement of the arts and sciences of our profession," a patently modernist gesture that culmi-nated in the Oscar, but also in the standardization of practices that came to define the so-called Hollywood style. Specifically, as Sands notes (though without further comment), the AMPAS produced a manual in

1931 titled *Recording Sound for Motion Pictures*—a topic, as I have argued, that, through the concept of the soundtrack, touches on the very frame of intelligibility in relation to which the AMPAS operated. In many respects, of course, the AMPAS was simply legitimating the practices that had emerged within the five major studios as they positioned themselves in relation to the Vitaphone breakthrough, an episode much analyzed within film scholarship but nowhere more thoroughly and cogently than in the work of Douglas Gomery. Recognizing that sound confronted U.S. studios with both the problem of translation (here the foreign language issue arises directly) and the problem of standardization (see chapter 1), Gomery, in "Economic Struggle and Hollywood Imperialism: Europe Converts to Sound," makes explicit what Sands does not, namely, that sound served as a decisive locus for the coordination of domestic and "foreign" industrial strategies. This coordination, vital in certain respects to the capitalist aim of vertical integration, did not simply standardize a certain technological system, it also displaced the infancy, the preverbal era, of the cinema. In other words, with the exportation of standardized sound practices, the cinema entered language, or as Fitzhugh Green famously put it, film found "its tongue." Hollywood presided over this transmutation, a posture reflected in *Recording Sound for Motion Pictures* and thus clarifying in what sense the AMPAS participated in a material transfiguration of the cinema with global consequence, indeed, a transfiguration with immediate implications for the links among language, film, and foreignness.

Certain aspects of the preceding point need to be drawn out. First, by stressing that the AMPAS's investment in "improvements in arts and sciences" finds expression in displacing the infancy of the cinema, I wish to explicitly suggest that this material transmutation reaches, as does the structure of the commodity itself, into the cultural practices of filmmakers worldwide. Resistance is not exactly "futile," but it is constrained to a degree that projects glaring light on "Western modernity at large," that is, on the social, economic, and cultural constellation that reframes "indigenous" practices even as quite unevenly developed realities adjust its focus. This is not a dynamic to be resisted or countered by simply recording indigenous sounds, whether these assume the form of dialogue or not. Or, seen from the opposite angle, if this last is indeed what is meant by resistance, then the concept desperately needs revisiting. In a certain sense, making a film now (even a no-budget digital film like *405*) means making a commodity that exhibits among its other features a sound-track, indeed, a soundtrack recorded in a manner designed for a certain kind of postproduction manipulation and eventual playback. Though often regarded as a tempest in a teapot, the controversy of digitalization is precisely a struggle over the cultural politics of standardization.

Moreover, if such claims are restated in the context established by the rules regulating the submission of foreign language films to the AMPAS, not only do they acquire additional substance, they illuminate rather acutely the link forged therein between film and language. After 1956, the rules contain the following language: "This Award shall be given for the best feature length motion picture produced by a foreign company with a non-English soundtrack, first released from January 1, 1956 to November 30, 1956 and shown in a commercial theater for the profit of the producer and the exhibitor." In requiring that foreign lan-guage films be three thousand feet in length, made by companies, shown in commercial theaters, and produced for profit, the AMPAS was implic-itly intervening in the domain of indigenous cultural practices not only to impose the capitalist logic of standardization, but also, in effect, to eliminate foreignness from the cinema, or put less polemically, to situ-ate foreignness on the soundtrack and in the speech of those "foreigners" recorded there.

It is useful here to invoke Bordwell's figure of the "straight cor-ridor," to clarify what is at stake in such an assertion. Introduced in *Nar-ration in the Fiction Film*, this vaguely architectural figure describes the relation between the narrative and the spectator sought by practitioners of classical Hollywood cinema. Without revisiting the controversy raised in the preceding chapter, let it be said that the "straight corridor," though characterized with rigor and subtlety, boils down to the insight that, for films seeking to make a profit for their producers through com-mercial exhibition in the United States, access to the product—in this case the narrative (or the film reduced to its narrative)—must be as direct and immediate as possible. What Bordwell calls narration, the delivery of the narrative, must be subordinated to this end, and all traces of "film work" must be effaced, that is, integrated into the task of producing the affective charge (whether "cerebral" or not) of the spectacle. Fine, but why reiterate such familiar points here? Because if foreign language films, precisely in order to be recognized by the center of the cinema ("the only Academy that amounts to a row of beans"), must be conceived with potential U.S. commercial exhibition in mind, then their makers are obliged, indeed compelled, to deliver their narratives by way of the straight corridor. This means that, virtually without regard to the narratives themselves, foreign language films must look and sound like the sorts of films perceived to be appropriate for commercial distribution and exhibition in the United States. I would go further. Precisely because of this central constraint on the organization of narration—or, as I prefer, enunciation—"foreignness" is obliged to gravitate toward the speech audible on the soundtrack. If we accept the notion that what is specific to the cinema is not the narratives it delivers, narratives that, after all, often derive from or convert into extracinematic forms, but the codes that have developed to link film delivery techniques to the apparatal constraints of the medium, then perhaps the polemical version of my point is closer to the truth: the straight corridor ushers, via the shortest route possible, foreignness from the cinema.

The point can be taken further still. Once expelled from the cinema, foreignness echoes, that is, it returns, as sound. As if passing through an inverted Ellis Island where, instead of names being made to sound less foreign, their sounds become the predominant site of their foreignness, the concept of the foreign language film functions, in effect, to drive a wedge between film and language. In other words (here more than a turn of phrase), once foreignness is reduced to the speech of foreigners, the vocal sounds delivered as dialogue on the soundtrack and translated in the subtitles, language is, as it were, spoken for. Instead of language, whether as concept or metaphor, having any relation either to the design or the construction of the corridor, it is surrendered, as

Derrida would doubtless insist, to the paradigm of speech and regarded as essentially irrelevant to any other aspect of the cinema, but certainly irrelevant to any conception of the codes operating to stitch the dialogue into the soundtrack and to cement the soundtrack and the image track together. As an indication of how fundamental this gesture is, note that many of those scholars we associate with the linguistic or semiotical turn in cinema studies figure among the most egregious oculocentrist theorists, suggesting that the "foreign mark" (to retrieve Barthes's characterization of Kristeva's work) made on film scholarship by the likes of Metz, Bellour, and Kuntzel (among others) was never foreign enough.

All this, of course, projects a rather different light on the debate with which the previous chapter concluded. Although my characterization of the insufficiently foreign mark made by cine-semioticians might lead one to conclude otherwise, the appeal made by Bordwell and Carroll to cognitive science or neoformalism is equally implicated in oculocentrism, not only because their works have tended to concentrate analytically on the image track but because their repudiation of the concept of language as a modeling tool, as a way to approach the cinema, is consistent with oculocentrism's subordination of sound to sights and, within this gesture, the reduction of language (as both phenomenon and concept) to spoken dialogue or speech. Thus, once language is understood as defined by the kinds of concerns a linguist might bring to bear on the analysis of speech, it follows easily that language brings very little if anything at all to the work of film analysis, because a film is not a speaker. In this sense, the attack on "enunciation," as based on a concept of language inapplicable to cinematic reality, becomes, no doubt unwittingly, a confirmation in theoretical guise of the frame of intelligibility within which the AMPAS constructed the concept of the foreign language film.

Native Speakers

In the scene from Alfred Hitchcock's *Marnie* that seeks, at least implicitly, to absolve Mark Rutland of the charges of stalking, vigilantism, and sexual harassment, there is an explosive and important exchange between Marnie and Mark. Signaling her impatience with what she clearly regards as "therapy talk," Marnie snaps, "Me Jane, you Freud?!" A rapidly escalating game of word association ensues. Her defiance ultimately gives way, and by the scene's end she is clinging to Mark begging him to help her. This confessional collapse certainly overshadows the line I have cited, but the latter retains an importance that deserves comment.

Marnie's designation of herself as Jane calls up, with an overtness that borders on clumsiness, the famous scene from William S. Van Dyke's *Tarzan, the Ape Man* in which Jane Parker's captivity assumes dialogic form. Set after Jane's first night in Tarzan's custody, the relevant segment is composed of fourteen shots. The dialogue unfolds as follows:

JANE [in medium two-shot with Tarzan high in tree]: Thank you. Thank you for protecting me.

TARZAN [in same shot]: Me?

JANE: I said, thank you for protecting *me*.

TARZAN [in same shot, now poking the knuckles of his right hand into her shoulder]: Me?

JANE [in same shot, shaking her head in nervous frustration]: No! I am only me, for me.

TARZAN [in same shot, with a face full of confidence]: Me!

JANE [while pointing to Tarzan]: No! To you, I'm you.

TARZAN [while pointing to himself]: You?

JANE [in reverse shot over Tarzan's shoulder, looking down and away, head shaking in utter frustration]: No. [pause] I'm Jane Parker. Understand? [then pointing to herself] Jane, Jane!

TARZAN [back in two-shot, and chiming in while resuming the poking gesture]: Jane. Jane. Jane.

JANE: Jane.

TARZAN: Jane.

JANE [in same shot, pointing at Tarzan]: You? [then pointing back to herself, and with a rising interrogative tone] Jane . . . [then pointing at him] You? And you . . . ?

TARZAN [in reverse shot over her shoulder, eyes widening in apparent comprehension and while beating on his own chest]: Tarzan. Tarzan.

JANE [in same shot]: Tarzan?

TARZAN [back to two-shot, while resuming the poking gesture]: Jane. [then pointing to his own chest] Tarzan. [repeated 6 times with accelerating violence]

JANE [in same shot]: Oh, please stop! Let me go. I can't bear this. Oh, what's the use.

TARZAN [in reverse shot over her shoulder, while gesturing to his open mouth]: Hoona? Hoona? [then while slapping first his belly, then hers] Hoona!

JANE: Oh yes, I am hungry.

JANE [now in a longer two-shot as Tarzan stands on branch]: Tarzan! Tarzan! Where are you going? Tarzan! Tarzan! Don't go without me. I'm afraid of her [Ooma, the maternal ape chased off at the beginning of the scene].

JANE [as she enters shot of right to left pan following Tarzan's departure]: Oh, I'm coming.

[The scene closes with an overlap dissolve.]

The visual syntax deserves separate comment, but it is important to note here that nowhere in the scene, indeed nowhere in the film, does the line "Me Tarzan, you Jane" actually occur. A "me" becomes a "Jane," and a "you" becomes a "Tarzan" (which, strictly speaking, is a reversal of the line parodied by Marnie, duly reflecting the link between English and the subject of enunciation), but that's about as close as the scene comes. However, like Jane, Marnie is Mark's captive, and Hitchcock's narrativization of the Stockholm syndrome as family romance obviously seeks to underscore its "popular" pedigree. Feminist scholars have drawn attention to the sexual politics at work in Hitchcock, but the link between Freud and primitivism, that is, Eurocentric racism, put in play here has perhaps been most emphatically underscored in Nandy's *Savage Freud*, a text to which I have already referred. Without rehashing these arguments, it is nevertheless worth supplementing them by concentrating on the grammatical mark of foreignness that is contained in the dialogue intertextually summoned by Hitchcock.[7]

Clarifying this requires the emphasis of two issues in particular. First, there is the matter of the suspended copula reiterated in *Marnie*. A competent English speaker might more properly convey the sense of "Me Jane" by saying "I am Jane" or even "My name is Jane," relying on the copular function in English to render "Jane" a nominative predicate of "I," the subject of the sentence. Indeed, this is precisely what Jane does in the original exchange. Thus, what the suspension of the copula signals, though not simply, is the fact that the sentence is either spoken by a non-English speaker or to a non-English speaker, specifically someone deemed incompetent in use of the language. When, through the substitution of Freud for Tarzan, this incompetence is looped through the chain: infant, unconscious, primitive, savage (whether noble or not), the copula takes on a special link to foreignness in the dialogue and on the soundtrack.[8] But what are we to make of the fact that, as noted, the line "Me Tarzan, you Jane" is absent from Van Dyke's film? I suppose one might cast about for other intertextual possibilities, for example, Joseph Newman's abysmal remake of *Tarzan, the Ape Man* from 1959, but more is to be gained, I think, from paying special attention to the gesturing that supplements the exchange between Tarzan and Jane Parker. At the point where "Jane" and "Tarzan" are actually articulated together and as proper names, Tarzan is poking his knuckles into Jane's shoulder and then pounding on his own chest. Pointing, as Wittgenstein might have said, supplements the missing copula. Tarzan, in seeking to cut through the entanglement of shifters while not yet being able to grasp the linguistic copula introduced by Jane ("I'm Jane Parker"), uses pointing and striking to convey (in the strict sense) "you are" and "I am." In this sense, that is, as Tarzan speaks and points/strikes, the line "Me Tarzan, you Jane" takes place, indeed, it takes the place of a copular function that is otherwise absent. Perhaps this is why the scene so strongly evokes the miscegenational copulation that the Hays Office would later censor. As Tarzan's pointing/striking accelerates and intensifies, the excitement that wells up in him and finally prompts Jane's line "Oh please stop. Let me go. I can't bear it" assumes a distinctly copulatory character. The maternal threat that closes the scene establishes a rivalry that supports such a reading. Given that one of the key dilemmas faced by Mark Rutland (an expert in "instinctual behavior," or, why not, "rutting") is Marnie's frigidity, indeed, a frigidity produced by her mother, it would seem that the very absence of the line "Me Tarzan, you Jane" is what rendered it attractive to Hitchcock. Frankly though, what is crucial is not immediately the evocation of "jungle fever," but the fact that the "native tongue" spoken by Tarzan is marked as one lacking the copular "to be." He cannot hear this in Jane's speech, in spite of the fact that the monosyllabic "me" drew more immediate attention than the polysyllabic, and therefore presumably more perplexing, "protecting" in her first line of dialogue. Setting aside the enormously fascinating questions raised by "hoona" and "Ooma," that is, the concocted language spoken by Tarzan and understood by animals, what remains of interest is the way "foreignness" thus appears figured in speech as a copular suspension.[9]

The second matter that bears emphasis here is the link between "foreignness" and copular suspension. This is not an association restricted to the representation of Tarzan's speech, who, after all, as Burroughs's story has it, has a native "competence" in English (with predictable colonial assurance Jane protests her father's callous dismissal of Tarzan's suffering by insisting, "but he's white"). In fact, the suspension of the copula is a prominent feature of what Michael Hilger has called "movie Indian." Though perhaps more typically associated with the liberal use of the adverb "heap" and the all-purpose, indiscriminately used suffix "um" (as exemplified, for example, in Disney's *Peter Pan*), movie Indian resorts to the same grammatical signal of foreignness. Consider, for example, the following scene from George Seitz's *Last of the Mohicans*, made only four years after the Van Dyke film. At its core is an exchange, awkward in its own way, between Cora Munro (daughter of British General Munro) and Uncas (son of Chingachgook, the last of the Mohicans). They are awaiting the arrival of Hawkeye and Cora's sister, Alice, after having been separated during a preceding chase. The scene unfolds in twelve shots.

UNCAS [in medium long shot with foursome]: Hawkeye bring sister soon.
CORA [in same shot]: I hope so.

UNCAS [traversing shot and sitting next to Cora]: Hawkeye find way, like Indian. Hawkeye same as Uncas's brother.

CORA [in two-shot, gesturing off-screen]: And the other one? Is he your father?

UNCAS [in same shot]: Chingachgook, Sagamore. Great chief of Mohicans.

CORA [in same shot]: And you?

UNCAS [in same shot reaches down to gesture at chest]: Uncas. [extreme close up of sign on chest] This mean Mohican chief.

CORA [back in two-shot]: Mohican? Are you taking us to your people?

UNCAS [in close up on face]: All my people gone. Killed in Huron war. Once, many warriors in our tribe. For many summer, this our hunting ground. [back to two-shot] Now, only Chingachgook and Uncas left.

CORA [in same shot]: You're all alone. So am I.

UNCAS: Hmm

CORA: My warrior died at sea.

UNCAS: He die chief?

CORA [still in same shot]: In your way of speaking, yes.

UNCAS: Then your son, like him, will be him chief.

CORA: Makes a nice dream sometimes.

UNCAS [in same shot, turns and reaches in bag, then quick cut away to disapproving glare of Chingachgook, then back to two-shot] Here. You eat.

CHINGACHGOOK [medium shot]: Mohican chief no wait on squaw!

Having circled around to Chingachgook imparting wisdom about beavers (the "Indian's sentinel"), the scene breaks off as a slapping beaver tail (clap stick?) announces the return of Hawkeye and Alice.

The resonances between this scene and the encounter between Tarzan and Jane are considerable. Although, strictly speaking, they articulate opposing narrative functions (Cora has been spared captivity, while Jane has fallen into captivity), the two scenes orbit tightly around what I am calling the suspended copular function. As Chingachgook correctly perceives, Uncas is "hitting" on the grieving Cora, and as the plot unfolds we learn that Cora and Uncas are indeed destined for a union that occurs only in death. In a scene that calls up "Little Sister's" rape-avoiding plunge in Griffith's *Birth of a Nation*, Cora joins Uncas at the bottom of a cliff in order to avoid Magua's lecherous designs. As their dying hands cross, the ring given to Cora by her dead "warrior" gleams up into the spectators' eyes. The "chief" their copulation was to have optimally produced and about which Cora liked to dream is terminally suspended, producing the interior motivation for the text's title. For it is with the death of Uncas and the children he and Cora might have produced, that Chingachgook does indeed become the last of the Mohicans.

Additionally, this narrative material is powerfully fused with the linguistic copula in Cora's response to Uncas's query about the status of her "dead warrior" when she answers, "In your way of speaking, yes." Here "your way of speaking" means both "in your world" and "in your tongue." Significantly, as the exchange makes abundantly clear, Uncas's tongue does not make use of the copular "to be." Like Tarzan, when asked his name, Uncas points to his chest (and the sign emblazoned there) and says his name. Indeed, every Indian of every tribe depicted in the film speaks in the same way. When the villainous double agent Magua introduces himself early in the film, he echoes Tarzan, saying, "Me Magua scout. Come see big white Chief Munro." Thus, the linguistic copula is not only suspended, but its suspension is thematized both in relation to miscegenational copulation (as indicated, Magua emerges as Uncas's rival for Cora) and in relation to "foreignness." It is important to note that, in Cooper's novel, the narrator spares us the sound of movie Indian by indicating that the reported speech of Chingachgook and the other Indians is translated, although the narrator cannot resist the temptation of calling attention to the "guttural" tone of Chingachgook's speech, declaring in a footnote that, in fact, tone is the vital element in Indian languages. What this brings to the fore is the degree to which the "foreignness" linked to copular suspension is not only "universal," that is, it is used indiscriminately to signal the "foreignness" of Africans, Indians, and as we shall see, aliens, but that this linkage is intimately linked to the cinema. In other words, there appears to be some sort of default mechanism triggered within Western cinema whereby, when "foreign" speech must be represented, and represented as both Anglo-phonically communicative and foreign, the linguistic copula drops out. Doubtless it was precisely this legacy whose end was celebrated (prematurely, I might add) in Kevin Costner's *Dances with Wolves*, where Native Americans actually conversed in Lakota, a language (actually a dialect of Dakota) in fact taught to the actors by academic linguists (Hilger 227).

As suggested, aliens have not been spared this linguistic strategy. Indeed, the very consummation of the tendency sketched here may well rest in the creation of the Klingon language spoken by the aliens from the Klingon Empire in *Star Trek: The Next Generation* in the films based on this series and in the various spin-offs, *Deep Space Nine* and *Star Trek: Voyager*. Developed by Marc Okrand, and now even taught at Auburn University, Klingon is a fully articulated language (it has both a lexicon and a grammar) that, when spoken on screen, is subtitled so as to convey the otherwise incomprehensible dialogue to Earthlings, but also—given the function assigned to subtitling by AMPAS—to convey, in fact literally to underscore, the "foreignness" of Klingon speech. True, there are many races of aliens included in the various *Star Trek* series—Vulcans, Romulans, Borg, and so on—and all of them speak in English, so while "foreignness" is not made equivalent to aliens (indeed the Federation, the group lead by English-speaking Earthlings, is constitutionally committed to a liberal form of anthropological multiculturalism), linguistic "foreignness" is nevertheless represented in the suspension of the copula.

Lacking fluency in Klingon I was fortunate to come upon the name of Mark Shoulson who, it turns out, is as native a speaker of Klingon as there can be. Noting that, in the *Klingon Dictionary* (Okrand), "we are Klingons" is rendered "tlhingan Mah," (literally "Klingons we"), I asked Shoulson about the apparent suspension of the linguistic copula in Klingon and received the following response:

> Your understanding of the copula in Klingon isn't "quite" right. We'll get into that. Yes, he deliberately wanted the language not to have a copula (like Russian, Hebrew, etc.). He's said that that was one thing he was

pretty adamant on, and was therefore flatfooted when they asked him to coin "To be or not to be" on one foot. Klingon doesn't have a copula, true. But its pronouns are used rather like a copula, so "tlhIngan Mah" may not sound quite so "verbless" as you might think. See, in third person, when it's "Qangor is a/the captain," the Klingon is "not" "Captain—Qangor" (or vice versa) like it would be in Russian, say. Rather, it's (HoD ghaH Qangor'e'): (ghaH) is the third-person singular animate (sentient) pronoun. And the -'e' suffix (normally topic or maybe focus) is mandatory in this construction. Perhaps its origins are something like, "It's Qangor, the captain" or some such. You can come up with various possible derivations. (e-mail to author, 29 September 2000)

Of the many important observations solicited by these remarks, perhaps the most immediately pertinent is the fact that, although Shoulson clearly establishes the limits of my understanding of the language, he concedes the crucial issue: "Klingon doesn't have a copula, true." Moreover, it is by no means insignificant that the linguistic models for Klingon are not only Eurocentric, but that they are perhaps the two most ideologically freighted languages of the twentieth century. Evoking alternately the "evil empire" and "the Jews," the "foreignness" built into Klingon cannot help but cast the Federation as a body politic torn by the conflict between Communism and Fascism, that is, capitalist Earth. However, unlike Tarzan and Uncas, who speak a broken English, Worf (a prominent and recurrent Klingon character) speaks fluent English. It is only when he converses in his native tongue that the suspension of the copula becomes audible. Doubtless, this represents a concession to the comparatively advanced character of the Klingon Empire (a concession motivated by the very codes of the science fiction genre) rather than a desire to break the fundamental link between "foreignness" and the suspension, or as Shoulson prefers, the reorganization of the copula. Apparently, in the future, aliens will have developed a language modeled on the speech of Tarzan and Uncas, much as if all of the television signals we have been broadcasting into the ear of the Other since 1947 had been interpreted as intergalactic language lessons. Tonto was no *tonto*.

Of course, most other instances of "movie alien"—for example, the famous line, "Gort, Klaatu Barada Nikto" (Gort, take Klaatu to the spaceship) from Robert Wise's *The Day the Earth Stood Still*—cannot easily be parsed for their copulas, but surely Klingon establishes the difficulty that greets one bent on interpreting the suspension of the copula as merely an index of primitiveness. Even if we insist that the Klingons are cast as "tribal," they read more like posthuman *Übermenschen* than neanderthals. A small point, to be sure, but one that bears emphasis, because otherwise the temptation is great to simply collapse "foreignness" into primitiveness, when in fact it is a rather sophisticated articulation with language that is at issue.[10] Of the two points raised by such an assertion, only one has been much attended to in the discussion of Tarzan, Uncas, and Worf. To shift then from a discussion of how "foreignness" is registered in the language spoken in a film to how film language is, as it were, made foreign, another pass over the scenes discussed above is required.

Attention must now focus on what has been called "the grammar of the shot," the visual syntax that articulates the copular suspensions I have emphasized. For example, in the scene from *Tarzan, the Ape Man*, it is not insignificant that a certain editing pattern underwrites its unfolding. As my transcription of the dialogue makes clear, there is an important oscillation throughout between a medium two-shot of Tarzan and Jane, and a shot reverse that adopts first Jane's perspective, then Tarzan's. The shot reverse has emerged as one of the unambiguous ways to convey to spectators "X is talking to/with Y." When, in the silent period, it was interrupted or framed by an intertitle, its grammatical function was almost too clear. Of course, it is also possible to convey the fact of a conversation through the use of the two-shot in which, no surprise, two people are shown talking. What is interesting about the scene I have described is the way this "grammar" interacts with the grammatical fate of the linguistic copula. On the one hand, the editing consolidates with requisite stealth the fact of an exchange that is failing but that is nevertheless taking place. After Tarzan mistakenly points to himself saying "You?" the two-shot within which they have been framed switches to a shot reverse over his shoulder in which Jane says, "No," shaking her head in weary frustration. In the same shot, she then delivers the line, "I'm Jane Parker. Understand? Jane, Jane!" Here, of course, the linguistic copula enters (though it can hardly go without saying that the syncope of the contraction assumes an otherwise unwarranted significance here), and it enters in its most conspicuous, that is, pronounced fashion. Immediately, there is a cut back to the two-shot in which the poking, the copulating, begins. One might say, therefore, that the grammar of the shot reverse enters to facilitate an exchange that is otherwise only slouching toward predication. The copular suspension interfering with predication and thus the exchange (ultimately, as Lévi-Strauss predicted, an exchange of a woman) is itself suspended in this shot, as if by that very coincidence motivating the reintroduction of the two-shot, that is, the shot in which Tarzan becomes Tarzan, Jane becomes Jane, and they become a couple.

It is crucial that the labor of facilitation appear, in contrast to the belabored exchange, familiar, that is, not foreign. Indeed, my argument is that it is precisely by stealthily effecting a coupling whose limits seem figured in the suspension of the copula, the "foreignness" of this suspension is exchanged with the Western-all-too-Western spectators. As a windfall, the grammar of the shot disappears into the "foreignness" whose conveyance it facilitates, thus striking up a deeply unsettled relation to that very "foreignness," a relation in which a certain Western film language becomes the purveyor of languages whose "foreignness" is there to be heard while, at that instance and through that act, becoming foreign to the very cinema in which this language emerged.

Not surprisingly, since this dynamic resonates strongly with the discursive logic teased out of Vogel's characterization of the "foreign language film," one finds some of the same ambivalence in scholarship concerned with the concept of film language. Consider, for example, Thorold Dickinson's *A Discovery of Cinema* from 1971. Written once he had retired from filmmaking and in the heyday of "cine-semiotics" (Metz's *Essais sur le signification au cinéma* had just appeared), Dickinson's study addresses itself to virtually all the issues broached in this chapter.

Notably, he not only discusses the advent of the concept of language as a description of the cinema, but, late in the book, he also warns against the danger of attaching "the language of one media to the study of another" (147), revealing that his grasp of the concept of language is subtle. Put concisely, he recognizes that language functions both as phenomenon (the analytic language credentialized in any given discipline) and as paradigm (the "model" used to describe the object of any given discipline). In an important footnote he writes the following:

> It was the French who first described cinema as a *langage*. The heresy arose out of the mistranslation of the word as "language." The French word for language is *langue*. *Langage* means speech, a way of speaking. *Le langage du cinéma* means a visual way of telling a story or making a statement: the phrase was never intended to lead to the study of grammar and syntax. (20)

In the body of the text, where the term "heresy" is first used, Dickinson is elaborating a distinction made earlier between film (a product tailored to sophisticated spectators) and movie (a product mass produced for the multitudes), drawing on Griffith's *Intolerance*. The claim is that language emerged as a compelling way to describe movies because these visually conventional products were script driven. A "scene" would be conceived and shot as if in a theater and then made visually interesting by introducing perfectly standardized edits. For Dickinson, *Intolerance*—even where it failed—was something else entirely.

What is of interest here is not Dickinson's perfectly conventional view of Griffith. Instead, what is striking is this "insider's" (Dickinson was both a filmmaker and a teacher/scholar) perception of the introduction of the concept of "language" within the study of the cinema. He refers to three crucial issues. First, and most obviously, is his reiterated use of the term "heresy." Derived from the Greek, where it denotes "factioning" or a taking of sides, the term has come to have the rather more specific connotation of taking sides against Rome, and the Roman Catholic Church in particular. For someone born in Bristol at the turn of the century (Dickinson may even have been Anglican) to stress the

French character of any given heresy obliges the otherwise simply over-determined character of such a gesture to assume both national and religious overtones. Thus, the French appeal to the concept of language is doubly "foreign": it is not British/English, and it is not Catholic. Though Dickinson does not go on to identify the precise profile of the "church" profaned by such heresy (presumably it would be the sect comprised of "film-," not movie-, makers), it is clear that he recognizes the gravity of the situation.[11]

Second, and this point follows immediately from the preceding one, Dickinson is keen to thematize the distinctly linguistic dimension of the heresy. Drawing attention to the distinction made in French between *langue* and *langage*, and tying the heretical act to a mistranslation, Dickinson complicates his invocation of heresy by suggesting it had something to do with the British reception of French theory, a reception in which one term, "*langue*," was confused with another, "*langage*." Given that, in the very appendix where he counsels against the drift of analytic languages, Dickinson goes on to urge film students to develop a "reading knowledge of English and French and if possible a third language" (148), it is clear that his linguistic clarifications are far from pedantic. Which is why, of course, the misleading character of his remarks may mean more than he says. As any careful, indeed French-speaking, reader of Metz would know, it is important not to translate *langage* as speech, for it is precisely in the French scene—about which Dickinson is apparently concerned—that speech is rendered as *parole* and thus contrasted with *langue*. As Metz famously put it, the cinema is "*une langage sans langue*." Yes, *langage* does have the connotation of "national tongue" or, as Dickinson says, "way of speaking," but that is not yet speech in the strict sense given the term by the theorists that mattered to Metz. What is important here is not, however, the perfectly predictable failure of translation. Instead, what matters is the way Dickinson, in the context of a denunciation of this particular heresy, implicitly though insistently moves to link speech and the cinema. When he insists that the French intervention was not intended to legitimate an interest in "grammar and syntax" but rather to draw attention to the "visual way of telling a story," he is clearly reorienting the cinema around the task of delivering, as he says, telling (the evocation of the "oral" is unmistakable), a story. Telling is obviously akin to speech, and indeed, Dickinson, in spite of his appeal to the visual, thinks of the film as something like a speech act. The fact that the telling of the story might rest upon visual "ways" (read: codes and conventions) that work to facilitate such telling represents precisely the perspective that deserves the characterization of heresy.

It is also significant that at the heart of this business lies the foreign language question. Insofar as mistranslation arises here as an issue, in fact, as *the* issue, it does so because languages foreign to one another have come into contact. In effect, what Dickinson says is that, due to the influence of a foreign language (French), a foreign/heretical language/ description has come to attach itself to the cinema, potentially obscuring the fact that the cinema is, insofar as it is, in its speech. Because Dickinson insists that "grammar and syntax" ought not apply to film (at a pinch, but only then, they might apply to movies), even though, as visual *ways* of telling a story, they obviously do, he can be said to be repeating Vogel's position, but now from the vantage point of the paradigm. Thus, the notion that the cinema can be studied as though it were a language is strictly foreign to a concept of the cinema that, conceived as essentially speech, functions to present spectators with what in the end are problems of translation, that is, confusing dialogue or simply subtitles that fall short.

The kinship this bears with Vogel's ambivalent posture can be clarified by elaborating the third issue raised by Dickinson's cited remarks, namely, the issue of enunciation. When clarifying presumably Metz's intentions, Dickinson contrasts, "telling a story or making a statement"; he invokes the distinction between statement and enunciation, where statement connotes the form and content of an expression and enunciation the act of making it. At one level, of course, he is simply making the standard move of accommodating the nonfiction film within the scope of his remarks. A documentary might not be telling a story, but it is certainly making a statement. It is certainly a film, and Dickinson himself made such films. However, in the context he has fashioned, especially in a context where his remarks have summoned forth the concept of *parole* without saying it, statement—by drawing attention to the verbs "telling" and "making"—puts the concept of enunciation in play. Who or what speaks without recourse to speech? Well, Dickinson to be sure, but it is not insignificant that his repudiation of an interest in grammar and syntax, a repudiation that puts the concept of the cinema in orbit around speech, indeed the speech act, is formulated so as to activate and suppress the concept of enunciation. Put more directly, for someone keen to translate *langage* as *parole*, the difference between telling (a story) and making (a statement) should have mattered more. The fact that this difference is put in play at all suggests that in the offscreen space of this discussion hovers a properly ambivalent relation between speech and enunciation, a relation that belies the confidence with which Dickinson corrects the British reception of French theory and renders the concepts of grammar and syntax as "foreign" to the cinema. Like Vogel, Dickinson knows that there is something syntactical at work not only in the cinema, but in its study. In trying to avoid saying this, he reveals that, in fact, the discourse he appeals to in order to make his point knows this better than he does.

Of course, Dickinson and Vogel are not alone in this dilemma. When, in 1974, the filmmaker and scholar James Potts brought the matter to a head by asking, "Is there an international film language?" he powerfully, though perhaps unwittingly, underscored the tenacity of the ambivalence discerned in Vogel and Dickinson. In fact, Potts draws attention to the "translation" problem posed by Dickinson, but ambivalence registers more palpably in his essay in the restless shifting of positions it charts.

Doubtless because it is framed interrogatively ("Is there . . ."), Potts's essay solicits the very attention I focus on it. The austerity of the "yes" or "no" called for by the title is complicated from the outset by the unmanageable tone of interrogation. To address this Potts begins "personally," almost apologetically (the mood of remorse is palpable), recounting work done by him in Ethiopia and Kenya as a filmmaker and educator. A past is created in this recounting. As he says more than once,

"I used to believe . . . ," going on to address first the existence of an international film language and then the value-free status of the camera. This establishes the position that his essay wishes to depart from: although he used to believe that there was an international film language, *now* he doesn't. Realizing that this unleashes two wild words, "international" and "language," he turns to address the concept of language as applied to film, drawing attention to Dickinson's characterization of it as heretical. Although it is clear that he wishes to distance himself from such a conclusion, the interrogative and remorseful tone of the essay, coupled with its reiteration of the theme of guilt ("How many of us are guilty" [75]; "We are all guilty" [78]), bring his discussion within the distinctly theological orbit of Dickinson's. What is important here is not, however, this alignment, but that Potts's desire to see the cinema as speech supports it.

Clearly impatient with Roy MacBean's anti-intellectual dismissal of semiology, Potts goes on to salvage (his rhetoric is distinctly archaeological) language, but in the guise of speech. This prompts a rephrasing of his opening question, whereby he begins to speculate on the existence of national speech patterns or styles, phenomena that at one point he calls "foreign film languages," providing this study with the referent for its enabling spoonerism. The development is important because it establishes that the more vexed term in his title is "international," as if the troubling part of the link between language and film was expressed in the French *langage*, that is, the notion of the language system at work within any national tongue or speech act. Pursuing this prompts an interesting reflection on national styles and specific camera technologies, a reflection whose rigors cause Potts to, as he says, "withdraw to my earlier position, that all we can really talk about is the *style* of an *individual* director" (80; italics in original). In the process, language as speech has given way to film as "private language," a development that, as Wittgenstein might have pointed out, allows him to cozy up again to MacBean.

At this point Potts's position has shifted from a repentant dismissal of international film language to a defensive and tentative affirmation of film as speech, to a defeated withdrawal into the antilinguistic notion of personal style or idiom. However, the consummate articulation of his ambivalence appears when the essay concludes. He writes:

> Film-making can be thought of as a form of universal speech, linking all individuals and communities, setting up its own average in terms of under-standing and interpretation: but we know that the same signs are not united with the same concepts—rather the signs which are apparently the same are often associated with different concepts in different cultures. . . . But I still prefer to think that film-making is a form of universal speech—not so much a "Visual Esperanto" as a developing visual language with a rich variety of dialects and idiolects which contain both alien and indigenous elements. (81)

Here, the figure of speech returns triumphant but with a new adjective in tow: the universal. In effect, Potts has backtracked to the position that resulted when, in fending off Dickinson and MacBean, he both established speech as the proper avatar of language in the domain of film and abandoned internationalism. Earlier disparaging remarks about the United Nations ("far from there being an international language of cinema, an internationally agreed UN charter of conventions and grammatical rules" [79]), grafted to a call for "linking individuals and communities," here blossom in the displacement of internationalism with universalism, a development Walter Benjamin would not hesitate to call the "aestheticization of politics." However, even as this unfolds, Potts hesitates, "but," "but," forwarding and rewinding over the join between film and language. Aware that "we are guilty" of imposing, at the international level, technical and aesthetic standards or expressive constraints through the dissemination of the collective apparatus of enunciation we call the cinema, yet preferring, wishing, perhaps even desiring that through this very imposition a new kind of "universal peace" (to invoke Kant) will prevail. True, these openly geopolitical themes are absent from Dickinson, but what both writers share is the struggle to conceal language as an apparatus of enunciation behind language as speech when cementing the former to the cinema. In this way, but in accord with different idiolects, they join in rendering language "foreign" to cinema. And while Potts's insistence upon the presence of "alien" and "indigenous" elements in the universal speech of the cinema is one with which I am in obvious accord—the very notion of a "bilingual" enunciation depends on the duality at stake there—this particular choice of vocabulary, calling up as it does both Worf and Uncas, clearly means more than it says. Perhaps it is where the "foreignness" of the link between language and the cinema is most blindingly illuminated.

Intermission

Before turning to the textual analyses, the comparative readings of Ousmane Sembene and Jorge Sanjinés that conclude this text, a few enabling features of these analyses require additional comment. Specifically, more needs to be said about bilingual enunciation and its relation to the unlivable conditions of postcoloniality. Although my aim here is primarily to clarify the terms of my reading, I will also, for those eager to know, spoil the ending by anticipating at least the concerns of my conclusions such as they are.

In striking out for the poetics of postcoloniality I have had Edouard Glissant's "poetics of relation" (*poétique de la relation*) in mind from the beginning. Although largely framed in terms of a theory of Caribbean discourse, the poetics of relation insists upon the theoretical principle of derivation, that is, the proposition that cultural identity is not given transcendentally, in advance, but that what identity there is arises in relation, in the multiple encounters among cultures and their languages. In *The Poetics of Relation*, he poaches a page from Bakhtin's playbook, arguing that poetry (not the novel) is uniquely and intensely stirred by what Bakhtin called the international encounters among languages. Arguing that this encounter is precisely what Victor Segalen meant by the "exotic," Glissant develops a poetics that places exoticism—the recognition of the moral and aesthetic centrality of the Other—at the heart of both Being and the word.

Numerous historical and political categories dot the maritime surface of his texts—the plantation system, exile, the colony, and so on—
but Glissant is careful not to, in his mind, reduce his poetics to such
events. While I see the wisdom of such a strategy, it has its risks. Specifically, if one wants to think through the link between poetics and politics, what are we to make then of what has appropriately been called
the politics of relation? Rather than tease out precisely how Glissant
belongs to what I earlier evoked as the derivation or sociogenesis of
poststructuralism from the conditions of postcoloniality, let me cut to
the chase by stressing that a specific form of relation defines the structural dynamics of a postcolonial poetics. It is necessarily, to preserve
the taxonomy of structure, diachronic and in that sense indissociable
from what Saussure would call linguistic variability. Crucial here is a
prior moment, one in which a relation is imposed and at the same time
denied. Initially, it is a relation of nonrelation, Fanon's "initial phase" of
colonialism. This is not the result of a distinction between reality (the
relation) and appearance (the nonrelation). It is the result of a relation
between groups who have unequal access to the means (cultural, social,
economic) by which to defer the crises that plague all identities. Indeed,
part of really breaking off or otherwise denying the postcolonial relation involves making the alterity alive within it belong to the Other; it
becomes the Other's responsibility. This does not mean that vicious
exploitation is not taking place; it means only that such exploitation can
be handled, managed, in effect, legitimated.

This initial moment is followed, both logically and temporally,
by an exceptional state wherein a new relation is forged—in the mode of
suspension—with the relation of nonrelation. The unlivable tenacity
of this suspended relation (and the antithetical meanings of the word
"suspension" are important here) derives from the way breaking off or
away from the prior moment has always already been actualized in the
nonrelation itself. How does one reclaim an "us" from a "them" when
the relation that produced this distinction only takes place once it is
too late, once the us and the them are, as it were, in suspension? Fanon
famously described the situation by insisting upon the fact that the

colonial subject lacked an Other, by virtue of occupying its place, by being the Other. As I will argue, the postcolonial condition cannot be reversed through a nostalgic recovery of the precolonial moment nor can it be endured as is. Precisely because it is the sort of relation it is, the postcolonial condition demands a future for which we lack the politics.

Jacques Derrida, in *The Monolingualism of the Other* (a text written in dialogue with Glissant and, even more directly, Abdelkebir Khatibi), allows one to forge the link between the poetics of nonrelation and language, ultimately, bilingualism. In its opening pages, this text is written in the form of a dialogue. His interlocutor is hostile (or is she or he hospitable?) and, though the matters aired are of some consequence (Derrida ridicules the Habermasean concept of "the performative contradiction," the idea that, because Derrida speaks repeatedly and persuasively of the truth, he must—contrary to the supposed tenets of deconstruction believe in it), more important is the textual function of the dialogue. It is a staged relation of nonrelation. As such, it works to establish that, precisely when we most see ourselves as "in dialogue," we are least in contact with one another. As is said, we talk past one another. This reiteration of his beef with Gadamerean hermeneutics is paired with a series of citations and readings in which the impossibility of translinguistic or intercultural communication/translation is front and center. Again, crucial here is the matter of function. This material works to establish the counterintuitive insight that language operates most effect-fully when its obstruction of understanding is the explicit topic of exchange. Taken together, the dialogue and the citations mime in textual form the paradox that animates the essay, that is, the prepositional gambit: "I have only one language, and yet it is not mine." Or, riffing off Hegel's maxim—my opinion (*Meinung*) is mine—my language is not mine.

In what sense does this miming take place? Most of Derrida's citations derive from Khatibi's *Amour bilingue* ("bilingual love," though translated into English as *Love in Two Languages*), a text written in both French and Arabic that situates love both in and in between the languages shared by the narrator and his interlocutor (a mother, a lover, a maternal tongue). Although, as with any text worth reading, it solicits more than one reading, the text can be said to posit love not as what is impossible, but as what arises in surviving the impossible communication between and across languages. Derrida, in citing this material and seeking to radicalize its implications—motivating, no doubt, his repeated expressions of friendship and affection toward Khatibi—makes it clear that one is, in effect, possessed by the language which is not one. It provides the frame, at once national and onto-epistemological, through which one thinks. In this sense it renders a certain dialogue improbable, if not impossible. It is not for nothing that the text opens by drawing oblique attention to the national encounter (French and German) at stake in the dialogue with Habermas. By the same token, the dialogic exchange—though presented in one language (French)—seems actually to be articulated either in a language not shared by the interlocutors or in several languages, only bits and pieces of which are mutually comprehensible. Derrida, in a moment of feigned exasperation, insists that, no matter how many times he might repeat verbatim a given formulation, it would always be misheard. In other words, precisely because we are each possessed by a language that is not ours, our dialogue is only potentially fruitful when we modestly seek to confront this very dilemma.

In radicalizing Khatibi's approach, Derrida is seeking to theorize the relation at work in bilingualism. Surprisingly, he pursues this through the concept of monolingualism rather than that of poly- or multilingualism.[1] Because his reasoning (yes, reasoning) matters to my own investment in bilingual enunciation, it bears brief elaboration. Predictably, the key point is that of the Other. In what sense is someone or something properly designated the Other always monolingual (or, for that matter, monotheistic)? There are at least two senses: first, the Other is monolingual because it is only in our encounter with another language, the Other's language, that we recognize, with humbling intimacy, that the language we have is only one among many. And second, the Other is always monolingual—and here, despite the obvious parallels, the allusion is Levinasian rather than Lacanian—because the language that, as it were, has us, has each of us and possesses us from a site of radical alterity, can only be named through some language or other, indeed through the *one* language we consult when making sense of Freud's question, "where do(es) *I* come from?" This illuminates, perhaps unexpectedly, the title of Derrida's essay, a title that pivots around an in/exclusive "or": *The Monolingualism of the Other; or, The Prosthesis of Origin.* In other words, in anticipation of the insight about possession and plurality, the "or" functions to make "the monolingualism of the other" say the same thing as "the prosthesis of origin," suggesting, indeed implying, that the Other is monolingual *because* the origin is "prosthetized."

The complexities here are legion, but let me draw out what I take to be the salient and, for my purposes, vital point. While it may be true that in any given geopolitical territory many languages coexist, the suspended relation of nonrelation at the heart of postcoloniality is one in which an other language, the language of the Other, usually because of its alignment with the state apparatus (the government, the schools, and so on) has redivided the linguistic universe in two. Once this realignment has made common cause with a denial of the relation itself—the colonizers wished only to relate to the same, that is, to those who speak their language, who talk their talk—it locates alterity first in the relation itself but then in the colonial subjects themselves. Bilingualism is the tactic of those who in surviving colonialism nevertheless speak within its legacy. It is a tactic aimed at drawing out not simply the monolingualism of the Other and returning the "gift" of alterity, but the logic of relation at work within the condition of postcoloniality. Put differently, if it made sense to think the colonial encounter in terms of class struggle (a story too well established to bear repeating), it was because, just as the capitalist mode of production had narrowed things down to the showdown between the bourgeoisie and the proletariat, so too had imperialism (the highest stage of capitalism) divided the colonial world between the colonizer and the colonized. Even if, as many anticolonial intellectuals were to insist (think here of the *négritude* partisans in particular), this reduction left too many disputes unaddressed, much less resolved, the structure of conflict—the friend/foe dyad—exhibits, from one moment to the next, a certain duple character. For me, beyond the linguistic "facts" to which it may or may not refer, bilingualism thus designates, conceptually, the structure of this conflict as it is put to work in cultural politics.[2]

But what then of enunciation? Perhaps unwittingly Derrida again gives us a place to start by both posing and staging the question of enunciation in the opening pages of *Monolingualism*. In particular, he places the word in the mouth of his hostile interlocutor, indeed at the very moment when said interlocutor is raising the specter of the "performative contradiction." He writes (in the voice of the Other):

> The moment you say in French that the French language—the one you are speaking in this manner, here at this very moment, the one which renders our words intelligible, more or less . . . —well, that is not your language, even though you have no other one, not only will you find yourself caught up in the "performative contradiction" of enunciation, but you will also worsen the logical absurdity, the lie, in fact, or even the perjury within the statement. How could one have only one language without having any, without any which is theirs? (3)

By saying that this "stages" the question of enunciation, I mean to stress that the passage, apart from putting in play the statement/enunciation pairing, makes a point of its deixis. It literally points to the here and now of its utterance yet does so in a text that complicates the identity of the "enunciator" through the structural device of the dialogue. This staging relates to the posing by suggesting that enunciation is not as simple as it might otherwise seem. Whose "here" is invoked in the text? Is it the one pronounced *ici*, the one pronounced *hier*, the one pronounced *here*, or all of the above? Do these all come from the same place, and do they refer to the same site? Regardless of how such matters might be resolved, the staging of enunciation, while clearly invoking its "collective assemblage," is also insisting upon its reflexivity, that is, the fact that enunciation puts statements in relation both to themselves and to their production as statements. By resuscitating Lacan's account of the Cretan's paradox, Derrida is associating enunciation not with the "other scene" of the unconscious, but with the otherness, the alterity, of monolingualism. Moreover, he is doing it in a way that urges us to think about the distinctive traffic between a text's saying and its doing enabled by its enunciative modes of reflexivity. In this, Derrida aligns himself, implicitly of course, with all those who have recognized how little enunciation has to do with a narrow disciplinary construal of linguistics.

Indeed, the emphasis here on reflexivity brings out a perhaps unanticipated link between Derrida's discussion and that of Metz in *L' Enonciation impersonnelle*, one that provides us with an important perspective on bilingual enunciation. If we recall that Metz sought to link enunciation with the semiological means by which some parts of a text talk about other parts of that text, in short with the codes and gestures of reflexivity, then Derrida's insistence upon the otherness of such monolingual talk prompts us to affirm, albeit from an entirely different angle, what I have called the split in enunciation. The film text is enunciated from multiple sites, or its reflexivity is not only multiple, but divided between conflicting semiological codes. However, here an important implication of Metz's discussion needs to be drawn out. When enunciation was conceded to linguistics and psychoanalysis, it assumed its own quasi-ontological status. Enunciation was enunciation and statements were statements. The deixis served as the *point de capiton*, the sole point at which the twain would meet. Rethought as reflexivity, enunciation touches its statements on many fronts. In fact, the very sorts of portals, frames, and apertures catalogued by Metz would appear to mark, within the film text, the interchanges across which traffic the sayings and doings of a text. As we have seen, this is the lesson of Derrida's staging of the question of enunciation. What this implies, of course, is that the alterity separating monolingualism from itself, an alterity splitting enunciation along the line dividing the Other and the One, is given specific content by the statements it produces. In other words, film texts making statements about the cultural politics of language (whether in their narratives or in their information), precisely through the mechanisms of reflexivity, give content to what might otherwise strike us as a blank or so-called purely formal process. At the same time, they make the question of enunciation, the who-sent-this-from-where-and-to-whom, belong to the statements put in circulation by the film text. Gone then is the ontologically secured rift between enunciation and its statements.

There is an additional implication for our approach to bilingual enunciation. If reflexivity opens up the sorts of intratextual traffic I have described, then reflexivity—especially in the grammatical sense of a verb sharing a subject and direct object—becomes subject to the languages put in conflict by the film's statements. It becomes important then to track how such conflicts put different grammars, different structures of reflexivity, in conflict. Indeed, the whole deep structure of languages can be made to assume significance from the stories in which such structure is made to matter. Thus, the so-called formal processes of shot selection and combination—processes typically conceived of as "universal" (consider here Roman Jakobson's effort to unfurl the canopy of metaphor and metonymy over these processes)—can take on specific semantic content, sense, if you will, by virtue of how enunciation is mapped into the narrative conflicts as modes of its reflexivity. What might constitute a "false match on action" cut in Godard and thus have the semantic content "anti-Hollywood" can, if put to work enunciatively, that is, if cast as a mode of the film's reflexivity, assume a quite different value in a film by Sembene, not because it is a film by Sembene, or made in Senegal, but because the technique is put to work in a text that poses the problem of cinematic resistance and critique. More on this anon, but for now let it suffice to insist upon a repudiation of the idea of the mere formalism or universal blankness of the signs of enunciation. Not only can they take on sense, but they can take on more than one sense, indeed, they can take on conflicted senses.

Needless to say, such a perspective requires that we take a rather particular approach to the analysis of narrative statements. While reluctant simply to revive the structural analysis of narrative as such, Roland Barthes has written usefully on the matter at hand.

> This fact [the lack of a properly linguistic analysis of discourse] is significant: though constituting an autonomous object, discourse is to be

studied from a linguistic basis; if we must grant a working hypothesis to an analysis whose task is enormous and whose materials are infinite, the most reasonable thing is to postulate a homologous relation between sentence and discourse, insofar as the same formal organization apparently regulates all semiotic systems, whatever their substances and dimensions: discourse would be one huge "sentence" (whose units would not necessarily be sentences), just as the sentence, allowing for certain specifications, is a little "discourse." (1994, 98)

As if anticipating the fancy footwork Derrida was to discern in Freud's *Beyond the Pleasure Principle*, Barthes traces here the difficulty of stepping beyond the linguistics of the sentence. As "The Language of Narrative" section of "The Structural Analysis of Narrative" unfolds (the source of the preceding citation), Barthes invites us to consider that narrative, as a discourse, is not only composed of sentences, but that it *is* a sentence. As several pointed allusions remind us, Barthes is thinking here of the approach Lévi-Strauss took in teasing out the "mythemes" of a text, analytic constructions that took the form of minimal (subject-verb-object) sentences. What interests me is that, as Barthes specifies, if such an approach can be applied to all semiotic systems whatever their substance and dimensions, then perhaps there is something to be said for thinking about the sequences and scenes that comprise films as sentences, sentences composed of shots that are themselves little sentences. One certainly senses something like this is at work when examining storyboards and shooting scripts, where events and episodes are often rendered in terse, even cryptic sentences, but sentences just the same.

If this hypothesis (as Barthes calls it) is fleshed out in relation to the recasting of enunciation as reflexivity, something remarkable and relevant is clarified. It becomes possible to treat the sentences comprising the statements of a film, not simply as produced in accord with grammars specific to different languages, but also one can begin to consider how reflexivity itself might be differently inflected by such grammars. In cases where the relevant grammars are quite different (consider here the difference, say, between English and Klingon), the modes of reflexivity, the marks of enunciation, are likely to diverge noticeably. In films that seek to narrate the conflicts among different communities of speakers, specifically communities antagonized by an aggressive politics of language, the intratextual traffic between statements and their enunciation will, almost by dint of necessity, register these conflicts in the conflicted modes of reflexivity. Tracking this and making it matter to the "stories" told by films is crucial to what I am calling the poetics of cinematic postcoloniality. Indeed, one might even go so far as to say that lack of attention to language at this level makes it impossible to analyze postcolonial *films*.

In contexts where films are screened before multilingual audiences, the bilingual enunciation I am calling attention to may actually be harder to discern (especially if the language competence and cultural literacy match the languages antagonized within the film) than in contexts where spectators are resolutely, even stubbornly, monolingual. There the conflicting modalities of enunciation are more likely to be perceived as signs of poor production values, inexpert storytelling, or pretentious vanguardism than anything else. In that sense, they are perceived but not discerned. In either case, something deliberate and specific about the assemblage of the films in question is at risk unless we are prepared to insist upon the need for concepts, for constructions of analysis, that foreground the political value of what is at risk. Although at a certain level it makes sense to say that the United States is a largely monolingual cinematic audience, Derrida's discussion complicates this in important ways. Answering him, perhaps in another sense provoking him, filmmakers have been probing the alterity of monolingualism but in ways that, when not simply lost to us, have been reduced to the odious concerns of niche marketing. Under such circumstances, the sentences organizing the narratives of Hollywood films seem "made in America," when in fact and in so many different ways (the traffic in international styles, the flight from fascism in Europe which transformed Hollywood, the tenacious, even banal, hybridity of popular media, and so on), such films are not American. They are distinctly un-American, but in ways we have deployed the category of the foreign to obscure. "Un-American" is a loaded and therefore provocative term in this context, alluding as it does to the Federal scrutiny of the U.S. film industry in the 1940s and 1950s. While I do not wish to insist upon an alignment between bilingual enunciation and the "foreigners within" (that is, Communists; that is, Jews), I do want to associate the misrecognition (to put it kindly) of enunciative bilingualism with the same sort of xenophobic and ultimately reactionary politics. At the risk of making a mountain out of a molehill, it is not without interest that the acronym for the House Committee on Un-American Activities (HUAC) had to be re-edited (from HCUA) in order to achieve a syntax or sequence that could be readily pronounceable in English.

A brief filmic example will help bring these remarks to a fitting conclusion. During the extended scene of the wedding reception in Sembene's *Xala*, there is a brief sequence that puts a number of the themes discussed here in play. The sequence, comprised of two shots and lasting no more than forty-five seconds, is the second of three such sequences, all of which, from different angles, probe the ambivalent conflicts at the heart of postcolonial Senegal. The first deals with middle-class Senegalese cynicism toward *négritude*, the third deals with the politics of representation, and the second deals with Godard. In the first shot three people are framed, two men and a much younger woman, seated on a lawn swing. As in the first sequence, the dialogue is conducted in French, the colonial tongue. The two men are aggressively, even competitively, flirting with the woman, complimenting her on her mouth, her hairstyle, and so on. As if to trump his rival definitively, one observes that she's the kind of woman he would rent a villa for a weekend to be with. "Weekend" is not rendered as *fin de semaine*, but as "weekend," in English." This prompts the rival to ask, in French, "how do you say 'weekend' in English?" The reply is interrupted by the arrival, in the same shot, of the *maître de cérémonie*, an imposing black woman who offers her services to the group. She is asked for a cigar. As she complies, the earlier question is redirected to her: "excuse me, my friend (*mon amie*), how do you say weekend in English?" To which she replies: "*le weekend c'est le weekend.*" Her reply produces some confusion, and as the two men confer, the woman makes her exit. In the second shot, the *maître de cérémonie* pushes the service cart toward the camera. Suddenly, we see her face break into a huge grin followed by her utterance of the word *shit*, delivered with a thick African American accent. Cut to third sequence.

No more than a gag, to be sure, but it is a deadly serious one. What makes it about Godard is, for those familiar with French cinema of the postwar period, the fact that *Weekend* is the title, in English, of one of Jean-Luc Godard's most important films of the 1960s, a film, in fact, that contains a sustained critique of the calculated underdevelopment of the Third World by the West. Although the sequence plays as yet another attack on Senegalese racism (the better-informed, multilingual African American clearly serving the comparatively ignorant Senegalese middle class), it also functions as one of many instances where the politics of language is put to work within the narrative statements of the film. Specifically, what is set side by side is a wry observation about the strictly colonial status of French (to the colonized even "franglais" is proper French, hence the question) and a somewhat more pointed comment about the English/American character of Godard's attack on Western empire. Roy MacBean, in a well-known study of Godard's *Vent d'est*, where Glauber Rocha, in a brief scene, is confronted about the nature of political cinema, has drawn attention to the tension between the European vanguard and the partisans of Third Cinema (Nichols, 91–106). In Sembene's brief sequence, we experience something of a rejoinder where Godard's profoundly ambivalent relation to American cinema is presented not only as a misreading of America (what about the language practices of African Americans?), but also—and therefore—as, with regard to the Third World, a gesture of complicity. As a result, the ante is decidedly upped for Sembene, who must find other innovations, other transgressions than those authorized by Godard to articulate a properly postcolonial Senegalese cinema. No doubt the place to start is with the strategy of the "cut away" gag, in which the geopolitics of the relation between language and cinema is bluntly stated. The fact that this scene segues directly to one in which a doorway—precisely the sort of frame

Metz reads as a reflexive and therefore enunciative marker—figures at the center of a deadlock over representation suggests that these statements are already circulating on and semanticizing the split plane of enunciation. Such, in any case, will be my argument in what follows. With this as a trailer, let us then turn directly to the comparative analyses.

CHAPTER 3

Ousmane Sembene's *Xala*

Limited Engagements

The idea of referring to the works of Ousmane Sembene and Jorge Sanjinés in, as it were, the space of a single sentence is not original. Their work has been compared by none other than Roy Armes in the "Cinema astride Two Cultures" portion of *Third World Film Making and the West*. True, four other filmmakers are discussed in conjunction with Sembene and Sanjinés, but Armes literally does place them side by side. However, having set his sights on the task of introducing the corpus of these filmmakers to an Anglophone audience, there is no sustained analysis of any single film, and this despite the fact that his discussion sets in motion the potentially useful figure of one's being "astride" two cultures. Through the concept of bilingual or split enunciation I aim, obviously, to make more elaborate use of Armes's rubric. In doing so I will attempt both to extend the distance between the present and an earlier reception of these films, when they were valued primarily for their "politics," yet avoid the kind of criticism that has been leveled against projects like Armes's by, among others, African filmmakers. This task has taken on a fresh urgency both because Sembene and Sanjinés represent the older generation that the current generation of filmmakers on their respective continents is now outdistancing (in the African context, one might think here of Flora Gomes, Jean-Pierre Bekolo, or Idrissa Ouedraogo), and because the postcolonial problematic, especially in the

Western academy, is energetically trying to wrap its paradigms around precisely the different differences that arise between the cultures of Latin America and Africa.

Perhaps the most condensed formulation of the issues and problems at hand occurs in Haile Gerima's contribution to N. Frank Ukadike's recent *Questioning African Cinema.* Appealing to his own concept of a "triangular cinema" (that is, the notion that the cinema is a social institution comprised by filmmakers, audiences, and critics), Gerima minces no words in criticizing the work of Western critics writing about African cinema. He writes:

> We have to make changes in this society because it is very hostile toward our humanity. If that is the case, and is the reason why we make movies outside of the mainstream, then we cannot imitate the establishment and claim to be transformers and arbiters of change. If the critic is in the Eurocentric tradition—i.e., a commentator upon the cultural product for the sake of just commenting—he is simply spurious. But if the critic engages in an activist role, then that individual is participating in the struggle as a warrior and not as an academic politician or pseudoscholar who exploits black political movements for personal gain and the limelight via newpapers and television. (270–71)

In bringing this line of reflection to a close, Gerima calls for the activist critic to participate in the elaboration of a "new cinematic order, including ideology and language" (271). With this he illuminates what it meant to modify "scholar" with the prefix *pseudo-*, at the same time that he complicates, perhaps irredeemably, the otherwise straightforwardly political category of "activism."

I do not wish to imply that Armes is the specific focus of Gerima's critique (after all, the former does devote a few kind words to the latter's work), but given that the above-cited remarks follow almost directly from a somewhat bitter reflection upon the fate of Third Cinema (or Third World filmmaking) in the Western academy, it is clear that Gerima is concerned about the role location plays in the tension between

commentary and activism. Though Armes and I live on different continents, we share this location. Because Gerima's remarks might therefore
be about me, some effort must be made to engage them. Pressuring the
concept of commentary is a good place to start. Clearly what Gerima
objects to is the criticism that fails to involve itself in the construction
of its object, that fails to perceive its stake in the new cinematic order.
I would argue that commentary—or even cinema journalism—fails to
do so as a matter of principle. To break with this tendency, as Gerima
says, one needs to become involved in the elaboration of, among other
things, language. This is no throwaway concept for Gerima. Indeed, he
and Ukadike discuss language for several pages, a discussion that culminates in the following flourish: "Cinematic language will not be invented
or forged in coffeehouses in New York with a few critics and film buffs.
The audience missing it and not getting it, getting it and not missing it
are critical ways of learning how to develop and transform our cinematic
language" (278). In other words, scholars who are not pseudoscholars
might both recognize the indispensability of the concept of cinematic
language and seek to involve themselves in its transformation, elaborating it in a way that acknowledges Gerima's triangle. This triangle's
structure is at once institutional and geopolitical. Ukadike, who invests
heavily in the Afrocentric concept of "oral storytelling," keeps coaxing
Gerima to accept the equation of language and orality, but, to his credit,
Gerima refuses to do so, insisting instead upon a conception of language
that encompasses the "echoes" of both speech and writing. Under such
circumstances activism would appear to become more complicated than
simply mounting the barricades or taking to the streets, and Gerima
gives one important reason for refusing to reduce the "activist" cinema
of the 1960s and 1970s to a politics devoid of a poetics. His refusal of
Ukadike's call for the recovery of oral narrative in African cinema, in
fact, could not be clearer.

By the same token, Gerima's comments are laced throughout with
heavy doses of heroic individualism, suggesting that, however seriously
one takes the concept of cinematic language, at some point it reduces
down to the philosophically dubious phenomenon of a "private language."

When, for example, Gerima rebukes filmmakers for starting out with the assumption that "film is told this way," he offers as counterweight the notion of personal comfort: "We should always be saying to ourselves, 'How am I going to tell my story in the way most comfortable to me?' because every time one tells a story, if it is comfortable to the individual, then he or she is closer to telling the story" (274). Here, all the important insights into colonialism, distribution, ownership, language, and so on collapse into an apology for creative narcissism, one that implicitly allows Gerima to again cozy up to the model of orality. If the bottom line is "If it feels good, do it," what is not legitimate? Why should Gerima, to invoke a now loaded example, feel shamed by his identification with Tarzan (see the *Framework* interview with Willemen)? I'm sure Van Dyke, if asked, would say that he was "comfortable" with the way he told his Tarzan story. This is a little unfair, of course, but it points to the necessity of following through on the repudiation of commentary by attempting to radicalize Gerima's own insights into the problem of African cinematic language. While it may be true that such language cannot be generated from an "isolated booth," it is also true that activist criticism is not well served by reducing the concept of film language to the affective equivalent of one's maternal (or in Gerima's case, paternal) tongue. Sembene, whom Gerima credits with "open[ing] the tracks and clos[ing] the holes in [his] consciousness" (259), provokes one to ponder carefully this very matter. Indeed his work demands that commentary give way to reading, to activism.

Though this chapter largely focuses on the textual analysis of a specific film—Sembene's *Xala* ("temporary impotence" in Wolof)—it is designed to pose and examine questions that range well beyond the interpretive problems raised there. In particular, I attempt to locate within the texture of *Xala* issues that pressure both the current theoretical preoccupation with the role of "national cinemas" in the politics of postcoloniality and the methodological foundations of a textual analytics derived from the European semiotics tradition. While it is clear that *Xala* engages the complexity of postcolonial nationalism by interrogating the "sexual politics" of African socialism (the tradition associated with Leopold Senghor in the Senegalese context), it is considerably less clear how this interrogation articulates itself in the conflict between French and Wolof—not merely as "tongues," but more crucially, as foreign film languages. In effect, this chapter seeks to delineate the ways Sembene, who has paid persistent attention to the politics of literacy, labors to articulate a mode of split enunciation that engages the radical bilingualism of postcoloniality in Western francophone Africa.

Now Showing

While in the United States, screening *Guelwaar* at the first Houston Pan-Cultural Film Festival in 1996, Sembene conducted a taped interview with Professor Hamid Naficy about his work, past, present, and future. Asked to forward a question, I proposed that Naficy follow up on a public exchange I had had earlier with Sembene concerning the importance of language in his films. In the transcript from the taped interview, this is what Sembene had to say in reply.

> Language is cinema. It can be political images, or . . . As soon as you have two human beings, if they don't speak there are problems communicating And people not only talk, but cry. Language is necessary. Let's say cinema is a universal language, but it also has its grammar, it has its metaphors . . . And it depends on each country, each culture.

Almost as if missing his own point, Sembene goes on to discuss the languages heard in virtually all of his films (*Black Girl*, Diola; *Mandabi*, French and Wolof; *Ceddo*, French and Wolof, and so on), but what gives one pause is the tension between the proposition (itself an important rhetorical gesture) concerning the universality of cinematic language and the observation that its grammar is subject to cultural, indeed national, inflections. Rather than treating this as a misunderstanding or confusion on Sembene's part, I will proceed as though this is precisely what he meant to draw attention to when, asked by Naficy to comment about the language in *Xala*, Sembene says, "a real insight into the French language." That is, instead of insisting that language cannot be subject to both the universal and the national (although this *is* the sort of thing linguists seek to capture in the distinction between, in French, *langue* and *langage*), why not treat Sembene's formulation as a version of Gerima's observation about "accents," that is, the particular way the universality of a technological medium of communication is joined to "one's identity, culture, and language" (Ukadike, 265)? In other words, what is called for here is a concept through which to think the contingent necessity of film language. As has been argued, that concept is the concept of enunciation.

If *Black Girl/La noire de . . .* (arguably the first black African film) is Sembene's first feature-length film, then *Xala* is his fourth feature film, one of three films he made in the seventies. I count myself among those who consider it his *chef d'oeuvre* to date. For those unfamiliar with either the film or the novel upon which it is based, a brief synopsis of the narrative will no doubt be helpful.[1] The film opens with what amounts to an overture during which we witness the expulsion of the French members of the Chamber of Commerce by a group of Senegalese *"hommes d'affaires"* in traditional dress. At the close of the overture a meeting among the newly installed members of the Chamber concludes with one among them, El Hadji (a man, indeed a Muslim, who has made the pilgrimage to Mecca), inviting everyone to attend a wedding reception for him and his third bride, N'Gone, to be convened later that afternoon. We then follow El Hadji as he gathers up his two other wives, Adja (the female Muslim pilgrim) and Oumi. During this itinerary we learn that a fundamental rift has opened between El Hadji and his daughter from his first marriage, Rama, who opposes the concept and the practice of polygamy. After the reception, during which El Hadji is offered two distinctly traditional invitations to guarantee his virility (one from a woman, the Badyen, which he refuses, and another from his male colleagues, which he accepts) he and his new bride, N'Gone, retire to her villa to consummate their marriage. Predictably, he is unable to. He has been stricken by the curse of impotence. Much of what ensues involves El Hadji's various efforts—both pathetic and comic—to determine the source of his curse and neutralize it. In effect, to become once again "*un homme*," a phrase El Hadji seldom utters without also holding up and shaking one of his fists. The two narrative strands of power and potency reconverge late in the film when El Hadji, who finally finds a *marabout* capable of relieving him, pays for his cure with a check that bounces (one thinks here of the dominant metaphor in Martin Luther King's address at the Lincoln Memorial in 1963). At this point, El Hadji's "extravagance" has undermined not only his credibility, but that of the entire Chamber of Commerce. His colleagues, all of whom were present at the reception, convene a meeting during which they vote to expel him, replacing him with a man, M. Cheli, we earlier see rob a peasant who has come to Dakar to solicit aid for his drought-stricken community. In the concluding episode, El Hadji, who has been stripped of both power and potency, is confronted by the source of his *xala*: a group of maimed and disfigured beggars led by a kinsman, Gorgui, imprisoned when El Hadji took his land in order to extend his own commercial ambitions. In the final shot we see El Hadji, stripped to the waist, covered with the spittle that this kinsman has insisted he endure in order to purge himself of his *xala*.

Ostensibly a parable about the body politic of neocolonialism, Sembene's film attaches its own enunciative syntax to a complexly articulated "immanent critique" of the postcolonial settlement in Senegal.[2] In what follows, I will endeavor to elaborate the structure and the necessity of this syntax by again appealing to the concept of bilingualism. In doing so I will be following initiatives taken by Teshome Gabriel, who has written an extremely provocative analysis of *Xala*, and Samia Mehrez, who, following Khatibi, has boldly theorized the cultural politics of bilingual textuality. The questions these initiatives permit us to pose, with regard to the status of semiotically inflected cinema studies within multicultural curricula, are at best latent in their work. It will therefore be my task to draw these issues out.

Most immediately, the issue of bilingualism asserts itself thematically in the gender antagonism between El Hadji and Rama. Significantly, Rama, who argues to her father's face that all polygamists are "liars," does so in Wolof, a regional, precolonial tongue she studies in school.

In fact, from the very first moment we encounter this dyad, it is presented to us as a linguistic antagonism: Rama only speaks Wolof (with one significant exception), El Hadji only speaks French unless it is expedient not to. Though it is tempting to fix the bilingual tensions of the film in the rift between the father and the daughter, it would be practically and theoretically compromising to do so. Significantly, Rama, whom Sembene himself interprets as a figure of the "new Africa," is split by an irreducible ambivalence. She appears to embody, in her actions (e.g., the cartographically staged confrontation with her father in his office) as well as her "props" (her scooter, her jewelry, the posters in her room, and so on), what Luce Irigaray—in an expression to which I have already appealed—calls the "sex which is not one." In other words, Rama exudes a kind of bilingual energy, a mixed signal, in the distinctive way the film's narrative statements entwine the politics of gender and the linguistically inflected struggle against colonialism in her character.[3] In a startling anticipation of the tenets of postcoloniality, Rama's failure to identify with herself as a woman (she sees that "man" interrupts her psycho-social relation to herself, to "her" identity) and her failure to identify with herself as Senegalese (she sees that the French reorient all the differences that had organized the terms of national identity) are made to interact as a condition of her own agency. In other words, it is because she can neither be woman nor Senegalese, and because this dual impossibility articulates different differences (gender and nation), that she sees herself as someone who can make, rather than "be," a difference. Just the same, the narrative statements constituting her character constitute her as split.

Similar fissuring is projected into the character of El Hadji. Because, in the confrontational scene, the French-speaking polygamist's speech is read almost immediately as duplicitous, what might otherwise seem to be little more than a serendipitous allusion to the language of enunciation is given considerable weight. So much so, in fact, that Sembene goes on to elaborate the imputed duplicity of El Hadji by dramatizing his contradictory relation to *Kaadu* ("the voice," or "word")—the only Wolof daily in Dakar, begun by Sembene himself as a way to counteract the illiteracy that hindered the reception of his francophone novels and prompted his turn to filmmaking in the first place. In ways that are perhaps distinctive to Sembene, allusions to the journalistic mediation of the voice become, through the general problematic of cultural mobilization, references to the filmic medium itself. In the French context, Godard's use of a copy of *Cahiers du cinema* in *A bout de souffle* might serve as an analogy.

Immediately following the traumatic scene (to which I will return) where El Hadji and N'Gone are blocked from consummating their marriage due to the former's impotence, we are led to El Hadji's dry goods store in the heart of Dakar. The scene opens with a predictable series of establishing shots and cutaways as we watch El Hadji's secretary, Madame Diouf, open for business. Almost immediately a hawker enters and hustles her, saying, in Wolof, "*Kaadu, Kaadu,* the only Wolof daily. Would you like one?" As if familiar with this routine, the secretary nods, pulls out her coin purse, and buys a copy. Here, El Hadji, as her employer, is cast as part of the socio-economic mechanism that creates a literate, petit bourgeois clientele for the people's voice. In spite of his antagonism toward his native tongue, El Hadji's drive toward economic self-determination is shown to have created conditions for the preservation and invigoration of Wolof. No doubt, the taxes he and his secretary pay help fund the courses Rama follows at school, courses whose very existence index the ravages of colonialism.

As this scene unfolds—it centers round El Hadji's admission of impotence to, and his plea for help from, the president of the Chamber of Commerce—a very different relation between El Hadji and *Kaadu* is constructed. Troubled by the beggars and townspeople who have gathered in front of his store, El Hadji asks that the president call a security force to remove this "*déchet.*" The President agrees. As the officers arrive, they begin indiscriminately rounding up everyone, including the hawker of *Kaadu.* What gives this episode its particular poignancy, however, is the fact that, immediately prior to it, we have witnessed the theft perpetrated by M. Cheli. Moments after this theft (and the attack on Senghor's failed response to the ongoing drought could not be more pithy), the peasant is approached by the hawker of *Kaadu*. Instead of buying the newspaper, the peasant explains his predicament. He would like to buy the paper, but he has no money, unlike, of course, Madame Diouf. Immediately, the hawker offers not just to listen to the peasant's story, but to publish it in *Kaadu*, with the aim of galvanizing public opinion around the injustice that has befallen him. When both the hawker and the robbed peasant are subsequently rounded up in the name of public hygiene, El Hadji is positioned vis-à-vis the people's voice, just as his antagonism with Rama would lead one to expect. Instead of fostering conditions for the preservation of *Kaadu*, he is shown to be actively, though "unconsciously," involved in its suppression. In addition to the important narrative details elaborated here, it is worth noting one additional aspect of these events. Since the entire thematization of the people's voice is framed within a discussion of El Hadji's *xala*—which also happens to be the name of the film we are watching—it would seem that the narrative question of literacy in one's "native tongue" touches directly upon the motivation behind Sembene's own turn to film as a more potent form of political mobilization. In effect, an analytical connection is established here, as in the case of Rama, between a split relation to one's own tongue and the techno-cultural problem of anti-colonial agency.

What is vital, though, is that Sembene does not permit us to read this as a contradiction, where one relation to Wolof is disclosed as fundamental and the other derivative. To do so would amount to eviscerating the bilingualism that is fundamental to Sembene's cultural politics. The refusal of such a reading is narratively played out when, in the scene where El Hadji is expelled from the Chamber of Commerce, he defends himself—and our sympathies are clearly with him—using the very vocabulary of Rama in her earlier attack on him as a polygamist, by denouncing his accusers as "liars." Significantly, he asks to address the deputies in Wolof but is prohibited from doing so. If El Hadji's suppression of *Kaadu* were to constitute his "real" position, it is not likely that Sembene would permit his duplicitous status as polygamist to ring true when applied to his colleagues. Of course, in the strictly linguistic register of the film, this split relation to the native tongue is thematized as an antagonism between French and Wolof. It is not by accident that, when El Hadji requests the security force that "coincidentally" rounds up the hawker, he does so in French, and given that his conflict with Rama structures much of the narrative (the substance of her critique virtually haunts his character), it seems warranted to conclude that the refusal to privilege either of El Hadji's two relations to "the voice," coupled with Rama's figurative return to the precolonial future, is an explicit invocation of the irreducible bilingualism that attends the struggle to dismantle neocolonialism; Sembene's rather traditional linkage of masculinity and control over the voice, notwithstanding.

In Samia Mehrez's work on Khatibi, bilingualism is read not only as a thematic preoccupation, but also as an enunciative practice; the language of Khatibi's text keeps shifting back and forth between Arabic and French. This means that in order to elaborate this problematic in the context of a reading of *Xala*, the enunciative moments of filmic bilingualism must also come into focus. Rather than pursue the angle opened by Teshome Gabriel, who articulates the specificity of Sembene's film language by appealing to the concept of *sem-enna-worq* (wax and gold)—an Ethiopian poetic code that organizes the allegorical function of verse—I want, in keeping with the theoretical commitments laid out in chapter 1, to indulge in a more semiotically inflected analysis of Sembene's bilingualism.[4] What prompts this is my conviction that, while Gabriel's approach illuminates how Sembene uses comic tropes to articulate certain ideological insights in an allegorical manner, it does not provide us with much of a framework within which to extend the struggle against colonialism into the analytical paradigms that organize cinema studies in the postcolonial metropoles—a serious shortcoming if we recognize the specifically international character of colonialism and the necessarily split character of the struggle against it within a postcolonial context.[5]

To proceed it is useful to recall that, in Metz's meticulous though ambivalent reflection on the applicability of language paradigms to the cinema, he decided not only that film is rather more like speech (*parole*) than a national tongue (*langue*), but that shots are like sentences, not words. In this he agrees with the remarks of his mentor, Roland Barthes, discussed earlier. Though he later modified this position somewhat, his whole influential schematization of the "syntax" of enunciation in the narrative film, the very prototype of ciné-semiotics, derived from this notion of the sentence/shot correlation.[6] What attention to bilingualism in *Xala* requires is that, at the very least, we take a look at the way "sentences" or, in this case, "shots" are formed in Wolof, the speech or voice of the people, as well as in French, the voice of the colonizers and the Senegalese middle class. Now, I claim no fluency in Wolof, but even a cursory study of the syntactic aspects of its verbal syntagm reveals the persistence of nominal sentence structures supplementing the attenuated presence of the verb "to be."[7] For example, to say in Wolof, "I am a child," (*xale laa*) one says, literally, "child me," where the pronoun is modalized in a way that traces the absence of the copula. Since the final purgatorial scene of *Xala* makes it abundantly clear that the drama of El Hadji's identity as a neocolonial man is what has been driving the enunciation of the narrative, it would seem reasonable that many of the "sentences" articulated by the film would conform to the unusual (at least from the point of view of its Romance partner, French) nominal sort that the syntactic properties of Wolof require, especially given the persistent attention paid throughout the film to the voice and the enabling conditions of anticolonial agency. The reflexive interchanges or portals that fold and refold the film make such elements even more prominent, more unavoidable, than they might otherwise be.

Of course, French syntax makes comparatively little use of the nominal sentence. Thus, when tracing the bilingual enunciative procedures of *Xala*, it is important to delineate the interplay between shots that concatenate according to the logic of the copula and those that do not. In fact, I will argue that the specific texture of *Xala* derives from the dense bilingual interplay between French and Wolof "shots." As we saw in chapter 2, it is precisely around the suspension, the withholding, of the copula that the mark of the foreign is registered for those tutored, as Daniel Dayan once famously put it, by Hollywood. Here, the foreign is aligned with Wolof (not French). To help concretize this reading, consider the following twenty frames from the shot sequence that institutes the onset of El Hadji's impotence.

First, let me clarify what is meant by the logic of the copula at the level of enunciation. Typically, shot selection in Western cinematic discourse is driven by a desire for continuity, so much so in fact that even oppositional cinemas in the West often pin their claims to alterity on a compulsory denial of continuity alone. To secure continuity, one follows a complex code that regulates, among other things, action and composition within the frame, camera position, sound levels, and narrative space. Since the syntactic function of the copula is to make the predicate follow upon or from the subject, I would argue that strict continuity editing is irreducibly driven by the logic of the copula, a logic that, at the level of narrative statements, is called "scene hooking." Thus in our examples, the first two shots (Figures 1 and 2) are concatenated according to this logic. We have first a typical establishing shot, the wedding party approaching the nuptial chamber down a short hallway and concluding with their arrival at the bedroom door, followed by— through the convention of a match on action cut—its entry into the bedroom. The two shots could be transcribed as "They are going to the bedroom." followed by "They are in the bedroom." But as this scene unfolds, the enunciative logic of the copula is persistently both instituted and disrupted. In fact, the narrative act of copulation that fails to take place here is fully signaled in the enunciation of the very

Figure 1

Figure 2

scene where the film enacts the trauma of its own name—*xala*.[8] In the subsequent shots, I want particularly to draw our attention to Sembene's use of false match-on-action cuts to invert and (con)fuse narrative space and, even more significantly, his use of black-and-white photographic stills (clear instances of what Metz calls reflexive or enunciative markers) to slow, if not actually stall, the continuous forward motion of the film image. My point is not that these gestures are more fundamental or authentic than the thematic critique of neocolonialism, but rather that the enunciation of *Xala* opens onto this critique in a way that gives what might otherwise be regarded as mere technique a distinct political valence. Enunciation here becomes radically bilingual, in effect, cobbled together out of shots produced in Wolof and in French, and this constitutes a decisive supplemental aspect of the critique of neocolonialism. In effect, the "impotent" stasis of the unlivable present is mimed or repeated in the production of this statement.

The two shots I have discussed inaugurate a sequence that extends from the end of one day into the beginning of another. In spite of this temporal cohesion, the action is pointedly situated on an unfathomable threshold between today and tomorrow. Significantly, Sembene chooses this naturalized inscription of continuity (the diurnal rotation of the Earth) as the site for his intervention, as if to underscore the range and ideological importance of his analysis.[9] Once inside the nuptial chamber, El Hadji is immediately directed into the adjoining bathroom in order to prepare himself (Figure 3). His action of entering has now been displaced, the shots articulating it have, in effect, retracted one another. Syntactically, the motion picture is beginning to stall. Once El Hadji has left the room, leaving N'Gone and her aunt (Yay Bineta, the Badyen or "mistress of ceremonies") alone, Sembene frames them within a triad of figures where the daughter is doubled by

Figure 3

her photographic image, which is mounted behind her on the wall (Figure 4). Predictably, N'Gone is being counseled by her aunt on how properly to conduct herself as a wife ("Don't raise your voice" and so on), while she is being prepared as a sight for her husband. Her wedding veil and gown are peeled off and mounted on a tailor's dummy that is situated next to a shelving unit topped with another photograph of the bride in casual and distinctly Western clothes.

Figure 4

As this scene of the bride's unveiling unwinds, there is a cutaway to El Hadji before the bathroom mirror preparing himself for his triumph (Figure 5). The crosscutting suggests a thematic parallel that Sembene relentlessly mines and undermines. I am referring, of course, to the status of the bride and groom as images and thus to the politics of gender as it surfaces within the enunciative domain.[10] The critical tenor of Sembene's approach to this parallel is embodied in the distinction he draws between the mirror and the photograph. To delineate

Figure 5

the terms of this critique and clarify its relation to *Xala*'s bilingualism, it is necessary to return briefly to the problems posed by the nominal sentence.

In Benveniste's influential discussion of the nominal sentence, he established what distinguished it from the so-called verbal sentence.[11] At the core of this distinction was a functional description of the verb. Instead of defining the verb as a process rather than an object, Benveniste defined it as a structure having two aspects: one, variable (the semantic details of tense and person); the other, invariable (the correspondence between the expressed details and the fact attested). The nominal sentence exhibits only the latter of these two aspects, which is to say not only that it is atemporal and impersonal but that it cannot relate the time of an event to the time of its discursive recounting. For this reason, Benveniste concluded that the nominal sentence lent itself well to the genres of the maxim and the parable. One might also be tempted to say allegory.

Returning now to the mirror and the photograph, it is worth stressing a couple of things. First, within the discipline of film studies, the mirror has a privileged analytical status in that it has come to serve as the dominant metaphor for the screen and by extension the cinematic apparatus itself.[12] Thus, at stake in the parallel of the mirror and the photograph is the enunciative apparatus as such. Secondly, in a way that resonates strongly with critical positions in feminist film theory, Sembene's parallel associates the mobility of the image with masculinity and the immobility of the image with femininity; El Hadji figures in the mirror, N'Gone in the photograph. Our immediate inclination to seize upon this as evidence of how Sembene's critique is mired in tradition must be tempered by our awareness of his commitment to Rama in the narrative struggle with El Hadji. In order, however, to protect this moment from a reading in which it would be simply denounced as a contradiction, it is vital that the link between immobility and atemporality be underscored. In other words, the mirror/photograph parallel is also a site where, in addition to the apparatus of enunciation, the French/Wolof interplay is stake. This can be clarified by returning directly to the film.

In the shots that ensue after the cutaway to El Hadji before his mirror while N'Gone is still receiving marital counsel, we witness a most peculiar staging of the relation between her body and its photographic representation (Figure 6).

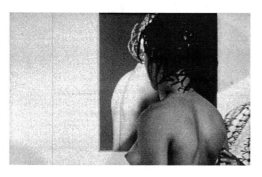

Figure 6

This staging is enunciated so as to give the content of the sentences/ shots involved a distinctly nominal character. If we recall that at this moment N'Gone is preparing herself as the object of El Hadji's lustful gaze, it is significant that she is shown as virtually a-mimetically fused with the photograph, as though her motion-picture body were capable of simultaneously projecting its own negative still. This effect might accurately be phrased as "N'Gone this" instead of "This *is* N'Gone." The immobility of the photograph is thus enunciatively absorbed as an instance of nominal syntax, a pattern more intimately associated with Wolof than with French. Significantly, the final shot in this sequence

(Figure 7) shows El Hadji separating himself from his fleeting mirror image, entering the shadow of the camera, and returning to the bedroom. Instead, however, of reentering the nuptial chamber, Sembene interrupts this match on action cut by cutting to the following morning when N'Gone's aunt and a friend arrive to consecrate the rupture of her hymen. This abrupt temporal

Figure 7

compression reiterates narratively the atemporality of the photograph, thus amplifying the sense in which it marks the suspension of the copula, of the copulation, that has, literally and figuratively, been cut as the world turns.

In the shots that articulate the events of the following morning, the enunciative work begun the night before is continued, though with certain modifications. This implies, I would argue, that the bilingual strategy is neither restricted nor accidental. From the point of view of the narrative, the sequence we are scrutinizing embodies El Hadji's humiliation, his loss of gender identity, in that his *xala* becomes public knowledge through the agency of his in-laws. Thus, here the political thematics of power and potency reach the catastrophic cusp where the body and the body politic begin to parasitize one another.

Returning to the disorienting match on action cut that displaces El Hadji's reentry with Yay Bineta's arrival (Figure 8), it is important that we sustain our attention to the photographic image or, more gener-

Figure 8

Figure 9

Figure 10

ally, to the volatile mix of stasis and motility in the image. Although the action is now clearly "outside" and out of the range of N'Gone's photograph, Sembene resuscitates the key coordinates of this material by using his confusion of the bedroom's boundaries (the door that opens to admit El Hadji, admits his in-law from the front gate of the villa) to project the photographic theme onto the *boubou* of Yay Bineta's companion. As the two women gather at the front door (Figure 9), the screened photographic prints of female busts (one white, the other black) almost appear to perforate the *boubou*, reestablishing the nominal syntax, but now in the form of what might be characterized as bas-reliefs reaching through the friend's body from the white background of the exterior wall. As if to secure this association, Sembene introduces yet another time-compressing, false match on action cut where, instead of entering the foyer, we witness the two women enter the nuptial chamber (Figure 10), making it appear that the two women have moved upstairs directly from the front door. In effect, the space of the house is disappearing as the secret of the *xala* is disclosed.

Sembene exploits the (con)fusions produced here to reopen the problems posed by the photograph in the earlier scene. As the aunt leads her companion through the bedroom door, a new configuration of images and bodies is staged. N'Gone's aunt is framed so as to position her within the doorframe but, more importantly, against a photograph hung in the hallway, a photograph that, through its depiction of starkly chiseled masculinity, immediately calls up the photographic pantheon of revolutionary heroes (such as Cabral and Samory) found in Rama's bedroom. As indicated earlier, to the right of this photograph appears the one of N'Gone in casual Western dress. With the marked presence of the veil (albeit a wedding veil), this configuration of photographic images—N'Gone naked, male national figure, N'Gone clothed—evokes Frantz Fanon's nationalist metaphor of "unveiling" that Manthia Diawara claims has introduced a new mytheme (that of the "daughter's liberation") into West African traditions of popular narrative.[13] While this certainly encourages us to sustain the political reading of the sequence, the syntactical argument is better served by drawing attention to how this same configuration extends the spatio-temporal confusions begun with the false match on action cut out to the courtyard gate.

The hero's photograph is not actually in the bedroom. It is in the hallway (or perhaps even in the bedroom of another home, Rama's). But the configuration deftly shifts the latter into the former, an effect that is given temporal inflection as Yay Bineta reprises her quasi-nominal positioning before the photograph of her niece (Figure 11), as if to insist upon the overlap between these two otherwise distinct moments. This is almost overstated in the subsequent shot (Figure 12), where she crouches down beneath this very photograph to inspect the sheets.

Figure 11

Figure 12

Sembene's tenacity shines forth here because it is in this same shot that the spatial fusions signaled in the photographic images on or in the *boubou* last seen against the villa's exterior wall are now added to the configuration of images defining the "interior" (?) space of the bedroom. The two female busts now appear to rise up off the white wall upon which N'Gone's naked image is hung, and in spite of the narrative time that has passed, the boundary between yesterday and today remains as hard to pin down as the spatial location of the walls of the villa.

To seal this development Sembene moves to problematize the space and time of his own diegesis, thus taking up the mirror's evocation of the cinematic apparatus. In the final shots of the sequence (Figure 13),

Figure 13

we see the dejected couple framed against yet another photograph. Given the syntactical and thematic context of the sequence, the fact that this photograph is cropped by the viewfinder so as to appear unviewable does not only reiterate the general problem of the missing, or cut, copula, but it does so by specifically drawing attention to the spatial limits of the frame itself. Something "withheld" appears to disappear into the off-screen space above the frame, into the uncanny space of the nondiegetical. Significantly, through a final false match on action, Sembene allows the bilingual tensions of the sequence to invade the enunciative mechanism of his film as a whole.

In the dialogue that dominates the soundtrack during these shots, Yay Bineta concludes her tongue-lashing of El Hadji by gesturing for him to retire to the bathroom, gather his things, and leave. This is shot as if to say, "He is getting up, opening the door, and entering the bathroom" (Figure 14). As the bathroom door closes, there is a cut to El Hadji, fully clothed (the temporal compression is severe), exiting, not from the bathroom nor even the bedroom, but from the front gate, where he traverses the scene of the reception. This shot sequence, as with all the other false match on action cuts, cancels the predicate established at the beginning of the "sentence," suspending the copular function of the enunciation. Sembene deepens the bilingual effect of this particular suspension by suddenly reintroducing music on the soundtrack, music that in fact forcibly attenuates the dialogue. What we hear as El Hadji exits the gate is immediately familiar. It is the music and voices from "yesterday's" reception.[14]

Figure 14

Figure 15

Of course, the irony here is unmistakable. But more important, the effect created rebounds directly upon the space of the diegesis because this sonoric material was so strongly marked as diegetic in the context of the reception (complete with what amounted to a short promotional video for the "Star Band of Dakar"), whereas this time around it is conspicuously nondiegetic, as though the film, like the villa, is starting to loose its spatial organization. Thus, the problematization of the villa's space is directly imbricated in the destabilization of the narrative space of the film, and, as a result, the diegesis stands forth as a screen that looms up from the Senegalese urban landscape. The soundtrack in this final shot appears to share the same space as the off-screen space evoked by the photograph above the couple, a "somewhere" apparently controlled by the *griot*/filmmaker, but which in fact is an unstable effect of the bilingual syntaxes that evoke, without fixing, its presence. Once again, tomorrow has failed to come, and the motion picture seems caught in some perverse stall, advancing without predication. Is this not precisely why it deserves the trauma of its own name?

But how are we to assess the political significance of such a suggestion? If the film itself self-consciously marches under the banner of impotence, is it not draining off the very energy (assuming, for a moment, that only men have a stake in this struggle) its critique of neocolonialism presupposes? This is a concern no doubt invited by the fact that some of these same enunciative strategies appear in the films of various European "new waves" whose politics are, at best, inconsistent. Yet it is important to recognize not only that Sembene explicitly attacks these traditions, spoofing, as I have observed, Godard's *Weekend*—a bilingualism neutralized by the official scandal of *franglais*—but that he resituates them and turns their effects to different purposes.

The enunciative suspension of the copula detailed in the sequences analyzed here ought to be understood in terms of the syntactical effects of the nominal sentence, the eruption of Wolof in the montage. The point is not to paralyze critique, but to link its possibility to an interplay of voices that undercuts the phallogocentric design of insurgency ("impotence" as a general characterization of the Senegalese middle class in the neocolonial context) while simultaneously risking its parabolic or allegorical recuperation. In other words, the atemporality that Benveniste saw as earmarking the nominal sentence for use in parables, and which I am associating with the spectacular (con)fusions of the traumatic scene, causes the cinematic syntax of Wolof to verge on the dogmatic, a quality virtually indistinguishable from the phallogocentric. But this is precisely what is crucial about bilingualism in *Xala*: the imbrication of sentences/shots that start to copulate and then break off. Without this mix, it would be impossible for the space of the diegesis to engage its own limits since, as Benveniste argued, the nominal is typically barred from the register of discourse. In fact, it is the irreducible, multi-grained texture of the enunciative voices that not only enables the specifically filmic critique of postcolonialism, but threatens to disappear when such a critique is sought exclusively in a reading that sifts the film narrative for "wax and gold."

To conclude, I will formulate the implications of this reading by sounding them in the context of a reprise of my opening themes. By examining the text of *Xala* from the angle presented here, it becomes evident that, if we fail to engage the level of filmic enunciation, not only do we risk surrendering film analysis to a multicultural curriculum dominated by a narrative paradigm, but we risk misunderstanding a fundamental aspect of the colonial inflection of cultural multiplicity. What emerges insistently in *Xala* is a critique of neocolonialism in Senegal that refuses not only the precolonial past and the postcolonial present, but also a future that imagines that an absolute gulf might separate it from the present and the past. In this way the film as a whole repeats the temporal problematic of the traumatic scene. Rama is as conflicted in her desire to move forward by rejecting polygamy *and* French as is her father who embraces these same phenomena. Though it is true that Sembene stresses that socialism in Africa cannot proceed without a political transformation of the social division of gender, he does not authorize us to conclude that the people of Senegal are eager to voice its social contradictions in the vocabulary of Euro-American feminism. The fact that these perspectives are woven into the very enunciative texture of the film is what requires that film analysis not lose touch with this meta-narrative dimension of the cinema.

An instructive comparison can be drawn with Sembene's recent film, *Faat Kine* (a female given name) from 1999. Separated from *Xala* by more than two decades (during which state power shifted away from Senghor for the first time since independence), the new film is nevertheless something of a remake of *Xala*. Indeed, more than a remake, *Faat Kine* is actually an inverted rearrangement of the film. For this reason, sustained discussion of it sheds important light on my reading of the earlier film.

The narrative of *Faat Kine* centers around the eponymous female protagonist. Like *Xala*, the narrative braids together two prominent strands: one, the story of Kine's children's (Aby, the daughter, and Djibril—Djib, for short—her younger brother) successful completion of the university entrance examination, the infamous "bac" (baccalaureate); and the other, the story of her children's efforts to find Kine "*un partenaire*" (as Djib provocatively puts it), a husband. The plot resolves the matter of the "bac" almost immediately (Aby redeems the previous year's failure and Djib passes with the equivalent of honors), but it weaves the meaning of this event tightly into the subsequent efforts to find Kine a husband. As if organized around the etymological resources of the term "baccalaureate" the film builds its narrative energy out of the concept of the "bachelor," the unmarried male, but also the degree one receives upon successfully finishing a certain educational program (here, university or college, there, high school). The side upon which these two dimensions of the "bac" meet is established in the unfolding of the narrative, a perfunctory reconstruction of which will be helpful for those unfamiliar with the film.

The film opens in traffic. Faat Kine is dropping her children off to learn the results of the national university entrance exam, the "bac." As they speak, in French, the radio ("Senegal National Public Radio—the top station") comments diegetically by broadcasting a story about the challenges posed for African youth by Western technology. Several scenes contain this internal radiophonic commentary (again, à la Godard), and, while I will not indicate them all in this summary, this is an important structural and enunciative feature of the film. After dropping her kids off, Faat Kine drives to the Total (surely not irrelevant) gas station, where she works as the manager. Several plot details are presented here. Two important men are introduced: Jean (an uncle of her son) and M. Goye (a philosophy professor from the local *lycée*, the estranged father of Aby). M. Goye is introduced through a flashback where we learn that Faat Kine failed to pass the "bac," having been expelled from school on account of her pregnancy. We witness Jean re-extending his, at this point ambiguous, "invitation" to Faat Kine, and we learn via a telephone call during M. Goye's visit that the kids have passed the "bac." In addition, this scene introduces the language politics familiar to us from *Xala*, though here there is no easy alignment between language and gender. Faat Kine speaks Wolof to a flower vendor and to the disfigured beggar, Pathé; French to Jean, M. Goye, her right-hand man, M. Sogne, and her various customers and friends.

What complexity is suggested in these linguistic politics is consolidated upon Faat Kine's return home where we meet her mother, Maamy. Maamy primarily speaks Wolof, and she is a devout, but tolerant, Muslim. I say "primarily" here because, as a Muslim, she has also mastered a few phrases in Arabic. But also—and I will return to this—there are several borrowed terms that dot not only her speech (for example, "bac"), but the speech of several other characters. The following pattern is observed: French dots Wolof (see preceding example) and English dots French (for example, Aby refers to her mother as "superwoman"). Understandably, Faat Kine only addresses her mother in Wolof. The flashback that interrupts this scene plays brilliantly on this linguistic borrowing, informing us both about the traumatic origins of Faat Kine's family and profession and fusing the two sides of bachelorhood. Upon learning of her pregnancy and expulsion, Faat Kine's father, in an abusive rage, attempts to scald her with a pot of boiling water. Her mother, Maamy, shields her with her own back, which is hideously burned as a result. Thus, the "bac" neither mother nor daughter competed for is inscribed in the "back" scarred when Maamy so indebted her daughter to her that she has since been unable to find the right "partner," that is, to cease being—in a term made popular by *The Dating Game*—a bachelorette.[15]

Soon thereafter an important rift opens between Faat Kine and her children. As they plan for the upcoming "boom" (huge party) to celebrate their achievement, Aby announces her intention to go abroad (to Canada) rather than attend university in Dakar. As voices are raised, Aby tells her mother that she wants to avoid the fate of becoming a gas station manager, and surely that is what the "bac" allows one to do. Predictably, Faat Kine is crushed, both guilt-stricken and angered. As if interpreting this scene, the subsequent extended scene between Maamy and the grandchildren—played over a game of Mancala—concentrates on the matter of finding a partner for Faat Kine. Here we learn two things: first, that both Aby's father, M. Goye, and Djib's father, the now-destitute Boubacar Omar Payone or BOP, are deemed absolutely unsuitable partners for Faat Kine by both children. And second, of the next tier of potential suitors, the children's uncles, only Jean is deemed—especially by Djib—suitable. Little do they know, unlike the audience, that Jean and Faat Kine are already "involved." Maamy implicitly gives the plot her blessing, acknowledging that Jean's identity as a Catholic as well as his status as a widower are problems that will have to be overcome.

The remainder of the film fills in the details—we meet BOP both in flashback and in the present, we meet Faat Kine's "posse," Amy and Mada; we watch Jean throw Djib and Aby out of his office after hearing their proposal; we see Aby acquiesce to her mother's wishes regarding study abroad; and we learn that Pathé has been incarcerated for having murdered both his wife and her lover—leading up to the celebratory "boom." In the final scene, under the auspices of the Club of Utopia and Prospectives (Djib's fledgling political organization), all three potential suitors of Faat Kine show up for the party. There is a climactic scene where Djib confronts both M. Goye and BOP, refusing to humble himself before them while vigorously defending his mother's honor. He rallies the guests—a transparent allegorical embodiment of the young Africa referred to on the radio in the opening scene—and they, under the approving gaze of Maamy and with fingers snapping, expel the two fathers and their friends from the party. Jean then arrives and is welcomed in. After a few intimate dances, Jean and Faat Kine retire to her bedroom, where she beckons him to make love to her. The final shot is an extreme close-up of Faat Kine's bare left foot flexing in apparent satisfaction.

The question raised by this summary, namely, in what sense is this a remake, much less a rearrangement, of *Xala*, doubtless imposes itself with no small urgency. I grant that the claim may seem far-fetched, not least because *Xala* is such a "boys" film, while *Faat Kine* is in a certain sense a "chick flick." However, what strikes me is that, much as though Sembene composed with the seashells thrown by the *marabout* in *Xala*, *Faat Kine* contains essentially the same "narratemes" (including, I would say, that of gender) as the earlier film, but arranged in a way that addresses the changed political circumstances of Senegal. Consider the following: The title character, Faat Kine, could be said to have as her counterpart Madame Diouf from *Xala*. Recall that we meet Madame Diouf as she opens up El Hadji's place of business on the day following his debacle with N'Gone. She is installed in a space very much like that of the Total gas station. True, she is a subordinate, but it is in this sense that the narratemes are re-arranged. Faat Kine's relation to M. Sogne is an inverted reiteration of El Hadji's relation to Madame Diouf. In other words, it is as if Sembene came back to *Xala* and asked: what sort of story would result if *she* were the main character? It would not be a story about impotence, it would be a story about birth control, safe sex, and infidelity. Indeed, the problem here is not about failed copulation, but about promiscuous and unguarded copulation. The long discussion between Faat Kine and her posse about the importance of condoms in the era of HIV/AIDS makes this very clear. This is not to say that the political valences of the link forged in *Xala* between middle-class power and sexual potency are sacrificed, it is just that middle-class power is linked not to potency, but to fidelity, monogamy (and therefore marriage) to be sure, but also faith. *Faat Kine* supplements *Xala*'s meditation on polygamy with a meditation on polyandry and promiscuity.

No doubt the strongest associative link forged between Faat Kine and Madame Diouf concerns the role their respective establishments play in the public sphere of Dakar. In the preceding reading of *Xala*, much was made of the ambivalent relation established by Sembene between El Hadji and *Kaadu*, "the voice." Similar points can be made about the relation between Faat Kine and the newspaper boy who parasitizes her clientele. This figure appears on the periphery of several scenes, but becomes central late in the film when M. Sogne, struck by a front-page story, succumbs to his hawking and buys a paper. In this he repeats Madame Diouf's purchase of *Kaadu* early in *Xala*. To give this event all its accompanying gravity, Sembene stages it so the newspaper boy has two francophone papers draped on each arm: one, the national paper instituted and maintained by Senghor, *Le Soleil* (the sun), the other, *Le Temoin* (the witness/observer), a kindred spirit of, say, *The New York Daily News*, not a tabloid, but close. M. Sogne purchases *Le Temoin*. Brandishing it, he rushes in to Faat Kine's office repeating, "It is not possible!" In a cutaway close-up we see, over Faat Kine's shoulder, the tragic story of Pathé, the disfigured invalid we met in the first gas station scene who, it is reported, killed his wife and her lover in a fit of jealous rage. This prompts Faat Kine to send, via one of her employees, a meal—indeed, a meal BOP earlier accuses Faat Kine of having refused him—to Pathé in prison. Promiscuity and adultery touch base.

There is here an important reiteration and elaboration of the issues raised in *Xala*. First, like the episode of M. Cheli's theft, *Le Temoin* is presented here as working the beat of the urban underclasses. However, it is not doing so in Wolof. Gone is the theme of fostering literacy in one of the several indigenous tongues spoken in Dakar. In its place is the presentation of a new proximity between something akin to the local tabloid press (decidedly not the national press) and Wolof. Pathé speaks to Faat Kine in Wolof, and later, when she mistakes one of his compatriots for him, this scene too transpires entirely in Wolof. Indeed, in this later scene, we see in full-screen close-up a rare instance of written Wolof. What emerges here then is a linguistic politics that recasts ambivalence as translation. *Le Temoin* translates the experience of Pathé into French and makes a Wolof speaker matter to the francophone, Senegalese middle class. The cost of this translation is official degradation, a degradation nevertheless mocked throughout the film, although not, it must be said, without ambivalence. When narratively thematized, as in Maamy's complaint about Djib's having fallen under the amoral influence of television, the official national media is held in contempt. When structurally or enunciatively active, as with the radio in the opening scene, the national media is omniscient, even *griot*-like. Negotiating and thus establishing the poles of this ambivalence is a scene when, after a bitter disagreement between Faat Kine and her children over her need for a partner, Adele, Maamy's *bonne*, turns on the television to catch the end of a segment devoted, apparently, to promoting the virtues of a prosthetic hand. Western technology here reaches out from and through the screen to comfort the anguished family but with a warmth as pathetic as the prehensile grasp of the robotic mechanism on display. Prosthesis of origin indeed.

Of course, the special link forged between Pathé and *Le Temoin*, especially as effected under the auspices of someone routinely referred to as Kine (Sembene, who learned the craft of filmmaking in the Soviet Union, would not be a stranger to the term Kino for the cinema), is somewhat overdetermined in the African context. Once referred to as the "Napoleon of cinema," Charles Pathé and the company founded by him and his brothers represent a decisive point of reference in the history of French cinema. Pathé was the first French firm to take control of marketing Edison's phonograph and kinetoscope, initially serving as an exhibitor but later becoming involved in production and, most importantly, global distribution of its own films. By 1908 in the United States alone, Pathé was selling twice as many films as all the U.S. film companies combined, with production facilities in Russia, India, and Southeast Asia. In addition, Pathé developed an early coloring technique, using stencils, and, perhaps most importantly, developed the first weekly newsreel, Pathé-Journal. If it makes sense to link the culture of imperialism to the international reach of early media networks (print certainly, but radio and the cinema as well), then it makes sense for Sembene to evoke this legacy through the character of Pathé, a character whose twisted fate—one in which the monogamy otherwise sought in the film goes awry—is reduced to a news story, a *fait divers*. More than a passing allusion, this evocation puts in place a relation between not only cinema and journalism, but between two cinemas: the enabling cinema of French colonialism and the cinema of postcoloniality, the cinema, the *Kino*, on display in something named *Faat Kine*. The casting of Pathé, not as the subject but as the object of the news, depends on a historical binary reiterated in the film, indeed a binary linked to the reflexive, that is, enunciative, texture of the film.

In a scene that has its counterpart to one in *Xala*, specifically the third in the series of gags discussed during this book's Intermission, Sembene frames the encounter between anti- and postcolonial Africa at the entrance to a bank. Arriving for a meeting with the bank manager, Faat Kine is accosted by one of her colleagues (Alpho, another station manager), who hustles her for a loan. The heat of their exchange is temporarily dissipated when the bank manager and his associate arrive. As the group passes through the Tati-like glass doors, the manager is buttonholed by Faat Kine's desperate colleague. Alpho explains that polygamy is crippling him financially and that his station will collapse without a loan, not unlike the desperate pleas of El Hadji toward the end of *Xala*. Unimpressed, the bank manager demurs, which provokes the line "you are the embryo of liberal neocolonialism" from Alpho. Ushering him out through the glass door, the bank manager replies, "And you, you are an African from the colonial period." A beggar woman who had earlier accosted the group returns to hound the dejected Alpho soon after his exit.

In the scene from *Xala*, the representative of the state and the representative of the people stand stalled at the doorway that frames their encounter. Here, the African from the colonial period—presumably a man who tragically invests in polygamy as a mode of nativist resistance to colonialism, a man who refuses to use birth control and cannot separate fertilized embryos from power—is ushered back across the threshold by a banker. This version of the old Africa/new Africa binary is an ambivalent one, and even if its structural integrity is sound, this only accentuates its ambivalence. It is hard to imagine Sembene casting the lot of postcolonial Africa with the indigenous representatives of finance capital, and yet the bank manager not only trumps Alpho, but Alpho's scorn for the beggar woman—what Spivak might call "the poorest woman of the South"—rings true. She is implicitly chastised for failing to discern that not all comprador Senegalese are the same. One senses here a complex political calculation that is ultimately only hinted at, one having to do with the sort of economic independence championed in *Guelwaar*, but that in *Faat Kine* is unambiguously linked to the entrepreneurial initiatives of Third World women.[16] Against Spivak and others who have called into question the politics of such initiatives (and the international credit policies that facilitate them), Sembene seems to be suggesting that postcolonial Africa lies at the end of a road other than the one paved by the African socialism of Senghor. Nevertheless, the scene insists not only upon the historical binary, but it associates this binary with the framing device itself, the window through which we see the present and the past darkly. In this sense a transparency, a portal, is opened between the narrative and the enunciative syntax of *Faat Kine*.

To spell out the significance of this portal, and clarify what light is shed upon *Xala* by this comparison, the scene from *Faat Kine* that virtually restages its counterpart from the earlier film deserves comment. It begins at the closing party, the "boom" celebrating Aby's and Djib's academic triumph. The party in *Xala* is the wedding reception that culminates in the failed copulation of El Hadji and N'Gone. True to the logic of rearrangement, several motifs repeat: the whitewashed walls of the villa are punctured by portraits, the villa has an inner court-yard traversed by guests, dancing is much in evidence, sexual aids are proffered and refused (both condoms and Viagra), and so on. In particular, however, the traumatic scene in *Xala* is essentially reshot (much as though Sembene was taking a page from Fassbinder's or Gus Van Sant's playbook). For this reason, the differences assume tremendous importance.

First, there is the nature of the transition being effected. We are not passing from today to tomorrow, but from the film to the cinema, that is, to the auditorial space where credits are accompanied by music, houselights, and the slow dissipation of the serial community called the audience. As I have indicated, the film concludes on the close-up of Faat Kine's foot with the inaugural Kora theme effecting the transition between a final black screen and the rolling of the credits. Second, there is the time elapsed in the sequence. It goes by in nine brief shots. As one can see, the first of these (Figure 16) reiterates the first shot in the sequence from *Xala* almost exactly, directly soliciting the comparison I am elaborating. But from that point on everything is different,

Figure 16

Figure 17

including the concluding suspension of the copula. Perhaps most importantly, there is no bilingual toggling between the reflexive mechanisms of the mirror and the poster. Instead, as is clear in Figure 17, both Jean and Faat Kine appear in her mirror. They are accompanied by mobile images of themselves. More particularly, though, Faat Kine appears both as an image and as a reflection, while Jean appears only in the mirror. Although there is no toggling, the poster is not absent. Here, though, it appears as the wall hanging against which Jean is shot turning, as had N'Gone, to engage his lover. As this shot begins, Jean's back is actually reflected in the mirror and thus superimposed upon the wall hanging—a wall hanging, as has already been noted, that doubles as the scarred bac(k) of Maamy. Back to back, framed between the framed "bacs," Jean and Maamy touch. In addition to having the most tenacious questions about Jean, Maamy is the one largely monolingual figure in the film, two details that complicate any effort to read the relations figured here as "gyno-social" (modeled, obviously, on Sedgwick's "homosocial"). While this places the difference between Wolof and French squarely in the scene, it does so in a way consonant with the more attenuated linguistic politics of the film in general. Gone is the counsel, in Wolof, to be submissive, and in its place is the daughter's desire to select precisely that man her mother's traditional reservations rendered a most dubious suitor.

Enunciatively, the mirror prevails. It repeats the camera's framing of the actors/characters within the sequence. Bilingualism is recast here not as a syntactical rhythm, a toggling, but as the spacing within a shot whose complexity lies entirely in its *mise en scène*. Each of the shots in the sequence subordinates itself to the task of confronting the viewer with this associative detail. They are all, even the slight zoom of Figure 18,

perfectly Western in composition and execution. As a result, the copular suspension, active within the enunciative syntax in *Xala*, simply reappears not at, but *as* the end of the film. Like death on the classical stage, Jean and Faat Kine's lovemaking, after first fading into the background, disappears into the final black screen. The last back? Con-

Figure 18

trolling this is the nature of the traffic passing through the reflexive portal between the narrative and the enunciation of the film. As we have seen, the film mounts a narrative in which the antagonism between Wolof and French, while caught up in the historical binary that makes postcoloniality unlivable in West Africa, is not defined by it. There is a sense in which this antagonism has been metabolized, incorporated, by the Senegalese middle class. Obviously, Sembene has not given up on the political centrality of the social division of gender, nor has he given up on the importance of language in the political field, but he has transformed his thinking about the poetics of a postcolonial cinema, a task begun already with *Ceddo*, the distinctly anti-Islamic film that immediately followed *Xala*.[17]

How might we account for this, and what significance might it be given? Obviously, between the mid-seventies and the end of the century, much has happened in francophone African cinema. With the appearance of precisely those francophone directors who figure so prominently in Ukadike's collection, the level of formal and/or linguistic innovation has risen dramatically. None of Sembene's films has the snazzy visual texture of Jean Pierre Bekolo's much-lauded *Quartier Mozart*. But the bar has not simply been raised, its function has been transformed. For Sembene, it is not simply a matter of imagination or innovation, it is also a question of how one's products circulate and whose sensory palate must be stimulated to attract the attention of an increasingly global market. In his famous 1995 address to FESPACO, Sembene compared the cinema to night school, insisting—in a way that would warm the heart of Raymond Williams—not that film production ought to figure in the curricula of night schools, but that the cinema is part of a popular pedagogy. If it, too, presupposes an absent literacy (as had been the case with the novel), then it risks abandoning, if not losing, its clientele. Moreover, it is clear that the national political changes that foster or menace night school—for Sembene the transition (such as it is) from Senghor to Chiouf—have only aggravated the problems of African socialism in the postindependence context. Because this is itself one of the proper subjects of a night school education, it must figure in a cinema struggling with its own fraught relation to colonialism and its aftermath. A poetics must be forged that is adequate to the delivery of this twisted lesson. On the one hand, this is why Sembene will not let linguistic politics go. On the other hand, this is where it seems appropriate to challenge the solutions he has worked out since the 1980s. What seems so clear about the decision to remake/rearrange *Xala* is Sembene's recognition that it still belongs to the postal present of Senegal. What troubles me is the retreat from the project of a bilingual enunciative syntax, a project that, while it may have less to do with lived linguistic politics of Senegal, has a great deal to do with the poetic politics of the cinema. Coming to terms with this is the stunning achievement of *Xala* that *Faat Kine* allows us to wrestle with so clearly.

Thus, it is not enough to respond thoughtfully to the intricate contradictions of "the other's" critique of neocolonialism, though beginning to do so more consistently would attenuate some of the worst excesses of the current fetishization of an ultimately vapid alterity one finds in official multiculturalism. It is also important that we permit our readings, especially of films whose "national" character is defined by the *intra*national fissuring produced by colonialism, to broach the theoretical problem of the paradigm that has come to define the very logic of enunciation within cinema studies. After all, part of the urgency that drives the "native" interrogation of neocolonialism, derives from the way it silhouettes our blindness to the intricate ways people are antagonized by the struggle over their unlivable identities. We need, in effect, to reverse Roland Barthes's revision of Saussure where linguistics, as a latent theory of cognition, was used to engulf the field of semiology. This is necessary not in order to arrive at the ultimate metalanguage that will permit us to approach all cultural systems as the same, but rather to reopen the question of whether the science of linguistics participates in an insidious form of the Eurocentrism that we have learned to mistrust in its other manifestations. However, just as Rama cannot denounce the sexism of polygamy without invoking the language of those who embrace it as tradition, we cannot study the cinema without drawing upon the very categories that have made the task of constituting multicultural curricula so urgent. While these situations are by no means symmetrical, the antagonisms they share nevertheless partially define the contested terrain of the global struggle over the legacy of colonialism. Precisely because the "never again" that has become virtually synonymous with condemnation of the Holocaust applies equally to colonialism, can we not afford to treat the past as lacking what we want the future to be free of? The concrete struggle against Eurocentrism must therefore risk repeating those aspects of the past that enable us to struggle with and against it today.

CHAPTER 4

Jorge Sanjinés's *El coraje del pueblo*

One of the effects of Roy Armes's placing Sembene and Sanjinés side by side under the editorial rubric of filmmakers who work "astride two cultures" is that their positions and the cinemas that articulate them are rendered structurally homologous. Armes does not argue that the cinemas of Senegal and Bolivia (as embodied in these "engaged" filmmakers) are the same, but he was writing at a time when some of the most immediately pertinent debates within postcolonial studies were just getting under way. Specifically, he was unable to avail himself of the scholarship that addresses itself to the applicability of the postcolonial paradigm outside the Asian and African contexts. This is work that has in certain ways dominated the second decade of postcolonial studies, the 1990s, and because its questions are both generally urgent and immediately relevant, they deserve sustained attention at the outset of this chapter. To put the matter bluntly: is the comparison at the heart of this study coherent and therefore viable?

As my evocation of the 1990s makes evident, there is a substantial literature to consider here. Because there is never world enough nor time, and because his inclusion in Gyan Prakash's anthology *After Colonialism* (1995) indicates his centrality to the applicability debate, I will avail myself of J. Jorge Klor de Alva's work as a representative (all caveats acknowledged) statement of the theoretical and political issues. Specifically, I want to draw on "The Postcolonization of the (Latin) American

Experience: A Reconsideration of 'Colonialism,' 'Postcolonialism,' and 'Mestizaje'" (in Prakash 1995) both to air what is at stake in this debate and to clear the spot where I will set up my reading of Sanjinés.

Klor de Alva's paper is in many ways a rejoinder. It addresses criticisms directed to an earlier iteration of the argument ("Colonialism and Postcolonialism as [Latin] American Mirages" from 1992) and does so in ways that have more than passing bibliographic interest. But first, the later paper. In building to its combative and embattled conclusion, namely, that "neither postcolonialism nor decolonization can be said to have ever taken place in the Americas" (270), the essay involves itself in three important problems: One, what is meant by the term "colonialism" and does that meaning bear properly on what is understood by postcolonialism? Two, how does the intricate relation between the fact of *el mestizaje* and the meaning of colonialism affect postcolonialism? And three, how did intellectual and even academic politics (what Angel Rama might call the politics of *los letrados*) affect the applicability of the concept of colonialism to the Americas in general and Latin America in particular? Along the way, other important matters are raised, notably that of how we (First World academic intellectuals) might distinguish between colonialism and imperialism in a way that would be useful both to the study of Latin America but also to postcolonial studies in general. As we shall see, these matter perhaps more to me than to Klor de Alva. Plainly, there is much here to hold the interests of stakeholders in the debate over the pertinence of postcolonial studies in the Americas. I will sketch the positions taken by Klor de Alva, and in the end, take my distance from certain of his solutions, especially those that ally him with a more typically North American investment in exceptionalism.[1]

With regard to the matter of the meaning of colonialism Klor de Alva avails himself of both history and philology. Most basically he is concerned to show that, in an earlier, precontact moment (notably that of the Roman Empire), a colony was little more than an administrative settlement. Its purpose was not to facilitate control or domination, but to protect imperial interests abroad by sending, in the Roman example, veteran soldiers to live and work in territories occupied by the empire.

Later, a colony came to designate precisely a relation of domination where a small group of foreigners sought, through economic as well as cultural means, to control an indigenous population and project or otherwise extend the interests of a metropolitan, and typically national, center. This shift, and the historical arc on which it is plotted, is what obliges Klor de Alva to conclude that colonialism, *strictu sensu*, did not take place in (Latin) America. Why? Because, by the time colonialism came to mean the foreign domination of an indigenous population, there was no indigenous population left to dominate. It had either been decimated by disease or reproduction. (Here, by the way, is where Klor de Alva's interest in *el mestizaje* enters the equation.) Thus, what was fought as the war of independence was by no means an anticolonial struggle, but rather a quarrel between different sectors of an empire, one differentiated from the other by the largely "hybrid," but certainly not indigenous character of its population.

This establishes an important insight, namely, that when debating cultural politics in Latin America one needs to confront squarely the fact that, unless one is dealing with indigenous peoples and their interests, one is not actually engaging the complex legacy of a belated colonialism. I used "belated" in the Freudian sense of an event that happens for the first time, again. Klor de Alva gets at this through his discussion of, largely, Latin American intellectuals who, in the course of the nineteenth century in particular, began to provide histories for emergent national identities that produced a legacy of colonial domination where there wasn't one. Or, at least there wasn't one in the second, now proper, sense of the term. Here, through a subtle reading of its deployment by said intellectuals, Klor de Alva is able to show how *el mestizaje* emerged as a fetish, one capable of effecting the casuistry whereby a radical principle of heterogeneity became a homogeneous, transnational essence. While he does not go on to examine the consequences for the postcolonial notion of hybridity of this conceptual precursor's fate here, he certainly could, reminding us all in the process of a piece of genealogical detail that would certainly appear to impinge significantly on the applicability debate.

Because Klor de Alva sees postcolonialism as essentially derived from the positions staked out by these Latin American intellectuals (typically, but not necessarily, on the Left) he bases his repudiation of its applicability upon the undigested errors it incorporated from the belated history of colonialism in the region. Like others before him, he is suspicious of the "post-" especially when, per the terms of his analysis, its moment would fall in the gaping belatedness that marks colonialism itself. Would the "post-" fall before or after the "again" that defines the staggered onset of colonialism? One senses that Klor de Alva realizes that there is more here than meets the eye, but he does not go looking for it. Instead, he settles for the scandal of insulting his hosts (in this case, Prakash) by underscoring how regionally circumscribed their version of the postcolonial project truly is. Nevertheless, what convinces me that this is something of a pose is the fact that, unlike the earlier iteration of the piece, here Klor de Alva creates space for the concept of postcoloniality, a concept intimately related to postcolonialism, but obviously not subject to the same self-defeating strictures. Specifically, by paralleling the categories of structure/colony and poststructuralism/postcolonialism he signals that the temporal and spatial problems haunting the "post-" of postcolonialism are precisely the concerns of poststructuralism, an intellectual project both he and I associate with the emergence of the concept of postcoloniality. Because this is where the comparative project I am embarked upon assumes much of its coherence, Klor de Alva's construction of the concept of postcoloniality bears brief elaboration.

> From a postmodern/poststructuralist perspective I agree with Fernando Coronil, among others, that postcoloniality does not need to follow from an "actual" colonial condition. . . . The dismissal of the modernist view of history as a linear (teleological) process, the undermining of the foundational assumptions of linear historical narratives, and the rejection of essentialized identities for corporate units leads to a multiplicity of often conflicting and frequently parallel narratives within which postcoloniality can signify not so much subjectivity "after" the colonial experience as a

subjectivity of oppositionality to imperializing/colonizing (read: subordinating/subjectivizing) discourses and practices. . . . That, I believe, is the way postcoloniality must be understood when applied to U.S. Latinos or Latin American hybrids. (245)

Aside from the way this establishes a clear distinction between postcolonialism and postcoloniality, it also grounds this distinction in a contentious account of the actual, indeed the very sort of account that would presumably fall under the general rubric of the undermined "foundational assumptions" of linear historical narratives. Where, one might wonder, is Klor de Alva situating the actuality, the ground, of his own distinction? Such complications notwithstanding, by implicitly contrasting a specifically anticolonial resistance with a general, though unelaborated, concept of oppositionality, Klor de Alva both makes an important concession (maybe a certain strain of postcolonialism is applicable to the Americas after all) and yet also begs the central question, namely, how are we to think the political logic of anticolonialism (and presumably postcolonialism) without appealing to something like the concept of opposition? Did the Caribes confront but not oppose Columbus and Las Casas? What must oppose mean if that is the case? When did opposition assume the meaning that radically distances it from the moment of contact? When did that meaning return, in effect, to redefine that contact, for the first time again? In other words, this might well constitute a fatal concession in that it introduces precisely the term that appears to scramble the neat oppositions from which the essay otherwise derives its critical force. In addition, what are we to make of the way Klor de Alva puts the distinction between colonialism and imperialism in his affirmation of the applicability of the concept of postcoloniality?

As Klor de Alva's probing meditation comes to a close, it worries deeply over the distinction between colonialism and imperialism. However, in the citation the distinction is used, almost in passing, to establish that postcoloniality opposes both, though differently (presumably, anticolonialism only opposes colonialism). Faithful to the strategy of parallelism that underwrites much of the essay, Klor de Alva links colonialism with subordinating and imperialism with subjectivizing, suggesting of course that the oppositionality of postcoloniality bears on both subordinating and subjectivizing. What this illuminates, if obliquely, is the condition of what I have been calling the unlivability of identity. Whether or not we accept the claim that imperialism alone subjectivizes, what is important here is that opposing it postcolonially means recognizing both the inhospitable character of one's lived circumstances, and the fact that the subject's life is radically other. One cannot live one's life anymore, and in this sense oppositionality pairs contestation and displacement. These implications of Klor de Alva's discussion I find both compelling and useful. However, as he maneuvers imperialism into the historical schema with which he approached colonialism, linking it to colonialism's association with foreign control, he lets something important, about Latin America in particular, slip. Specifically, in the work of Latin American intellectuals, the critique of imperialism has for a long time tended to mask the claims of anticolonialism. In other words, the concept of imperialism, while it may have radicalized the concept of colonialism by insisting upon its relation to domination, has also tended to fold the concept of colonialism into that of imperialism, where the North/South struggle almost entirely overrides the ongoing national conflicts between *los mestizos* and the ethnic formations that, regardless of how distant they may be from their precontact ancestors, nevertheless do not speak Spanish, do not practice Christianity, and do not regard their class affiliations as fundamental to their political identities. Thus, while Klor de Alva is certainly right to index the relevance of postcoloniality to a distinction between colonialism and imperialism, he sacrifices much of the former's critical force by not articulating the way oppositionality might bear on the fraught relation between colonialism and imperialism, especially as it is lived out in the Latin American context.

In saying this, I have no interest in throwing the proverbial baby out with the no less proverbial bathwater. On the contrary. What is deeply pertinent about Klor de Alva's analysis is that, through the concept of postcoloniality, it both clarifies and overcomes problems that might otherwise lie at the heart of my study. By arguing that Klor de Alva fails to articulate fully the links among postcoloniality, imperialism, and colonialism, one is not thereby committed to repudiating his account of the applicability of the postcolonial problematic to Latin America. It does, of course, entail paying heed to the complications I have identified, and it is precisely this mode of attentiveness that I will attempt to sustain in the readings that follow. Specifically, I want to explore here how the intellectual and political tension between colonialism and imperialism engages the enunciative dimension of the cinema of postcoloniality. To do so, it will be necessary to think carefully about the various modes of bilingualism active in films produced within Latin American cinema. Obviously, not all films are equally relevant here, and it is precisely my concern to foreground those films where indigenous tongues interlace with Spanish (the case of Brazil reminding one how difficult it is to generalize about Latin America) that led me to the work of Jorge Sanjinés. By reading this work carefully, it will become possible to consider how different political histories (in both senses) articulate themselves in different enunciative modes, thereby underscoring from a different angle the importance of the concept of enunciation to the discipline of cinema studies.

Filming in Tongues

As is implied by its title, this chapter will largely focus on the textual analysis of a specific film, Jorge Sanjinés's *El coraje del pueblo* ("the courage of the people"). While justification for this focus is provided in what follows, I do not aim to invoke it as an excuse for avoiding discussion of others of Sanjinés's remarkable films. On the contrary, as in the case of my discussion of Sembene, both precision and clarity will require me to consider at least two of his works at some length: *Yawar Mallku* ("the blood of the condor") from 1969 and the comparatively recent *La nación clandestina* from 1989. And while *La nación* will function here much as *Faat Kine* did in the preceding chapter, as an illuminating contrast to the earlier film, the focus will properly remain on one film,

El coraje. In insisting upon this, it becomes easier to establish what the concern for a poetics of postcoloniality brings to a corpus more typically valued for its anthropological or sociological evidence than for its semiotic texture. Here, of course, I want to side with critics of those who theorize the cinema simply as the means by which to get to another end. More often than not, under such circumstances, one is compelled to say a little about many things in order, finally, to talk at length about something else altogether. Armes toys with this approach—after all, he has set himself the task of producing something like an academic survey— and while he never quite gives into it, he leaves the figure of one's being "astride" two cultures relatively undifferentiated at the level of the film work. Both Sembene and Sanjinés deserve better

El coraje is Sanjinés's third feature film. It was made in 1971 with the help of an Italian television production team, and thematically it returns to the concerns of *Aysa!*, a short film about miners made in 1964 under the auspices of the Bolivian Cinematographic Institute. *El coraje* is based upon the brutal suppression of a strike at the Siglo XX mines by the Barrientos government in 1967. Although the film goes to remarkable lengths to articulate the popular memory of this event with near documentary fidelity, it nevertheless assumes narrative form. For those unfamiliar with either the massacre of "*el noche de San Juan*" or its representation, I offer the following synopsis.

The film opens with what we later realize is a framing device. In the first sequence we see a large and tumultuous group of people descend a mountain slope and traverse a plain. They are led by María Barzola. A small platoon of soldiers opens fire on the group killing María (among many others). This event, set in 1942, initiates a series of similar atrocities that serve as the context for the massacre at Siglo XX, but it also represents the naming of the space where it unfolds in that the plain becomes known as "the María Barzola" in commemoration of the courage depicted in this scene. The footage shot here is later recycled in the closing sequence, and we realize that, in addition to having mastered the rigors of organic form, Sanjinés has framed his entire film within this event of naming the space of its representation.[2]

Through a compilatory montage we move from 1942 to 1967, tracing a virtual archipelago of atrocities. Then, by means of strategically selected vignettes, we are exposed to the conditions of daily life in the Siglo XX mining camp. In an extended sequence composed of several scenes, we witness a bitter and divisive confrontation between "*las mujeres de Siglo XX*" (led, significantly, by Domitila Barrios de Chungara) and first the grocer, then the commissary supervisor, where, in addition to learning that there is nothing to eat in the mining camp, we learn how the politics of gender figure within the class struggle at Siglo XX. Women are on the front lines both in militancy and misery.

In the confrontation with the supervisor, we are introduced to one of the key narrative elements in the film. In a moment of defensive exasperation, the supervisor accuses the women of mounting a "political strike" as opposed to a protest, the clear implication being that, if their presence is motivated by "politics," as opposed to something as concrete as "misery," then not only is their action illegitimate, but it then deserves whatever retaliatory response it receives. The film, of course, proceeds to reveal the falsity of this distinction, not by underscoring the hypocrisy motivating it but by showing that the alliance between the strikers and the guerillas around Che Guevara is selective and clearly a result of management's refusal to recognize the political character of unmitigated misery. In establishing the falsity of this distinction, the film oscillates back and forth between representations of events (acts of torture, futile efforts to locate *desaparecidos*, and so on) leading up to the massacre and the stories of survivors who incarnate the link between the moment of filming and the event motivating the film. This micrological enunciative texture at once anticipates and complicates the framing device noted earlier. Through the voice of Professor Eusebio Gironda Cabrera, one of the survivors, we are presented with the "film's" analysis of the irreducible role of North American imperialism in the destruction of Bolivian labor unions in general and the miners' unions in particular. His perspective is resoundingly echoed in a later meeting where the miners shout, "*Bolivia libre? Si! Colonia yanqui? No!*" clearly indicating that the question of postcolonialism in Bolivia is not about Spain, but about the United States—precisely, one should add, as Klor de Alva has argued.

The massacre, which has been anticlimactically foreshadowed throughout, then follows. The festivities of *el noche de San Juan*, which include drinking, dancing, commiserating, and promising, are obliterated by an attack organized around the struggle over a warning siren activated by a few armed miners that the army wants to silence (in order to keep the casualty rate high and the profile of its intervention low). More than one hundred people are killed. The film concludes with a eulogy to the dead and a condemnation of those responsible (including the then-current president), with the final scene returning us to the plain of María Barzola and a final freeze-frame that, like Sanjinés's immediately preceding *Yawar Mallku* (his second feature film), leaves the dialectic at a standstill.

Though it may seem contrived to do so, I want to broach my reading of this film by situating it in relation to the difference that, according to Sanjinés, separates it from *Yawar Mallku*. In an interview with the magazine *Triunfo* given in 1977, Sanjinés explained,

> The peasants resisted a work like *Yawar Mallku* because of its formal structure. We asked ourselves what had happened, in that this film did not function in the peasant context as it had in the petty-bourgeois one, and we discovered that it was a strictly cultural problem. We needed to search for a coherent language with the capacity of conceiving itself collectively, in conjunction with a collectivist culture, and little by little we began encountering solutions.

In detailing these solutions he added,

> We think that the form of filmmaking must result from an attentive observation of the people's culture. In this way we began to feel, for example, that the "close-up" ("*primer plano*," was also an obstacle to the clear comprehension of our propositions. We noted that already formally the film distanced people from reality, it created obstacles for them. For this

reason we now use wide shots, general shots, which give popular actors the greatest freedom of action and impede the authoritarian manipulation of montage that is characteristic of bourgeois cinema." (Sanjinés 1979, 155–56)

Though the film to which Sanjinés is contrasting *Yawar Mallku* is not *El coraje* (he is referring to *El enemigo principal*, which followed *El coraje* by three years), it is clear that, as he says elsewhere, "a qualitative leap" separates *Yawar Mallku* from *everything* that comes after it. Moreover, the formal concerns emphasized by Sanjinés here apply to *El coraje* rather obviously. But finally the issue of applicability is not what is important. To my mind, there are two formulations in these citations that are particularly suggestive and that therefore solicit an attentive reading if we are to make headway in our understanding of foreign film languages. First, there is the equation implicitly drawn between form and language, an equation given further weight by a long discussion of film language in Sanjinés's essay "Problems of Form and Content in Revolutionary Cinema" (in Chanan 1983) where he underscores the exemplary achievement of *El coraje* in articulating a film language of the people. Secondly, there is the characteristic insistence upon linking film form and "*la cultura de un pueblo.*" As my title suggests, it is this complex and ambitious link between film language and the people's culture that I find intriguing and well worth pursuing in a reading of *El coraje*, a film made with respect for this link explicitly in mind.

But first, what might be said about the film language in *Yawar Mallku?* Although it might make sense to follow through on Sanjinés's observation, made elsewhere, to the effect that his language is largely modeled on the neorealist codes of Rossellini and de Sica, more instructive is careful consideration of a scene from *Yawar Mallku* that, by virtue of its content (the shooting of several indigenous characters by the army), certainly should have worked for the peasant audience but apparently did not. It is a scene comprised of two sequences, and it constitutes an early moment in the plot. The sequences are distinguished dramatically between the anticipation, and then the execution, of the execution.

The first sequence is comprised of thirteen shots, the second of twenty-seven. Although twice as long, the second sequence actually takes up less of the entire two minutes and six seconds of the scene, indicating that the duration of the shots and the rhythm of their combination changes dramatically. One important, perhaps crucial, result of this change is that something only implicit in the first sequence becomes only too explicit in the second. Indeed, it becomes so explicit as to become puzzling and for that very reason directly pertinent to the matter at hand: the film language of *Yawar Mallku*.

In the fourth shot of the first sequence, where the film's protagonist, Ignacio (the "condor" or Mallku, that is, the chosen leader or protector of the village) and two companions are being led up into the mountain to their execution, something very Soviet interrupts the neorealist cast of the scene. Specifically, Sanjinés, through the position, stability,

Figure 19

Figure 20

and angle of his camera, essentially recreates an early sequence from Sergei Eisenstein's *Alexander Nevsky:* the sequence in which the "Mongol host" is descending upon Nevsky's fishing party, and Eisenstein and Tisse (his cameraman), who have otherwise been busily rooting the Russians in and on their land, frame the Mongols as teetering on its very edge (Figure 19). In Sanjinés's shot (Figure 20), the victims, the soldiers, and the presiding officer lumber up the rock path, moving right to left and, due to the camera position and angle, reconfiguring the rectangle of the screen as the parallelogram of the tractor tread of a tank. What might otherwise have been merely an intertextual allusion, however, is given considerable weight in the second sequence. In a textbook illustration of what Eisenstein understood by the montage cell of the shot, Sanjinés renders all the ugly violence of the execution in the selection and combination of shots, some of which are only slightly more than ten frames in length (see, for example, Figures 21–24). Within seconds, nine shots report, bodies fall and writhe, wounds are clutched, soldiers reload, and then suddenly the impassive sublimity of the mountain valley is restored. *Psycho* might also come to mind here, until one recalls that Eisenstein, with his stunning treatment of the Odessa Steps in *The Battleship Potemkin* or, perhaps even more pertinently, with his rendering of the machine gunner firing on/in the crowd in *October*, is Hitchcock's precursor and teacher here. The entire scene assumes even greater shock value than it might otherwise have because this moment in the plot falls at quite a different point in the story. In fact, we have only just been introduced to Ignacio, whose drunken ramblings in an earlier scene tell us everything we need to know about this execution but before we are prepared to hear it. In effect, Ignacio is shot (in fact, mortally wounded) by the Bolivian army working in

Figure 21

Figure 22

Figure 23

Figure 24

conjunction with the U.S. Peace Corps in retaliation for Ignacio's attack on a clinic that, under the guise of providing gynecological care to indigenous women, is in fact sterilizing them.

What is then puzzling about Sanjinés's appropriation of the enunciative syntax of Eisenstein is the way it ends up in alignment with the depiction of the power of his political enemies. Even without knowing anything more about the subject matter of *Yawar Mallku* than what motivates the shooting of Ignacio, it is clear that the film aligns itself with, if not communism, then certainly an unflinching Left critique of North American imperialism. Given that, one might expect Eisenstein's visual vocabulary to resonate more widely in the film and certainly not be confined to articulating the self-serving brutality of the Bolivian army. Although puzzling, perhaps even troubling, a few things need to be said here. First, there is Sanjinés's acute sense of audience. While it is true that this awareness only comes to him after the fact, he does recognize that, while Eisensteinian montage might "say something" to the petit bourgeois members of his audience, it certainly says something quite different (if anything at all) to the "people" with whom he seeks to align his cinema. In effect, the function of this visual vocabulary, as the evocation of a specifically politically charged bilingualism, would be lost to, as he calls them, the peasants. As if committed to Benveniste's concept of "discourse," where a sender and a receiver are put into relation in the utterance, Sanjinés concludes that the film language of *Yawar Mallku* is not language after all, or at least it is not language in the sense that he uses the term.

Secondly, there is the matter of strategy. Aside from the issue of the efficacy of the language involved, there is the question of what may or may not have complicated the bilingual gesture presented in the scene. The larger story to which Ignacio belongs is one he shares with his brother, Sixto. Once wounded, it is to him that Ignacio's wife, Paulina, turns. Sixto has long ago abandoned the village and has gone to work in the manufacturing sector of La Paz. While not fully proletarianized, Sixto exhibits a strong working-class consciousness. In the course of struggling to find blood for his brother (whence the film's title), he effects something of a fusion between his class consciousness and an emergent indigenous consciousness, one that is politicized in a way quite different from Ignacio. This, especially in the context of Sanjinés's corpus, would appear to stand very near the core of the statement made by *Yawar Mallku*, and as such it suggests that there may have been more to the strategic evocation of Soviet montage than first meets the ear and eye. In other words, given that Sanjinés is seeking to forge a Marxism that does not foreclose the colonial problematic (as defined by Klor de Alva), and given that this problematic is most vivid for him in the language politics of the region (as we shall see), then perhaps it was not only important but necessary to cast Eisenstein's visual vocabulary as an enemy of the people. This, of course, suggests a different kind of failure, in that it opposes one language to another, remaining resolutely within good and evil, rather than forging an effectively bilingual enunciation. Eisenstein achieves reflexivity—through intellectual montage—by making the phenomenal surface of the film emerge as the purveyor of its narrative effects. This fuses language and surface in a way that, I would argue, makes Sanjinés's task infinitely more challenging. When everything becomes discourse, variations and inflections are engulfed. This may not, I will concede, be the precise way to formulate the strategic character or aspect of Sanjinés's dissatisfaction with *Yawar Mallku*, but it gives us a way to understand why the question of language(s) survives the break that enables *El coraje*.[3]

Clarifying this will require me to pressure the concept of language that organizes Sanjinés's approach to the form of revolutionary cinema more explicitly. This takes us immediately to the discussion of *El coraje* and the problems it poses with regard to several concerns sketched in my opening remarks. Despite the fact that semiology, during the period when Sanjinés is working out his notion of a popular filmic language, has deeply transformed the way film theorists debate the pertinence of the linguistic paradigm in the cinematic domain, there is little evidence that the term "language" resonates in this way for him. Predictably, this is due to convictions rather than ignorance, for Sanjinés is remarkably well informed about film theory and practice throughout the world. Contrary to what an acknowledgment of such convictions might lead one to assume, Sanjinés does not reject the notion that the selection and combination of shots is where the linguistic paradigm bears directly on the practice of filmmaking, although at times he does seem to shift his focus from the structure and texture of the "imaginary signifier" to the traditions or genres of cultural expression. It is clear, for example, in the citation from *Triunfo*, that enunciative preference is deliberately given to wide-angle establishing shots and long takes, and this is done with an eye toward expressing the revolutionary content of the film in the proper visual vocabulary. But what is equally clear, and I think more problematical (if not even contradictory), is Sanjinés's apparent belief that the film language of the people is something like the realism discovered by the Lumière brothers and later championed by André Bazin, good Europeans if there ever were any.

Consider Sanjinés's following remarks from "Problems of Form and Content." After stressing how both *El coraje* and *El enemigo* used peasant actors and historically accurate locations, Sanjinés writes,

> The peasants used the filming to break the silence of oppression and speak openly, saying to the judge and the boss in the film what they wanted to say to their counterparts in reality. At such moments cinema and reality came together. They were the same thing. In the evident external circumstances artificiality was clearly present. But the cinematic fact was fused with reality through the people's act of revelation and creation. (quoted in Chanan, 35)

In elaborating the consequences of this view at the level of enunciation, Sanjinés repeats the claim that, in order to secure involvement of the peasant spectator and to stabilize a collective protagonist, it was necessary to minimize close-ups, excessive camera movement, and short takes.

When close-ups do occur, "these never get closer to the subject than would be possible in reality," for to do so would "brutally impose the director's point of view, imposing meanings which should arise from the events themselves" (quoted in Chanan, 36).

The problem here is not primarily Sanjinés's somewhat fanciful extrapolation of what Antonio Gramsci would call "the organic intellectual," nor even the peculiar way he conflates the passivity of the film technology with the activity of the people, as if the long take has no imaginary, and therefore ideological, value. What I find odd is the way he implicitly aligns the speech of the people (the breaking of silence) with the formal syntax of realism, without really confronting the irreducible multiplicity of the people's speech, and this from a man who otherwise insists that the form (i.e., language) of filmmaking must arise from an attentive observation of the culture of the people. As Sanjinés himself has stressed, the peasant population in Bolivia is divided equally between Aymara and Quechua speakers, many of whom can also speak, or at least understand, the colonial language of Spanish (1979, 112).

In fact, in a provocative and insightful attack on "leftists" in Latin America, Sanjinés argued,

> The devaluation of our culture comes from *los conquistadores* and the Spanish colonizers, and this has been handed down in the republican epoch and has now been passed on to us. Many leftists underestimate this culture; they are unfamiliar with it, they underestimate the richness it has, both in terms of contents and potentialities, and this is extremely serious. Many leftists continue to be racists. The political vanguard, of either petty-bourgeois or bourgeois extraction, ignores our culture and does not continue to speak the language of the majority of the people. Such is the reality, the majority of the population has a culture which does not correspond with the culture of this minority that heads the movement of the left. . . . Anyone, no matter how far to the left they are, who does not speak the language of the people on *el altiplano*, or who is unfamiliar with this culture, would be as much an outsider on *el altiplano* of La Paz as would be a Spaniard. This is tragic. (1979, 151)

Significantly, Sanjinés goes on here to disassociate himself from *"indigenismo,"* making it clear that his point, like that made by Klor de Alva, is not to indulge the fantasy of a return to a precontact moment as the objective of a political transformation of Bolivian society. Rather, what emerges here is his keen sense of the need to recognize the plurality of tongues that constitute the language of the people. And yet, this is precisely what strikes me as odd. One would think that someone who understood the link between language, culture, and the cinema as clearly as does Sanjinés would recognize that, if the very form of revolutionary filmmaking is to arise from an abiding exchange with the people, then cinematic realism—with all its investments in monologic immediacy— is not enough. A *cine junto al pueblo* cannot simply show Quechua or Aymara and Spanish in relation to one another, cannot, for example, simply have a stationary, wide-angle shot of a peasant and a Spaniard conversing and failing to understand one another. The point would presumably be to integrate this linguistic and cultural relation into the act of showing it, in effect to produce and cultivate what I have been calling a mode of bilingual filmic enunciation.[4]

But what precisely might be at stake in the implicit concept of an Aymaran or Quechuan film language? Sanjinés gives us important clues here. In fact, I think he understands more about this situation than he realizes, a situation that, I will argue, has prompted him to misrecognize the nature of the "qualitative leap" between *Yawar Mallku* and *everything* that comes after it, a misrecognition triggered by the conflicted ways that Latin American intellectuals live and seek to oppose the contradictory configuration of colonialism and imperialism.

As we have seen, Sanjinés regards the syntactic interplay between close-ups and other shots as problematical. In fact, in his remarks to *Triunfo* he characterizes the close-up as fundamentally alienating to peasant culture in Bolivia. Elsewhere he has sharpened the ethnic and ultimately political character of this point. Because of the psychological connotation of the close-up (it is typically used either to frame the face as an indexical map of the character's thoughts and feelings or to isolate a psychologically charged detail—think of the heroine's handbag in

Marnie), Sanjinés treats it as a key syntactical device in the repository of
an *auteurist* cinema, a form of filmmaking intimately associated with
Europe (France, in particular) and North America (Hollywood, in particular). One might reasonably conclude then that the alienating effect
of the close-up is due to its syntactical status within a predominantly
white, unabashedly Eurocentric film culture. As we have seen, the point
is not that the close-up is itself problematical, for to assume this would
be to misunderstand the very concept of syntax in the cinematic field.
Rather, the point is that one must avoid using the enunciative pattern-
ing through which the close-up secures its psychological status. But
what does this mean, and how might such avoidance articulate with the
bilingualism of the Bolivian people?

This is where things get really interesting. Given the divide Sanjinés perceives between *Yawar Mallku* and everything that comes after it,
and given that this divide is understood as indexed directly to the level
of syntactic alienation experienced by popular audiences, why is it that
in a film like *El coraje* one still finds the syntactic device of the close up?
In a particularly significant sequence, for example, where the full complexity of the Bolivian army's relation to the miners is crystallized, we
watch as two soldiers crouch behind a stone wall, one firing upon people
in the street. In a series of six shots, most of them medium shots, we
are presented with a confrontation in which one of the soldiers is shot
by the other for refusing to fire upon the people in the street (a motif
that returns in *La nación*). As he is shot, we get a full-frame close-up of
a badge on one soldier's jacket. It identifies him, or at least his jacket, as
a "Jungle Expert" (in English), suggesting of course the presence of U.S.
military "advisers" in the Bolivian army.[5] The close-up here functions
in the typical manner of highlighting, from a patently "unreal" focal distance, a significant detail, at least one designed to have a psychological
impact on the audience. The dialectical reader will no doubt hasten to
point out that this close-up is used in a manner that duly reflects its content, namely, an act of aggression against the miners, which is certainly
not to be overlooked. In this sense, it succeeds better, or is at least less
charged with ambivalence, than the execution scene from *Yawar Mallku*

discussed earlier. However, if I have drawn our attention to this particular shot, it is because, of the numerous close-ups that provide *El coraje* with its enunciative texture, this is perhaps the *least* problematical one. Far more typically, Sanjinés appears willing to exploit the close-up for all of its standard narrative potential, and yet one wonders whether this is all there is to it.

In what sense or to what degree, then, does this film actually realize the qualitative leap that allegedly separates it from *Yawar Mallku?* To be sure, *El coraje* is organized around a collective protagonist, the people, and it was "scripted" in collaboration with them as an explicit articulation of popular memory. Actual survivors were called upon to re-enact, to re-stage, their survival. But, in terms of form, in terms of film language, is there any clear indication that a leap has been executed? I think there is, but to grasp it, one has to flesh out the cinematic discourse within which Sanjinés is operating, where, in effect, his aim is being defined and deflected in two separate directions.

If we follow the cues given us by Sanjinés, then we can organize the film language around broad categories of shot distance. On one side we have everything in the medium to long (including aerial) range, or what Sanjinés calls "the objective," and on the other, talking heads and close-ups of varying length, all of which he refers to, predictably, as "the subjective." Let me hasten to add that, though this arrangement might seem to invite the characterization "bilingual," I do not think this term yet applies. At best here we are working with, as was suggested by my remark about the "Jungle Expert" close-up, two dialects of the same film language. What we need is a syntactical practice that actually fuses the objective and the subjective in a manner that underscores their distinct linguistic derivations. Such a practice presents itself in Sanjinés's ingenious appropriation of the zoom.

A standard instance of mobile framing, the zoom, by virtue of the structure and mechanics of the lens, articulates two positions: the wide angle and the telephoto.[6] One can move in either direction and at many different speeds. As a mobile framing it is intimately tied to the control of screen space, where it is quite literally capable of redrawing the boundary between what is on and off screen, a boundary that ultimately reaches to the very limit of the diegesis itself. In this sense the zoom is radically reflexive, making the screen itself mime the viewfinder whose selectivity appears upon it. While one certainly sees zoom shots used in Hollywood narrative cinema, its more typical application has been in so-called independent and ethnographic filmmaking, both instances of attempts to work on or at the limit of Western film culture. Especially as concerns ethnographic practice, the zoom shot fulfills the dual syntactic function of focusing attention on what then become telling "factual" details and of varying the texture of the image track, often for patently promotional effects. The truth must never be boring. Such effects and details inscribe a visual sign of nonintervention in that the zoom allows one to get closer to an event without actually moving, without, so the story goes, interrupting the unfolding of what is being filmed. Significantly though—and this seems important to Sanjinés—when one zooms forward from wide-angle to telephoto, the experience is not that of approximation. Instead, what one sees in the collapsed spatial relations of the telephoto image (where the foreground and background appear merely superimposed) is in effect our distance *from* the event as part of its visual definition.

This matters to Sanjinés—faithful student of Brecht that he is—because, as he says in "Form and Content," distance permits reflection. The zoom, both because it allows us to approach from a distance and because it, paradoxically, is less invisible than cutting while achieving some of the same effects, represents the ideal syntactical device of a revolutionary cinema. In effect, it reproduces in the visual character of the film the dialectical proximity between the people, as guardians of popular memory, and the film crew that Sanjinés saw as so crucial to the work of Ukamau (the film collective of Sanjinés, Oscar Soria, and Ricardo Rada) after *Yawar Mallku*. But in what sense can the zoom in *El coraje* be said to articulate itself as a non-Western film language? This is the really the crux of the matter. To resolve it, I propose that we turn to the film itself and consider a couple scenes through which we can frame the terms of my proposition.

The two scenes I want to examine are in many ways typical, but they recommend themselves because of their function in the plot, such as it is, and because of their thematic preoccupation with the thorny matter of the spokesperson, in this case, Domitila Barrios de Chungara. As concerns the plot, we are dealing here with the beginning of the episode evoked in my synopsis where *las mujeres de Siglo XX* (the double entendre is far from insignificant) confront first the grocer and later the commissary supervisor. It is here that the social division of gender is knotted with the political question of the protest itself: is it or is it not "political"? The issues raised by the presence of Barrios de Chungara are thorny because they crystallize the dialectic of the individual and the collective, thus challenging someone committed to breaking with the politics and aesthetics of individualism in the most direct way possible. In fact, I would argue that the very possibility of a cinema *junto al pueblo* rests upon one's ability to embed personal testimony within collective experience without resorting to typification or psychologism.[7]

What I want to draw attention to in the scenes is the contrasting ways in which Sanjinés enunciates the close-up. My point is that there is a distinctly bilingual dimension operating here. In the first scene, comprised of six shots, we are situated in the interior of the Barrios de Chungara home. In a medium long shot we see her approaching the door of her home (Figure 25). In a second medium long shot, rotated ninety degrees, we see her enter. Then, in a close-up, we see a shelving unit cluttered with pots and pans. Food is conspicuously absent (Figure 26).

Figure 25

On the soundtrack we hear Domitila talking in Spanish about her father's belief in the equal rights of women. This close up is actually a telephoto shot that we recognize when the camera gently zooms back to reveal Domitila and one of her children in the foreground. It is certainly not accidental that, in a subsequent scene, this entire set-up is recreated, but an official portrait of Simón Bolívar replaces the subject of the shelving unit with Domitila and her child seated beneath it. In the fourth and fifth shots of the initial sequence, both medium close-ups, we witness an enunciative syntax that follows a very familiar pattern. Abruptly, without transition, we simply cutaway to two children engaged in activities (Figures 27 and 28). These are coded as "telling moments"; her children do what they can to amuse themselves under the circumstances. These shots stand out starkly from the telephoto close up that was almost immediately reconfigured as a wide-angle shot reframing both the objects shown and our visual access to them. In the sixth and final shot of the initial sequence of the scene, we begin with a cut to a medium shot that then pans left to right, revealing the domestic space and its occupants, coming to rest on Domitila. As she turns to address us, there is a slight zoom in and a craning downward of the camera that then comes to rest at her level

Figure 26

Figure 27

Figure 28

(Figure 29). Although her voice, which is now discussing her involvement with the "housewives committee," has continued on the soundtrack, it is strictly nondiegetic. We see clearly that she is not speaking her words.

Figure 29

Figure 30

Figure 31

As if to "correct" this, the next scene, comprised of nine shots, begins with a close-up on Domitila who is criticizing someone off-screen to the left (Figure 30). Her voice is now synched to her lips. This sequence is set in the interior of the *pulpería*. Although there is a massive spatio-temporal condensation here, it passes virtually unnoticed because we are so accustomed to this enunciative vocabulary. We establish the subject in one shot, and then, in a revealing close-up, we hear her story, her words. As this scene unfolds, particularly in shots two, three, and nine (all considerably longer takes than any of the others) we again witness Sanjinés's use of the two types of close-ups. In shot two (Figure 31) for example, which begins as a medium two-shot of the grocer and his assistant framed against bare shelves, their idle scale in the middle foreground, there is a slight left to right pan and a tracking back that sets up a precipitous and abrupt zoom that singles out the face of a woman, just as she begins vehemently ticking off all those items that are missing from everyone's shelves. They are heard but not seen. This telephoto close up (Figure 32) flattens her against the wall, giving us access to her testimony and criticism, but at the price of this visual inscription of our access.

Shot three then answers with a cutaway medium close-up that centers on yet another woman who aggressively pursues the tongue-lashing of the grocer. Then, so the audience recognizes that we are indeed confronting the problem of the "spokesperson"—a theme made explicit in a slightly later scene—we zoom back to reframe the three women with Domitila at the center, and then zoom in on her as she resumes her criticism (Figure 33). Here, she is not flattened against a wall, as was her *compañera*. Instead, she is visually blended into the collective. The solidarity is graphic.

Once there was meat, butter, olive oil...

Figure 32

It is significant that the women resist every effort made by the grocer and his assistant to either erase the difference between

If you don't complain we'll go to Catavi...

Figure 33

them ("we are workers too") or to reduce this difference to a gendered "complaint" ("it is always the same women"). As the ninth and final shot makes clear, they want the grocer to accompany them to the commissary assistant's office not just so that he might actually answer the door, but so that the grocer and his assistant can redeem themselves and prove that their explanations are not simply patronizing rationalizations. What is remarkable about the ninth shot is the choreography of the camera that is utilized to give the zoom close-up its cultural and political meaning. The shot begins as a medium shot of the grocer and his assistant (Figure 34). As the quarrel intensifies, the camera pans and then tracks around behind the two men so that their backs visually block (blacken and obstruct) the space between the camera and the women (Figure 35). At this point the dispute has polarized into a gendered accusation and a

Figure 34

Figure 35

provocative invitation, but it is the men's bodies that have displaced the middle ground. As the sequence comes to a close, the camera, through a series of dramatic movements, tracks hurriedly out from behind the men, and as all three "spokespeople" talk at once (an important sonic articulation of graphic solidarity), it executes a final zoom that frames the third *compañera* in a telephoto medium close-up. The scene concludes as she pounds her fist on the countertop.

What I want to draw attention to here is the way the zoom not only functions to approximate without cutting, but how, in this shot, it acquires the special value of a process obstructed by the recalcitrance of the grocer. Literally, the zoom can only be used here when the camera is moved so as to remove the men from the middle ground their position (in both senses) has rendered inaccessible. In this sense, what might otherwise be regarded as an empty enunciative strategy is brought into association with the content of the dispute itself. The point here is not that the zoom close-up is "on the side" of the women. Rather, it is caught up in the field of politicizable contingencies organized by the interests at stake in the miners' struggle.

This said, I want to push beyond the obvious observation that, by using the zoom, Sanjinés is in effect editing in the camera, or put another way, he is flattening the distance between the scene of directorial control—the editing room—and the scene of the profilmic events and in *this* sense producing a *cine junto al pueblo*. This is of course true, but we need to remember that he uses both types of close-ups, and that it is precisely the interrelation, or dialogue, between them that needs to be situated within the interests at stake in the struggle. To proceed here I think we need to consider in what way the telephoto close-up and the zoom engage the language of the people, in this case Aymara.

In the debates that raged around the introduction of the linguistic paradigm within cinema studies, at least one issue seemed fated to remain uncontroversial, namely, that film language had little to do with speech and certainly nothing whatsoever to do with national tongues.[8] In effect, while there might well be a *plan américain* (a medium shot, typically of people), this had nothing to do with the English spoken in America. As we have seen, this was because the linguistic paradigm was understood to bear upon *langue*, not *parole*. It has been my contention throughout however that, precisely because the debates around post-colonialism have obliged us to recognize the subtle Eurocentrism of the structuralisms that conditioned them, it is time to revisit and probe this received wisdom. Though there is much to reflect upon here, I will pass by the issue of locating the very notion of "language system" in the West to take up the distinctive syntactic features of Aymara, the indigenous language predominantly spoken in the region of the Siglo XX mines from which Sanjinés took the title of his first film on the Bolivian miners, *Aysa!*.

I stress the syntactical issue for the following reasons. First, because syntax qualifies as a matter of language structure and thus avoids the stricture that earlier had neutralized this line of reflection within film studies. But second, and even more importantly, syntax is one of the key points of intersection between language and filmic enunciation. For example, it is now commonplace in film studies to characterize a shot/reverse pattern, that is, the way one typically and correctly enunciates the statement "these people are communicating," as a piece of film syntax (see chapter 2). Although I am no more a speaker of Aymara than of Wolof, even a cursory analysis of the former's syntactic system reveals some striking features. According to Martha J. Hardman, a leading scholar of Aymara in North America,

> Aymara is a suffixing language, where exploitation of the rich variety of suffixes is considered a stylistic achievement. Obligatory grammatical structures are generally marked with suffixes such as inflectional verbal suffixes, case suffixes, or a special class of syntactic suffixes, leaving word order relatively free for stylistic play. (8)

Morphologically Aymara is composed entirely of roots and suffixes, the latter being particularly abundant in the domain of the verb, where they can inflect everything from tense to intentionality. In explaining the special class of syntactic suffixes that, as the preceding citation would suggest, come into play after all other suffixing is in place, Hardman observes,

> The syntactic suffix . . . turns a word into a sentence. All words occurring with syntactic suffixes are also grammatical structures without these suffixes . . . ; with the syntactic suffixes they may stand alone as sentences or in combination with other grammatical forms and are called "syntactic words." The syntactic suffixes . . . mark such sentence types as information question, yes/no question, personal knowledge, hearsay, reaffirmation, attenuation, conjunction or listing, exclamation, and surprise, politeness or doubt. (11)

When such observations are set in conjunction with two other general characteristics of the Aymara language, namely, the fact that all verbs are conjugated within a binary person system (who is acting upon, or in relation to, whom) and that the overriding preoccupation with respect or politeness in the language (there is only the equivalent of the *usted* in the Spanish *tú/usted* system) centers around preserving the distinction between human and nonhuman, then the notion of "syntactic words" (acknowledged to be linguistically odd by Hardman) emerges as more than simply a "special" case of suffixing.

If nouns and verbs can become sentence matrices through suffixing, and if this agglutinative quality of the language is cortical to its, apparently much coveted, syntactic openness and stylistic richness, then any effort to articulate an Aymara film language has to respond to such distinctive features of the language system. This is precisely what I propose to do in thinking about the use of the telephoto close-up in the sequences described above. It is worth remembering, therefore, that the traditional close-up for Sanjinés is problematical because of the way it both psychologizes (individuates) and unnaturally (but should we not now add "impolitely"?) traverses the distance that allows both us to reflect and *el pueblo* to represent itself. My point is that the telephoto close-up (and the zoom that manipulates it) functions rather like a "syntactic word": it not only orders visual signs without cutting; that is, it functions as a single "lexical" unit, but it inflects precisely those types of utterance associated with the syntactical word by Hardman, namely (and I will emphasize only those instances that are immediately relevant to the sequences from *El coraje* detailed earlier) questions, exclamation, listing, doubt, personal knowledge, and of course politeness (or its absence).

If we return briefly to the scenes in question, I think the following observations can be made. Though the entirety of the dialogue is conducted in the official national, and ultimately colonial, language of Spanish, the enunciation of both sequences oscillates between an occidental and typically Eurocentric film syntax and what I am proposing that we consider as an indigenous, if not strictly Aymaran, film syntax. If we consider how the zoom, for example, the one that constitutes shot three in the first scene, produces a syntactical relation between an equipment-laden shelving unit (a nonhuman) and Domitila (a human) as she works to comfort and feed her youngest child, or how the extreme telephoto close-up in shot three of the second sequence flattens the speaker against empty grocery shelves as she *lists* everything missing from them while nevertheless presenting us with a graphic reminder of our "reflective" distance, or, to take one final example, how the choreography of shot nine in the second scene visually and conceptually links the toady recalcitrance of the men and the obstruction of the zoom, then I think we can see how the Spanish dialogue is filmically enunciated in a language that, to the precise extent that it (code-) switches between close-ups like these, where, as I have said, our distance is engraved in their proximity, and traditional cutaway close-ups, as in shot four of the second sequence, is properly bilingual. Both tongues are filming.

There is an important thread running through this scene that gives the very absence of Aymara in the dialogue a decisive role to play in how one thinks about the bilingualism at work in the confrontation between *las mujeres* and the Spanish-speaking *mestizos*. It is a thread, perhaps better a vein, whose linguistic and political topography has been charted—dare one say "mined"—by the Peruvian novelist José María Arguedas in his text *El zorro de arriba, y el zorro de abajo*. What emerges— and the text deserves much more attention than it will receive from me here—is the means by which to understand an important scene in *El coraje*. In this scene the suspicions formulated by the grocer and his companion are confirmed when we witness a political meeting—indeed, the very one from which the line defiantly characterizing Bolivia as *una colonia yanqui* derives—that takes place deep within a mine. It is underground in all its overdetermined senses. Although the agitprop speeches take place in Spanish, this is the one extended scene in which Aymara is heard, exchanged in snatches, among the miners attending the meeting. What Arguedas clarifies, although the bilingualism with which he is concerned is forged between Spanish and Quechua, is the extent to which the binary above/below is both a physical and a linguistic typography. In other words, one hears Aymara in the mine, even though it ultimately gives way to Spanish, because that is where it has historically sustained itself, both as a language of exchange and as a language of protest. Thus, in the confrontation in *la pulpería*, the absence of Aymara underscores and undermines the exchange, giving a distinct but subtle bilingual cast to an otherwise monolingual episode. The very obstruction of the zoom by the gaping backs of the grocer and his partner creates the portal through which two moments and two levels of the film cave in upon each other.

To move this chapter toward its conclusion and a closing consideration of the comparison effected between the work of Sanjinés and Sembene, I want to revisit the matter of the "qualitative leap" reputedly separating *Yawar Mallku* from everything after it. To do so, it is crucial that we extend what might fall within this "everything" and include there one of Sanjinés's more recent films, *La nación clandestina*. My aim here is not the familiar Foucauldian one of editing the leap/break, but rather that of appreciating more fully what is at stake in this leap.

Like *Yawar Mallku*, *La nación* narrates the story of two brothers, one who has gone off, at an early age, to La Paz, the other who has stayed in Willkani, the village. Significantly, though, *La nación* is even more formally and enunciatively ambitious than the earlier film. While it may certainly be true that Bolivian audiences have extended the range of their visual and cultural literacy in the eighteen years between *Yawar Mallku* and *La nación*, it is clear that the issues confronting a *cine junto al pueblo* remain urgent. Indeed, the opening shot of *La nación* contains a printed (in Spanish) dedication: "Al Pueblo Aymara" (to the Aymara people), clarifying both the film's addressee, but also the extent to which what follows (the film) exemplifies what a cinema aligned with the people might look and sound like. Of particular interest to me, therefore, is how the syntactic device of the close-up is deployed in a film dedicated to the indigenous speakers of Aymara.

Because the story/plot relation is very complex– a complexity motivated within the plot—and because the film is in very limited international circulation, a brief reconstruction of the story is in order. The narrative centers around the four members of the Mamani family: mother, father, and their two sons, Sebastián (Sebasti, to his brother) and Vincente. For reasons largely due to the constraints of their meager circumstances, Sebastián is sent (virtually sold into bondage) by his parents to grow up in La Paz. His father offers Sebastián to a bourgeois *mestizo* he helps to ford a narrow river in the outskirts of the city. While in La Paz, Sebastián decides to repudiate his Aymaran heritage and change his surname from Mamani to Maisman (the oblique evocation of Asturias—*hombres de maíz*—may well be deliberate, as may the allusion to one of the survivors in *El coraje*), an act he commemorates by dancing in a carnival parade. Shortly thereafter he enters the army and is dispatched to disarm the indigenous community. In a tortuous scene Sebastián returns to Willkani and attempts to take his brother's rifle, provoking both his brother and his father to disown him, to banish him from the family. Perhaps out of resentment, Sebastián decides to offer his services to a paramilitary organization involved in the murder of communist dissidents. He is accepted, and he soon becomes involved in a raid. Because, at the moment of truth, that is, at the point where he has been ordered to shoot the dissident, Sebastián refuses to fire, his comrades turn on him, beating him severely and leaving him for the dogs. Disillusioned and miserable, Sebastián descends into drunkenness and despair until he is retrieved from a bar one day by Vincente, who has come to tell him that their father has died. They return to Willkani for the funeral, and Sebastián decides to stay and make a go of indigenous rural life. Soon he imposes himself on a young woman, marries her, and is elected as the "Jilakata" (the "condor") of Willkani. Against the protests of his wife, he decides to return to La Paz to work out a foreign aid deal to benefit the community. There, he falls in with a *droguero* with whom he decides to swindle the community by siphoning off half the aid and selling it for their personal gain. Needless to say, the swindle is discovered. Sebastián is chased into the mountains, caught, and confronted. In a devastating scene, his mother, repeating the gesture earlier carried out by his father, disowns him, and he is banished from the village. He returns to La Paz and decides that he must atone for his betrayal by offering himself in sacrifice to the community in accord with a traditional ritual, the Jacha Tata Danzante, he once witnessed as a young boy. As he gathers up the elements of the necessary costume, notably a huge, rather grotesque mask, a military coup erupts and shooting breaks out in the working-class districts of La Paz. Sebastián sets out for his village, encountering soldiers, a dissident on the run, and indigenous insurgents along the way. It is clear that he belongs nowhere. Upon his arrival in Willkani, he beseeches the village wise man, Tankara, to accept his sacrifice. Initially reluctant, Tankara relents. Sebastián prepares and the Danzante begins. As the procession winds up into the surrounding hills, it comes upon a group returning from a nearby mine where there had been a coup-initiated crackdown on the union workers. Vincente is among those returning from the mine. A noisy and acrimonious exchange erupts where two forms of sacrifice are put into contention, that of the fallen union supporters and that of Sebastián. Ultimately, Tankara prevails, convincing the community to allow Sebastián to proceed with the Danzante. He dances to his death. As his fallen body is borne through Willkani, Sebastián himself appears at the end of the procession. A freeze-frame of his troubled face concludes the film.

The plot unfolds by beginning with the period immediately following Sebastián's final exile from the village. A disciplined rhythm of flashbacks (leaping first to childhood and then moving forward) ensues in which, as we watch Sebastián prepare for and then carry out his sacrificial return, we are provided with the episodic details of the story. The triggering mechanism for this rhythm is a metanarrative scene in which we are first introduced to the wise man, Tankara. This brief scene opens and closes with the same image—Tankara framed in a wide-angle shot against a sublimely mountainous backdrop, his arms raised in supplication—establishing, in formal terms, the scene's necessarily Moebian character. As if calling to his muse, Tankara is cast as the film's enunciator, the source of its statements, but in that very call he is also deprived of this status. Nevertheless, what he lays out, in his distinctively grainy voice (E.T. with more rasp, less buzz), is the Aymaran theory of time. Speaking in Aymara, he provides us with the logic of the final scene by explaining that, for the Aymara, all time is synchronous with itself, "our past is in our present, it is the present, we live the past and the present at the same time." Thus Sebastián can witness his own death because he is present after the moment he is past. As we have seen in relation to Sembene, this would also appear to resemble the unlivable time of postcoloniality where one's past has already overtaken the present, just as the present has rendered even knowledge of the past impossible. If Tankara is indeed the enunciator manqué, then the function of the scene is to plunge the enunciative structure of the film into a politically fraught temporal paradox. The one is two. The then is both now and then.

This very aspect of the film has caught the eye of Leonardo García-Pabón, who, in "*The Clandestine Nation:* Indigenism and National Subjects of Bolivia in the Films of Jorge Sanjinés," provides one of the few sustained treatments of *La nación*. More specifically, García-Pabón not only addresses himself to the visual syntax of the film, but he attempts to correlate it with the Aymaran theory of time. In doing so he shares my concern to link film language and the infrastructure of speech. Thus, in dialogue with his analysis, I can clarify what the concept of bilingual enunciation brings to the table.

García-Pabón situates *La nación* at another break in Sanjinés's corpus. Arguing that *El coraje* begins a period of "political radicalization" (in this sense he agrees with Sanjinés's dating of the break), he closes this period with *Las banderas del amanecer* from 1984. *La nación* is the first film after this period, and García-Pabón characterizes it as a return to the concerns of his first two films, including, of course, *Yawar Mallku*. In doing so, he cues one to the fact that approaching the leap or break that inaugurates the period of political radicalization from the standpoint of *La nación* complicates matters in an interesting way. In a certain sense (indeed, is it an Aymaran sense?), *La nación* repeats the break by always already having reversed it. I will return to an articulation of the consequences of this.

In laying out Sanjinés's syntactic strategies, García-Pabón follows Pedro Susz in stressing the importance of the "integral-sequence shot." Derived from Sanjinés's own formulations about the importance of using camera movement and editing to fuse the spectator and the participant, the concept of the integral-sequence shot explicitly rejects, as we have seen, close-ups motivated by a need to interject or otherwise impose an authorial perspective. Although no mention is made here of the zoom, it is implicitly affirmed as a strategic piece of the integral-sequence shot. More curious, however, is the fact that García-Pabón never really works out how the, as he calls it, circularity of Aymaran time is active in this shot. True, one finds many shots in *La nación* where the camera circulates around the action, but in fact most of the most important articulations of the synchronicity of time occur through disturbing, even jarring, flashbacks and flash-forwards. This suggests two things: first, the link between Aymara and the integral-sequence shot actually remains to be forged, and second, that the implicit repudiation of bilingualism here needs to be questioned.

To pursue both issues in the context of the film, it makes sense to consider the status of the close-up in the visual syntax of *La nación*. Doing so instantly reveals that, contrary to expectations, there are not only numerous close-ups of varying focal lengths, but the zoom close-up is apparently absent. Although this might immediately suggest that Sanjinés has abandoned the bilingual enunciation of *El coraje*, such a conclusion is, in fact, unwarranted. Contradicting it is the presence in the film of a new close-up. Here are its properties. It begins with a fixed camera position toward which advances a character. As the character advances from medium to close-up, its form begins to fill the entirety of the frame/screen. Continuing through the focal lengths of the close-up the character's form actually blots out the viewfinder/frame/screen, producing in effect a fade to black. Here the close-up is so extreme that it overcomes the very optics of visual perception, leaving us with nothing to see but the rectangular hole in the auditorium. When earlier I mentioned the apparent absence of the zoom here, I meant to acknowledge two features of the new close-up. Although the optical distortions are slightly different, there is a zoom effect in the first portion of the shot where the character advances into the viewfinder. This is consistent with the "rules" of the integral-shot sequence. However, as the character's advance begins to precipitate the fade to black, there appears to be a supplemental zoom effect in maintaining focus up to the very point at which the character (or now some sartorial metonymy for it) vanishes into the realization of the fade. One might say, then, that in the new close-up, there are two zooms, one achieved by other means, the other at precisely the point where one's distance from the object can no longer be inscribed in the background/foreground relation.

All this would be of merely technical interest were it not for the fact that this new close-up is deployed to deliver not only decisive moments in the plot, but also literally to effect, via flashbacks, the plot/story relation, a relation we have already linked to the rigors of Aymaran time. Consider the following three scenes.

In the first of a mere seven shots, we see Sebastián advancing on his final trek to Willkani. He is shot from above and in deep focus as he

Figure 36

Figure 37

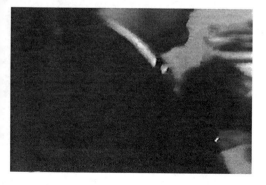

Figure 38

advances toward the camera. In the second shot, Sebastián is shot from below (Figure 36), the camera tracking back so as to maintain its distance from the advancing character. As the shot comes to an end, the camera halts. The character continues to advance, quickly filling the screen. The first instance of the new close-up is achieved (Figure 37). The flute theme that has accompanied every rendering of the trek home forms a sound bridge to the third shot, breaking off first through the heavy reverberation introduced on the soundtrack and then by the ensuing dialogue itself. In the third shot, the fade to black achieved through the new close-up is, in effect, reversed (a fade *from* black) and we find ourselves placed at the shoulder of a Hispanic bureaucrat who is interviewing Sebastián, who has presented himself as a candidate for the paramilitary organization run by the bureaucrat (Figure 38). This flashback takes us from the present of the trek to the past of Sebastián's final expulsion from the Bolivian armed forces. It does so by lining up two temporal moments, one itself a turning point, and the amorphous portal created by the full-screen close-up, the fade to black. The auditorial presence of the screen itself offers up the present of the

screening to this temporal chias-
mus. The third shot is considerably
longer than the preceding two and
is marked throughout by the circulating camera central to the integral-shot sequence (Figures 39 and
40). It concludes when the presiding bureaucrat proclaims that "we
will teach you how to treat communists." The fourth shot flashes for-

Figure 39

ward to a slightly later moment
in the homecoming trek. As with
the first shot, it captures Sebastián
from above as he approaches a ruin
site not far from Willkani (it is
later characterized as a place where
Vincente and "Sebasti" played as
children) (Figure 41). The camera
cranes down to reiterate enunciatively the darkened (indeed blackened) portal through which Sebas-

Figure 40

tián passes carrying his grotesque
mask. An approaching thunderstorm hastens Sebastián's progress,
and the camera tracks and "stoops"
to follow him into a mud-brick
shelter. As the camera approaches
the portal, the same new close-up
effect is realized (Figure 42). The
screen is engulfed by the camera's
proximity to the blackened interior. Once "inside" all shot-length

Figure 41

discernment becomes impossible. We have joined Sebastián in the
camera obscura.

Figure 42

Figure 43

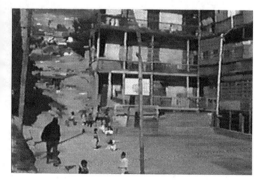

Figure 44

As before, the next shot begins as this darkness is dispelled by the violent throwing open of a door, only instead of this door opening onto the aftermath of the thunderstorm and the resumption of the trek, it opens into the home of a "communist" that Sebastián and his cronies have broken into (Figure 43). In effect, another flashback. True to their formal rhythm, this one captures a slightly later moment in the past than the preceding one, but its structure is identical. As before, this shot unfolds faithful to the integral-shot sequence with the camera winding its way in around the chaos of the flushing and abduction of the "communist." The last two shots depict the execution of the "communist" and the attack upon and abandonment of Sebastián for refusing to fire on him. Because they take place outdoors and at night, the ambience of obscurity associates both shots with the darkened interior of the shelter without actually returning there. Indeed, the shot following shot seven leaps further ahead in the flashback (the temporal compression is severe) to the day Vincente arrives in La Paz to inform Sebastián of their father's death (Figure 44). One could follow this out to the point at which we again flash forward to the trek (an astonishing scene, during which a desperate and pointedly nonbilingual dissident is gunned down by the soldiers who have been pursing him throughout Sebastián's trek), but what is important about the new close-up can be clarified on the basis of its two uses in the scenes described above.

First, it seems appropriate to stress the way it not only links to, but in a strict sense articulates the Aymaran sense of time. If it makes sense to say that the filmic paradox of the flashback (the fact that the advance of the film effects a retreat through time) conforms to Tankara's observation "our past is in our present" (setting aside for the moment the matter of what such words can mean if the sentence in which they appear is not nonsense), then it also makes sense to say that the new close-up, specifically in the way that it effects flashbacks and flash-forwards, articulates an Aymaran sense of time. In this sense, the newness of this close-up lies in the very fact that it does not compromise the integrity of the integral-sequence shot. In fact, since the latter is never clearly linked to the Aymaran sense of time, might it not even make sense to say that the new close-up, much more explicitly than the integral-sequence shot itself, constitutes what might be called *un cine junto al pueblo?* The question is rhetorical, but it invites us to pose another, far less rhetorical one: if there is a difference between *el pueblo* and, to refer again to the opening shot, *el pueblo Aymara*, then is the enunciative bilingualism sacrificed to producing a visual syntax consistent with the Aymaran sense of time come at too costly a political price? In other words, does the new close-up, precisely to the extent that it caters to an indigenism that Sanjinés is otherwise wary of, not abandon too quickly the general oppositionality both Klor de Alva and I associate with postcoloniality? It is clear that the new close-up, precisely as it effects passages, transitions between Sebastián's failed and humiliating attempts at assimilation, and his sacrificial drive, puts Spanish and Aymara into conflict with each other. However, unlike *El coraje*, there is no enunciative or syntactic registration of this difference. All other close ups in *La nación* are of the sort that slot easily into the logic of the integral-sequence shot. In effect, *only* Aymaran is spoken here.

This is a bit of an exaggeration—surely there is something important about the way the new close-up enunciatively reframes, literally, the auditorial space itself—but it helps me draw out something important about the comparison I am making between Sanjinés and Sembene. If Klor de Alva is right to argue that there is something quite wrong about the applicability of the concept of postcolonialism to the Latin American situation and that this has something crucial to do with way the concept and event of imperialism has displaced the colonial problematic, then perhaps this helps us understand why—even for someone as committed to critiquing the unfinished business of colonialism as Sanjinés obviously is—recognizing the indispensability of a politicized bilingualism is so difficult. To an extent, I am conceding García-Pabón's point about the relation between the integral-shot sequence and Aymara. But in addition to complicating how that might be worked out, I am also suggesting that what this sacrifices is a bilingualism crucial to the poetics of postcoloniality. If oppositionality is more than a mouthful, then it must insist upon and underscore the uneven and overdetermined forms of opposition active in the confrontation with the West. Sembene, who works in a geopolitical space where what he has called "metacolonialism" defines the very texture of daily life, has different reasons for embracing and/or repudiating such bilingualism. Indeed, as I argued in my reading of *Faat Kine*, what one sees is something like resignation in the face of a colonial legacy that has all but vanished in the myriad contradictions that render life in Senegal unlivable. Sanjinés, on the other hand, rushes the cinematic apparatus, trying to use its imperial reach, its status as an international medium of communication, to disseminate an experience of time, perhaps even of tense, that is both antagonized and endangered by imperialism. To be sure, both represent articulations of that general oppositionality Klor de Alva linked to the concept of postcoloniality, but what distinguishes them are the specific strategic conjunctures in which they are obliged to operate. Among the things that link (both descriptively and internationally) these conjunctures is the medium of the cinematic apparatus itself. How this uniquely modular instance of Western modernity is indexed to a confrontation given political meaning through either the imperial or the colonial problematic (acknowledging, of course, that such problematics can and do converge) is what sets the parameters of one's strategic (and tactical) thinking. On such a terrain emerges the poetics of postcoloniality. When articulated through the cinema, such poetics cannot avoid the conflicting instances of enunciation that arise as the syntactic constraints of an increasingly global popular medium get refunctionalized in speech communities where other divisions (at once linguistic and political) have preceded them. Chinua Achebe (1994), in resisting Ngugi wa Thiong'o's repudiation of the colonizer's tongue, established the frame within which a postcolonial poetics of the cinema can be specified. Edouard Glissant's poetics of relation is clearly a backup avatar of the same stance.

Coda: Alternate Endings

An argument that this text has attempted to sustain holds that in the absence of the concept of enunciation, indeed in the absence of a concept of the split in enunciation, one cannot think the specificity of postcoloniality in the cinematic domain. Resistance to such thought might well be characterized as what is at stake in the advocacy of narrative at the expense of enunciation, even or particularly when that is not the stated aim of such advocacy. As proposed in chapter 2, such maneuvers are the theoretical means by which foreignness is left to operate unchecked in both the North American film industry and in the border traffic circulating between it and the disciplines of cinema studies. Language remains not only the site of the foreign, but, by virtue of that status, language becomes that which is foreign to the cinema. It, like the supposed dead languages that cannot or do not copulate, becomes archaic. In the odious and baldly opportunistic jargon of the current U.S. regime, language in cinema becomes so "pre-911." This is misguided not only because novelty is a dubiously modernist and much overrated theoretical principle, but because such a view shuts those of us in the North out of so many of the film cultures we profess deep, multiculturally inspired interest in, cultures in which filmmakers are still heatedly talking about the urgency of articulating film languages cut to the size of their various political and poetical projects. Because the heavy hand of colonialism, imperialism, and now globalization assumes many guises, we must be prepared to recognize it in the hypocrisy of gestures, whether diplomatic or disciplinary, that embrace others precisely in order to avoid being transformed by them. This is how one might construe the perhaps unintended but nevertheless decisive consequence of the attack on enunciation. I hope—and this may, as Bloch said, be primarily for those without hope—that this study has located some of what is at stake in this attack. If, as Cherchi Usai so laconically puts it, "film history is based on the destruction of the moving image" (27), we do ourselves no service when we place film theory on the same footing. By giving up on the questions the concept of enunciation helped film scholars to pose, we risk precisely that. Is this what the revolution wanted: the global corporatization of content, form (technique and technology), and now disciplinary reason itself? I think not.

Notes

Introduction

1. Though implicit certainly in the section devoted to method in the first volume of *The History of Sexuality*, "problematization," for reasons worthy of scrutiny, is actually elaborated orally, that is, in several of the interviews given by Foucault late in his career. It is addressed in a 1984 interview with Paul Rabinow titled, "Polemics, Politics, and Problematizations: An Interview with Michel Foucault," now available in Rabinow. A more elaborate articulation of the concept—indeed, one that underscores the issues I have raised—appears in a 1983 interview with Thomas Zummer (consulted, apparently by Rabinow in preparation for the later exchange) titled, "Problematics," and now published in Lotringer. In addition to being a more elaborate formulation, the earlier interview does not mobilize the tired distinction between thought and politics, a distinction one might think Foucault, if anyone, would be more suspicious of.

2. Strictly speaking, one (even or especially a friend) might object, what is at issue here is poly- or multilingual enunciation. For reasons whose elaboration strikes me as premature, I think it is analytically important to hang on to the concept of bilingualism. For now I will simply observe that it, especially as deployed in the context of film analysis, captures and sustains the contradictions voiced in Derrida's characterization of monolingualism, "Yes, I have only one language, and yet it is not mine" (1998). Since in many respects these contradictions control the proliferation of difference signaled in the prefixes *multi-* and *poly-*, they render them, these prefixes, less than useful. Clearly, there is a great deal more to say about all of this.

3. Although the allusion here to Luce Irigaray is manifest, it clouds what is a profound and complicated issue, namely, the constitutive relation between so called French feminism and the epoch of decolonization in France. The "two" that lies behind Irigaray's "that is not one" points, through her essay on Simone de Beauvoir, "The Question of the Other," back to this maternal body, this prepropriative (to use Spivak's term) corpus. In doing so it reminds us that *The Second Sex* (1949) was not presented as a feminist, whether French or not, text at all. In fact, as is well known, de Beauvoir did not turn to feminism until the 1970s, a turn famously documented in the series of interviews she gave to Alice Shwarzer, one of which, "A Vote against This World," makes it clear that, precisely due to the failure of the French Left (both socialist and communist) to align unequivocally with the cause of liberation in Algeria, feminists were obliged to forge their own political identity and organizations. Although a full defense of the proposition will have to wait for another day, this distinctive way of articulating the "difference" the specificity of feminism in France has left its mark on virtually all factions (even de Beauvoir's detractors) of the movement. Thus, French feminism—which has been routinely assailed for its "idealist" cast—was not one because its specificity was organized within a France whose national univocity was fast disappearing under the ruins of empire.

4. Foucault's essay "On the Return of History" provides one with an instructive critique of the shibboleth that structuralism was ahistorical. Although Foucault's own status as a structuralist is a vexed one, in this essay he addresses himself to the charge of ahistoricism by considering how three structuralists, Boas, Trubetzkoy, and Barthes, engaged the question of history explicitly. His point is an important one, namely, that in order for the charge of ahistoricism to stick, a certain unthematized, and therefore untheorized, concept of history must prop up the charge. What is vital about Boas et al. (Foucault might also have referred us to that stunning meditation on historiography in chapter nine of Lévi-Strauss's *The Savage Mind*) is that they each conducted their research so as to problematize the concept of history at work in their chosen fields. This is far from denying history (as Foucault once put it to Tombadori). By the same token, the concept of history that emerges in Foucault's text, that of " serial history," is, all protestations to the contrary notwithstanding, deeply structural. It stresses "layers of events, multiplying" (429), and "multiple time spans" (430), where, almost in *Annales* fashion, the clear accent falls on the interrelations among differentiating elements. True, such commitments do not a structuralist

make, but they do suggest that structure is key to a certain rethinking of the concept of history, indeed one we associate intimately with poststructuralism.

1. The Return of Enunciation

1. Interviewed on *Good Morning America* (ABC) the day following the announcement of the proposed merger between America Online and Time Warner, Steven Case and Gerald Levin (the respective CEOs) both emphasized the need to overcome the "fragmentation" currently defining the mass communications sector, suggesting both that people were eager to overcome the inconvenience of media democratization and that this eagerness expressed a tendency latent within the globalization of mass communications as such. Tellingly, at least to me, Levin (reputed to be the more sagacious of the two) even went so far as to compare the merger to both "spring training" and "making a movie." Warner Bros., most would agree the studio largely responsible for the international emergence of sound cinema, is part of this merged corporate structure. Since those heady days, of course, the merger has undergone crisis after crisis, and although different principals are at the helm, the drive toward monopolization and vertical integration it heralded has only intensified. Consider in this respect the impact of the Telecommunications Act of 1996 (signed into law by Bill Clinton) that effectively eliminated controls on cross-media ownership, largely shredding the last remnants of the liberal public sphere.

2. Though it would take us far afield, there is an important point to be made here about the intricacy of the relation between the cinema and rail travel. Mattelart of course is content to stress the way technically reproduced art facilitated a certain traffic in culture. Art works could, like tracks, come to where one was. In 1935, Walter Benjamin characterized this as the means by which "aura" (the aesthetics of contemplation) was destroyed. However, both Wolfgang Schivelbusch and Paul Virilio have argued that if Benjamin is right it is because both the cinema and rail travel were part of a historical transformation of the human sensorium. In *The Railway Journey*, Schivelbusch draws on Freud's account of shock-inflicted neurasthenia—specifically the mental impact of repetitive trauma (everything from jostling and rocking to actual crashes)—to argue that rail travel "proletarianized" experience, rendering it at once "striking" and collective. Virilio, in *War and Cinema*, proposes that the experience of speed, the subordination of space by time made possible by industrialized forms of transportation, transformed the windshield into a screen on which enervated travelers

projected a scopophilic urge to consume the space their movement uprooted. Though neither writer refers to the other, it is a clear implication of their separate studies that the hierarchy of the senses dominated by the eyes undergoes an important modification during the nineteenth century. As if predicting the attention his work would later receive from film theorists, Freud, in "Further Recommendations in the Technique of Analysis," urged that analysands be encouraged to "say whatever goes through your mind. Act as if you were sitting at the window of a railway train and describing to someone seated behind you the changing views you see outside" (12:135). And this from a man whose own "phobia" of rail travel dates from a childhood journey from Leipzig to Vienna during which he had occasion to see his mother naked. The implicit fusion in Freud's counsel of the psyche and the passenger car vista no doubt reaches its apotheosis in Lacan's famous use of the anecdote of the boy and girl railway travelers in "The Agency of the Letter in the Unconscious" from 1957, where the rails are metaphorized as the very bar of signification. With Freud in particular, writing in 1913, one can say that the appeal of his expository analogy would appear to be predicated on a perception not just of the transformation sketched by Schivelbusch and Virilio, but of the place of psychoanalysis itself within it.

3. Another potentially useful way to think about the matter was formulated in a 1957 talk given by Alexander Kojève at the invitation of Carl Schmitt, "Colonialism from a European Perspective." In what Kojève characterizes as its "introduction" (at which, as is well known, he excels), he argues that socialism in the Soviet Union is one among three manifestations of contemporary capitalism. It produces surplus value from a laboring majority internal to the nation and uses the state to redistribute it. Colonialism—as his title suggests, the true object of his talk—is the third form of contemporary capitalism and as such presents the international community with its most pressing economic and political challenge. Drawing on Schmitt's onto-political distinction between taking (*Nehmen*) and grazing (*Weiden*), Kojève calls for a "giving colonialism" that, while clarifying the economics of cultural imperialism (much is made in the talk of Truman's Point IV, that is, the supplement to the Marshall Plan—itself a distribution mechanism for Hollywood—for "underdeveloped" nations), says nothing about the then current crisis in Algeria. Academic Left Hegelianism thus marches in sync with the PCF.

4. A particularly interesting articulation of such a position transpires in

the collective statement on sound written by Eisenstein, Pudovkin, and Alexandrov. Explicitly repudiating the Western and ultimately North American tendency to "adhere" sound to the image, the writers argue that the aesthetic character of the medium is at risk unless filmmakers recognize that sound is itself a material susceptible to semiotic modeling. Issued barely ten years after the revolution, this statement could be read as a formulation of the "high road" around the problem of "literacy" generated once it became possible to record dialogue in languages subject to national and regional constraints, a problem rendered acute by the numerous languages and dialects spoken with the borders of the Soviet Union. However, it is clear that Eisenstein is not opposed to sound—the position one might expect the entrepreneur or propagandist to take—instead, the writers argue for developing an approach to sound that might put linguistic diversity to work within a filmmaking practice expressly harboring "internationalist" ambitions.

5. Because it bears on a matter of later consequence, it is worth drawing attention here to Jean Rouch's "Man and the Cinema" from 1955 (collected in 2003). Considered by many to be one of the founding theorists of contemporary ethnographic film, Rouch displays in this essay a truly remarkable sensitivity to the problems of imperialism and language. Discussing that building block of visual literacy, the zoom, he writes: "The physical immobility of a tripod-fixed camera is thought to be compensated for by the wide use of variable-focal-length lenses (zoom lenses), which create an optical imitation of a dolly shot. But in fact, these lenses don't allow one to forget the unseen rigidity of the camera, because the zooming is always from a single point of view. Although these casual ballets may appear seductive, one must recognize that they only bring the camera and man together optically, because the camera always rests at a distance. Actually, this type of shooting more closely resembles a voyeur looking at something from a faraway perch, and zooming in for details. This involuntary arrogance on the part of the camera is resented not only a posteriori by the attentive viewer but also by the people who are filmed, because it is like an observation post" (38).

6. Attention must also be drawn here to Benveniste's contribution (1970) to the special issue of *Langages* on "Enunciation" edited by Tzvetan Todorov, "L'appareil formel de l'énonciation."

7. It is important to acknowledge here that the dialogue between psychoanalysis and the cinema was well along by the time Metz published *The Imaginary Signifier*. Indeed, as is often the case, this dialogue was fostered by and

among various cinema journals circulating during the period. I have already touched on the *Screen* debates, but just in the French context; one should also consult the pages of *Cahiers du cinéma* (which, by the way, went through its own editorial coup), *Cinéthique*, and *Positif*, just to name the more obvious sources. Metz, however, precisely to the extent that his academic position at the Ecole des Hautes Etudes allowed him to challenge and dislodge "filmography," deserves to be credited with making the fields of linguistics and psychoanalysis bear on the formation of the disciplinary object of the cinema. The ethical significance of this development is, of course, another matter.

8. In 1975, Louis Marin, in "Critical Remarks on Enunciation" (2001), was to frame these issues in terms of the problem of introjection, arguing that enunciation marked the hole or trap in a discourse where the speaking subject struggled not to be eaten by his or her own words. Although elaborated in terms of a theory of fiction, what his account clarifies is precisely the ontological complexity of the agent of speech. Moreover, Marin's is one of the few French syntheses, in the period, of the work of Derrida and Lacan, showing how their thought converges, perhaps unwittingly, on the vanishing present.

9. With the publication in 1996 of *Soft Subversions*, most of this material has now been translated into English. It appears in French in the first edition (Editions Recherche) of *La révolution moléculaire* in a section entitled "The Cinema: A Minor Art" (this is contemporaneous with Deleuze's and Guattari's little book on Kafka where the concept of "the minor" figures prominently). When reprinted by 10/18, this section was suppressed, as Brian Massumi has noted. Sadly, the editorial state of the first edition is something of a disaster. As will become apparent, I have been obliged to go back to the "original" publication of "Towards a Micro-politics of Desire" (*Semiotexte* 1:1) in order to find a complete version of the essay. For reasons that escape me, Guattari's British translator neglected to consult this material, preferring instead to garble the text rather than confront the editorial shortcomings of the French volume. This said, the translations that appear in *Soft Subversions* are considerably more reliable.

10. Here it is appropriate to make reference to the work of one of Metz's interlocutors in *L' Enonciation impersonnelle*, namely, Francesco Cassetti. This is chiefly because Cassetti has endorsed in his own way the concept of split enunciation and in a manner that has immediate implications for the status of the deixis in film. Specifically, in "Face to Face" (Buckland, 118–39), Cassetti argues that enunciation must be divided between an enunciator (his usage does not

conform to Bellour's) and an addressee, a point in fact emphasized by Benveniste in the passage from *General Problems* previously cited. Predictably, this obliges him to reintroduce the deictical category of the shifter in order to map the structure of enunciation. Used as a way to rethink the concept of interpellation, it is compelling, but it still resists opening up the concept of the split in ways that a general account of enunciation would require.

11. Although one needs to take such things with a grain of salt, it is relevant here to acknowledge that the longstanding ad campaign of none other than Landmark Theatres is organized around the conceit of the cinema as a "universal language." Part of the commodity advertising that routinely introduces features these days, the brief trailer, presents spectators with the phrase "Cinema is the universal language" in ten different languages. Significantly, this accompanies a montage of abstractions and charts a suggestive fluctuation between "cinema" and "film," underscoring, I would argue, the very dilemma the ad seeks to disavow. Landmark, it bears emphasis, is of more than passing interest because it is the United States' oldest art house chain (it acquired its flagship theater, the Nuart in Los Angeles, in 1974), and this is precisely the exhibitionary circuit through which U.S. audiences have most consistently encountered the "foreign."

12. Needless to say, Bordwell and Carroll are not enunciation's only detractors. During the 1980s several French journals were devoted to debating its linguistic and literary merits. See "Sur l'énonciation," a special issue of *Etudes Litteraires* (16, no. 1 [April 1983]), and "La Mise en discours," a special issue of *Langages* (70 [June 1983]), for sample statements. Additionally, it is worth acknowledging that Carroll in particular has engaged many of his own detractors, defending his views in ways that separate him from the strict "anti-theoreticism" advocated in *Post Theory*. Two exchanges are worth tracking. See Warren 1989 and Carroll 1992, but also see Carroll 1982 and Heath 1983.

13. Although doing even minor justice to its complexity would take me far afield, Ann Banfield's essay "*Ecriture,* Narration, and the Grammar of French" throws a serious wrench into the workings of Carroll's argument. By establishing that novelistic narration depends both on the *passé simple* and the neuter *il* of the third person (following here Maurice Blanchot), she confronts Carroll with the fact—and her empiricism is insistent—that narration since the nineteenth century is unthinkable without the absent agent of the third person narrator. Taking up Benveniste, she reverses the evaluative current of the essay,

insisting upon the importance of *histoire*, and while this leaves much to then say about a deftly recontextualized concept of enunciation, it suggests strongly that Carroll's contention about human agency and representation, especially as it bears on the concept of narration, is an invidious one.

2. Foreignness and Language in Western Cinema

1. This information derives from materials held in the archives of the Academy of Motion Picture Arts and Sciences housed in the Margaret Herrick Library. Much of it is dispersed. As such, it is not organized in a manner that conforms to the standards of bibliographic discourse. Nevertheless, the note-book "Entries by Country" can be consulted at the library in Beverly Hills, California.

2. "International" was dropped from the name almost immediately, indeed even before it was announced to the public, and this despite the fact that, at its inaugural dinner, none other than Cecil B. deMille toasted the formation of AMPAS by characterizing its power to "influence the mental processes of mankind" (Sands, 39). Moreover, in order to regulate the submission process for foreign language film entries, rules were developed that required the forma-tion of "organizations whose aims and purposes" mirrored that of AMPAS, and this only after an effort to involve the United Nations—through the good offices of M. Jean-Benoit Levy—were deemed inadequate. Thus, one might rea-sonably argue that—intentionally or not—"international" was dropped because it threatened to make the obvious explicit, namely, that in establishing an orga-nization designed to police the film industry in the United States, AMPAS was also shouldering the burden of "policing" the international scene, at least at the cultural level.

3. The practice of subtitling raises important issues. Already in 1944, when foreign language films were recognized within the "special awards" rubric, English subtitling was included among the traits of foreignness. Indeed, in 1978 when the Egyptian film *The Ascent into the Abyss* was deemed ineligible, it was because the print submitted had French subtitles. Though I have no evidence for this, Henzell may well have been hedging his bets by subtitling his film in English. Even if this is untrue, it draws attention to an important issue. If, as I have argued, foreign pictures present themselves to the ear, what is interesting about the insistence on subtitling is the way it shifts foreignness back toward the eye. In other words, and this would be especially true of a film like *The Harder*

They Come, the questions raised by the dialogue (Is this English, or not?) are settled, as it were, in the image, that is, at the foot of the image where one sees not merely the graphic traces of bad translation, but "foreignness." This is an effect consummated in *Star Trek: The Next Generation* where, precisely through subtitling, an entirely concocted language, Klingon, is made simultaneously foreign (alien) and *real* language. More about this later. Consider, though, the symptomatic importance of the fact that, in the year following the submission of Henzell's film, the rules defining the foreign language film award were revised so that the phrase "must have English subtitles" is in bold caps.

4. Missing as well is any acknowledgment of issues that have figured largely in film scholarship on foreign language films, namely, the fact that, during the 1950s, television was seen in Hollywood as pressuring the industry to screen products that preserved and underscored the distinctness of the cinema. Under such circumstances the U.S. market began to accommodate more "foreign" imports. Additionally, a new genre began to emerge. The "art film" was not only aggressively marketed to new audiences, but these audiences were invited to new exhibition sites, indeed sites that produced provocative new encounters between so called high- and lowbrow cultural constituencies. For a succinct yet reliable formulation of these issues, see Joseph Phillip's contribution to *The American Movie Industry* (Kindem). The "auteurism" solicited by the very genre of oral history here functions to make Vogel appear more than a little naive.

5. Nothing in Vogel's remarks suggest that he follows contemporary film scholarship, but the point I am raising has received considerable scholarly attention. Just to take an example that is close at hand, in *Ozu and the Poetics of Cinema*, Bordwell uses the revered Japanese director to exemplify, through Ozu's systematic violation of various principles of filmic continuity, what it means to develop an alternative visual vocabulary. He, of course, prefers the notion of style, but the point remains (Bordwell 1988).

6. At another point in his exchange with Hall, Vogel confirms the general point I am making, though from a different angle. Drawing attention to the fact that, in the rules regulating foreign language submissions, the status of subtitles shifts markedly, Hall asks whether the absence of English subtitles would hurt a submission's chances. In responding, Vogel explains that problems had arisen where, due to excessive exposure to what he calls "junk pictures" (presumably the spate of "B films" that flooded Europe after the war), subtitlers, in trying to conform to Yankee expectations, would fill their texts with expletives.

His point is that, even with subtitles, pictures could be disadvantaged, but what strikes me is his recognition—precisely in relation to the theme of subtitles—that, even in Western Europe, U.S. films were understood to be "made" within a "code of living" that needed to be both recognized and respected if a given foreign language film was to have a chance in the AMPAS competition. In the midst of this, it is not difficult to discern the outlines of the transcultural dynamic formulated with precision by Roberto Retamar when, in explaining the need to displace Rodó's appropriation of Ariel, he quotes Caliban's line from *The Tempest:* "You [Prospero] taught me language, and my profit on't / Is, I know how to curse."

7. Eric Cheyfitz, in *The Poetics of Imperialism*, has pursued similar matters by approaching Edgar Rice Burroughs's text (not the subsequent films) through the problem of translation. Although he is attentive to the language of the encounter between Tarzan and Jane, skillfully showing how it is used to naturalize the British aristocracy and its presence in Africa, he does not track the grammar of enunciation in the infamous "first date" scene. This prompts him to make rather different points about James Fenimore Cooper as well. Regardless, our studies have rather obvious implications for one another, especially given our shared interest in poetics and politics, as well as the film and fiction distinction that subtends it.

8. Although it would take us far afield, Hitchcock's allusion invites one to think carefully about the theme of acceleration. In both *Marnie* and *Tarzan*, the supplement of the copula, indeed the simulation of the copulation, is directly indexed to the speed of the poking or the speed of the word associations. Given that one of the earmarks of foreignness in the domain of speech is the lack of intelligibility that accompanies excessive speed (consider here what it means in English to be a "fast talker"), the thematization of acceleration may not be entirely random. Luce Irigaray, in her contribution to the special issue of *Langages* on enunciation (Todorov 1970), while not addressing the theme of acceleration, draws important, and in this context relevant, attention to the intercourse between women and the copula. For a more comprehensive treatment of the phenomenon, see Regina Pustet, *Copulas: Universals in the Categorization of the Lexicon* (2003).

9. It is interesting to note here that "ooma" shares some phonic and perhaps even lexical properties with "oowa," the word concocted by the author and linguist Anthony Burgess so as to allow the cave people in *Quest for Fire* to

say "alarm" or "danger." The implicit chain—mother, animal, danger (strangely familiar, yes?)—solicits precisely the sort of study called for below.

10. Obviously, my remarks here need to be supplemented by two additional kinds of study, perhaps studies whose elaboration they will stimulate. One would be a study of how, say, movie Indian is dubbed abroad. This might produce an interesting sketch of the field of permutations wrought upon other languages as they confront copular suspension. A telling example would doubtless be a Russian-language version of *Last of the Mohicans*. There is, of course, much important work being done on "multiple language version" (MLV) cinema, and a study of the sort I am calling for would supplement it in interesting ways. A second study would be a systematic examination of all confected movie speech, everything from the language spoken by Kubrick/Burgess's droogs in *A Clockwork Orange* to the grunt patterns uttered by Milton in W. C. Fields's *My Little Chickadee*. Describing the grammars of these various confections might well lead to a decisive insight into the *langue* of Western cinematic dialogue

11. I do not know whether Dickinson was present at the *Mostra del nuovo cinema* event that took place in Pesaro, Italy, during the mid-sixties, but it is possible that his use of "heresy" has Pier Paolo Pasolini's *Empirismo eretico* as its reference. Since Pasolini's book did not appear until 1972, that is, after the appearance of *A Discovery of Cinema*, this is unlikely, unless Dickinson or a colleague attended the festival. However, the fact that nowhere in his study does Dickinson acknowledge the existence of Pasolini, who, quite apart from having made some astonishing films (not movies), was also a provocative early semiotician of the cinema, may suggest that the reference is so charged as to go, as is said, without saying.

Intermission

1. Another important formulation of the matters at issue here occurs in Jean Claude Milner's *For the Love of Language*. Ann Banfield, his translator, draws attention to the idiosyncratically psychoanalytical character of Milner's discussion, without teasing out the distance between his project and that of Derrida's. Suffice it to say, and the link virtually leaps from the page in the French title of Milner's study (*L'amour de la langue*), what Derrida is wrestling with through the concept of monolingualism, Milner is pursuing through Lacan's concept of *lalangue*. What is gained there in the register of theoretical abstraction (*the* language that speaks *the* subject's relation to the signifier) is lost in the register of a

socio- or geopolitical linguistics that would track the signifier through the knots of language acquisition and imposition. So even as one hastens to demur on the question of whether he is indeed the most Franco-Maghrebean writer writing today, it is hard not to appreciate the value of this version of Derrida's resistance to psychoanalysis.

2. In his contribution to Khatibi's *Du bilinguisme* (later modified and reprinted in Arteaga's anthology *An Other Tongue*), "Bilingualism, Dialogism, and Schizophrenia," Tzvetan Todorov associates bilingualism with the politics of dissidence, proposing a parallel between the public/private split in what he calls "totalitarian" countries (such as his native Bulgaria) and bilingualism. He does this in the context of a complaint against the French champions of polyphony, and while I disagree with his "psychiatricization" of politics (schizo-phrenic bipolarity is invoked to call up the experience of being between lan-guages), I think it important to point out that even here the distinctive intimacy between bilingualism and the structure of political conflict is recognized.

3. Ousmane Sembene's *Xala*

1. I am working with a 16mm color print of *Xala*, distributed in this country by Cinema Guild, which runs 123 minutes. See also Ousmane Sembene's novel, *Xala*. All of the spellings of characters' names derive from the novel. For other sustained, and often remarkable, treatments of both the novel and the film, see Landy 1996; Gabriel 1985; Mulvey 1993; and, of course, Jameson 1986.

2. My characterization of *Xala* as a "parable" derives from Françoise Pfaff's path-breaking monograph on Sembene's work, *The Cinema of Ousmane Sembene: A Pioneer of African Film*. Though she, like many interpreters of Sem-bene, appeals to the notion of film language throughout her study, she does not pursue it in relation to the bilingualism she also observes in the corpus. As we shall see, doing so invites one to recast what might be at stake in the analytic evocation of the parable or, to recall an earlier discussion, allegory.

3. Sembene himself has stressed this correlation between gender and language. See Noureddine Ghali, "An Interview with Ousmane Sembene" (in Downing 1987). Irigaray's theorization of the essentially duple character of fem-inine sexuality appears in, among other places, *This Sex Which Is Not One*. Beyond simply invoking this association in order to illuminate the politics of bilingual-ism, I am drawing on the latter to give Irigaray's concept of "the lips" (which in their evocation of "mouth" also activate "tongue") a slightly less corporeal ring.

Although the pun only works in translation, it is worth emphasizing that when the lips separate ("When Our Lips Speak Together"), lip comes out. El Hadji's duplicity (Rama calls him a "liar") echoes in the "back talk" that identifies it. On a different level, the importance of language as a field of struggle within the context of African anticolonialism has been methodically laid out by Ngugi wa Thiong'o in *Decolonising the Mind: The Politics of Language in African Literature*. Surprisingly, Ngugi mentions Sembene only in passing, and in spite of his abiding interest in theater, he never discusses film, much less film language. This is also true of Ngugi's brief contribution to the recent conference devoted to Sembene's work, the proceedings of which have now been published. See Samba Gadjigo's edited volume *Ousmane Sembene: Dialogue with Critics and Writers*.

4. See Gabriel 1985. It is significant that the perspective adopted by Gabriel, with its concentration on the aesthetics of narrative, is taken up, more or less intact, by Marie Claire Ropars-Wuilleumiers in her discussion of Sembene's *Black Girl/Le noire de . . . .* I say significant because Ropars-Wuilleumiers is responsible for one of the most rigorously articulated practices of "textual analysis" in the last twenty years, a key feature of which has been precisely the painstaking delineation of the enunciative syntax that both she and Gabriel tend to subordinate to narrative concerns in their commentaries on Sembene. While this may have something to do with "respecting differences," neither explicitly argues the point. See Ropars-Wuilleumiers 1975.

5. See Mowitt 1992. There, through an analysis of the concept of Fanon's "position" (necessarily both location and tendency) during the Algerian war for national liberation, I tease out a topography of the "here" and the "there" that, while distinguishing the two, does not, however, separate them. Indeed, part of what constitutes the "unlivability" of postcoloniality is the fact that the urgency of the struggle here is misrecognized as the impossible priority of the struggle there. One of the significant risks taken by Hardt and Negri's concept of "empire" is that it produces a plane of immanence on which the here and the there matter chiefly as absolute singularities. Not only does this render the specificity of the there (for example, its version of the critique of globalization/financialization) irrelevant, it obscures the tenaciously national character of the here.

6. The discussion of Metz I am referring to takes place in the opening chapter of his justly celebrated *Film Language: A Semiotics of the Cinema*. What I nevertheless find troubling about the implications of this analysis can perhaps best

be clarified by revisiting Potts's use of them in "Is There an International Film Language?" (see chapter 2 in this volume). In effect, the "maybe" that answers the rhetorical question posed by this title completely reorients Metz's theoretical concerns about the aptness of speech as an object of scientific inquiry—concerns he inherits from Hjelmslev and Saussure—toward the more noble issue of cultural solidarity. While I support such solidarity in principle, it seems that we ought not sacrifice what are clearly enabling cultural and linguistic differences in the name of a stance that often has more to do with the vertical relation between masses and leaders than with the fraught character of the horizontal that constitutes the contradictory space of the popular. Metz, whose politics had later moved into the foreground, invites this sort of misappropriation by having placed too high a price on theoretical integrity at the expense of the conflicted specificity of his object.

7. My source here is Codu Mbassy Njie's *Description Syntaxique du Wolof du Gambie*.

8. My take on the grammatical and sexual copula has been deeply influenced by Gayatri Spivak's discussion of Woolf's *To the Lighthouse* in "Making and Unmaking in *To the Lighthouse*." Her own discussion has in turn been stirred by Derrida's resourceful reading of the "copular function" in his "The Supplement of Copula: Philosophy before Linguistics" (in Derrida 1982).

9. In the Western tradition, the figurative linkage between revolution and rotation dates back at least as far as Plato's *The Statesmen*. One might also argue, though, that in the African context, at least insofar as *The Egyptian Book of the Dead* warrants metonymic status there, the link between pharaoh and the sun's diurnal voyage across the sky stands forth as an important pre-diction of this figurative linkage.

10. There is, of course, a long and distinguished list of scholars—mostly women and certainly all feminists—who have delineated the complex role filmic enunciation plays in the cultural construction of the social division of gender. I do not mean to resist or avoid this work. However, since many of the perspectives mapped out within this theoretical tendency are still assessing the utility of the concept of "the gaze," I think it best to forego a direct translation of the bilingual or postcolonial problematic into a psychoanalytical one. Nevertheless, much of what follows has rather obvious implications for such a translation and, where warranted, I will try to underscore relevant moments. The later contrastive discussion of Sembene's more recent *Faat Kine* will produce many such

opportunities, but the forced choice between the sociological/anthropological as opposed to the psychoanalytical/philosophical subject must be overcome.

11. See Emile Benveniste, "The Nominal Sentence" (in Benveniste 1971). In Roland Barthes's "African Grammar" (in Barthes 1979), one finds a suggestively inverted account of the nominal sentence. In spite of his title, Barthes is actually not interested in African language practices. Instead, as is typical, he is interested in how "Africa" is constructed in the rhetoric of French journalism during the period of North African anticolonial insurgency. True to the general drift of *The Eiffel Tower and Other Mythologies* (in which the piece originally appeared), Barthes is bent on disclosing the linguistic workings of ideology. He does this by showing how French journalism tries to nominalize Africa by depriving it of both agency and temporality. Two things are worth noting here. First, Barthes makes it clear that French has to strain in order to achieve this effect, implicitly underscoring Benveniste's point (whose essay, curiously, he does not cite) about the comparatively attenuated presence of the nominal sentence in the Romance languages. Second, in Barthes's critique of the French press, it becomes clear that he sees how the imputation of nominal status obscures something crucial about the African situation. He does not go on to broach the question of bilingualism for reasons that are similar to those that hampered Metz's engagement with the cultural specificity of the cinema.

12. The relationship between the screen and the mirror has been so effectively institutionalized that not until fairly recently has it been recognized for what it is—an enabling disciplinary prop—and criticized. See "The Orthopsychic Subject: Film Theory and the Reception of Lacan" in Copjec 1995. It is not an insignificant detail, given the orientation of my own analysis, that Copjec's analysis does not break apart this relationship so much as it shifts the locus of the metaphor; the mirror is now actually a screen. In Metz's enunciative taxonomy, the mirror holds a privileged place, but he does not spell out the way its reflexive effect introduces the distinctly Eurocentric presence of cinema studies as a discipline into the texture of those films in which it appears. Copjec captures the disciplinary angle, but not the enunciative one.

13. I am referring here to Frantz Fanon's remarkable essay "Algeria Unveiled," from *A Dying Colonialism*. For Diawara's commentary, see "Oral Literature and African Film: Narratology in *Wend Kuuni*." Fanon's essay has, of course, been the object of significant criticism from various quarters. Two important feminist perspectives, largely influenced by Djamila Amrane's "Les

femmes algériennes dans la guerre" from 1982, are Marnia Lazreg in *The Eloquence of Silence: Algerian Women in Question* and Marie-Aimée Hélie-Lucas in "Women, Nationalism and Religion in the Algerian Liberation Struggle" (in Badran and Cooke). Fanon's graphic inscription of his knowing complicity with a certain colonialist masculinism eludes both of these writers but in ways that do not vitiate their criticisms of his rush to represent (as both portrayal and as proxy) Algerian women.

14. It is important here to draw out the crucial role played by the soundtrack throughout the film. Supplementing the spatial complications—the reorganization of diegetical and nondiegetical space and time—the soundtrack also importantly complicates our perception of the various narrative situations. Lyrics, typically delivered in Wolof, will draw out an almost superegoic voice, especially in El Hadji, and in doing so set up an important structural parallel between the voices and the music he hears, one that, in being shared with the audience, positions us inside a guilt that hovers somewhere between voice and instrument.

15. This association, contrived though it may appear, is forced upon us late in the film when the full-screen close-up of Maamy's blistered back from the flashback is provided its counterpart in a full-screen close-up of the cowry shell–bedecked wall hanging that decorates Faat Kine's bedroom. The wall hanging figures in a flash forward where we see Faat Kine putting a framed copy of each of her children's diplomas (the trace of their passage of the "bac") on either side of the wall hanging above her "bachelorette" bed. The three surfaces belong together—the parchment, the canvas, and the back/shield. If I stress this last connection between the back and the shield, it is to draw out the deep etymological link between *baccalaureate* as bachelor and bachelor as *baccalarius*, medieval Latin for *escuier* or, in English, *squire*, that is, shield bearer. All of which points, however obliquely, to the ambiguity of Faat Kine's gender identity. In a way that calls up the brilliant line from Sembene's *Guelwaar*, "he is a white back man," Faat Kine—who swears like a sailor, runs her station with an iron fist, exploits her sexuality for professional advantage and decides when and where she enters into relationships—is a female man. Doing justice to this insight will take me too far afield, but I do want to acknowledge my colleague Tom Pepper, whose study of the links between philosophy's repressed homosexuality and bachelorhood provides one with some of the key theoretical terms for doing so.

16. In *Guelwaar*, the problem of economic independence is addressed

through the figure of foreign aid—food aid in particular. Structured like a detective story, the film smuggles beneath its meditation on the encounter between Christianity and Islam a reflection on state violence, specifically the Senegalese state's involvement in the killing of Guelwaar. What makes Guelwaar expendable, as we learn late in the film, is that he is an outspoken and eloquent critic of the state's dependency on international food aid. In a brilliant deconstructive move, Guelwaar establishes during an impromptu speech that aid, instead of satisfying the need to eat, actually eats those who depend on it. In a closing climactic scene, portions of his audience descend upon an aid truck delivering grain to a local village, spilling its cargo on the road. This new spin on what, during the 1960s, Glauber Rocha had dubbed "the aesthetics of hunger" steers clear of any endorsement of private enterprise, but it insists upon the principle of economic self-determination or what earlier I referred to as "sovereignty." Already here, however, the national dimension of the problematic is fading, a process made explicit in *Faat Kine*, as we shall see.

17. It should be said that *Ceddo* complicates its anti-Islamicism in important ways. Most notably, in an important sequence, where the Ceddo (a tribal group otherwise resisting the "imposition" of Islam) are being given Muslim names, Sembene appears in one of his numerous, but irregular, cameos. He appears immediately after his own name, Ousmane, is given to someone else. Thus you have both what Bellour would call the enunciator acknowledging his relation to Islam while at the same time disavowing it, that is, showing that, to garble Desdemona, "he is not that name." Because Christianity is cast in no better light, it would appear that Sembene is clearly seeking to articulate his origin myth of Islam in West Africa in aggressively secular terms. Let us not forget that the reign of the spirit, as embodied in the Imam, is ended by a bullet shot by a woman.

4. Jorge Sanjinés's *El coraje del pueblo*

1. A subtle and considerably more thorough airing of the various issues involved here is to be found in Joshua Lund's "Barbarian Theorizing and the Limits of Latin American Exceptionalism."

2. The significance of this gesture becomes more apparent when, in consulting Domitila Barrios de Chungara's *Let Me Speak!* (1978), we learn that during the period of the filming of *El coraje*, women active within the MNR (Movimiento Nacional Revolucionario, the party of Paz Estenssoro) called

themselves *barzolas* and yet often took positions in opposition to the more militant women's organizations such as the "housewives committee." The issue here has to do with a struggle over popular memory and the significance within that struggle of naming, or language, more generally. Through his opening, Sanjinés clearly situates the cinema squarely within this struggle. I will return to the issues at stake here at various points in the body of this chapter.

3. In referring to Eisenstein's "visual vocabulary" as a Soviet encroachment, I realize that I would appear to be complicating, if not abandoning, my approach to bilingual enunciation. In other words, shouldn't I have written Russian rather than Soviet? True, and here I am making a concession to the conventions of cinema studies scholarship. However, I do want to insist that a systematic study of the links between Soviet montage and the severe attenuation of the linguistic copula in Russian might bear significant fruits. If Roman Jakobson is right about the linguistic power of the relation between similarity and contiguity, between substitution and combination (let's not forget that the cinema is one of his examples), then the impact on the perception of similarity of a grammar that inhibits one's use of "to be" might well help explain why the abrupt juxtaposition of images and sounds—the very paratactic texture of a certain modernist internationalism—has more to do with deep structural qualities of Russian than one might immediately assume.

4. Carlos Mesa Gisbert's discussion of the Bolivian Cinematographic Institute (ICB) in "Cine Boliviano 1953–1983: Aproximación a una Experiencia" (in Sanjinés 1985) frames the issue here in a useful way. According to Gisbert, the ICB was formed in a political context—the assumption of state power by the MNR in 1952—where one of the burning questions of cultural politics centered on the status of Bolivia's Indian populations. In a manner that calls to mind the *négritude* movement in Africa, the ICB began sponsoring film projects that sought to reclaim the Indian heritage as a vital aspect of Bolivian national identity. Though most of these projects were documentary in character, many of the most talented young filmmakers in Bolivia, including Sanjinés, began their careers under the auspices of the ICB. For this reason, one might fully expect Sanjinés to be more explicitly focused on the linguistic articulation of Indian identity, since, according to Gisbert, he was literally learning how to assemble shot sequences in a context where a general commitment to the national reclamation of Indian cultures was at the head of the institutional agenda. By the same token—and this constitutes a profound historical irony in some ways—it

was precisely in seeking his independence from the ICB that Sanjinés, but also Ruiz, really came into his own as a filmmaker of and for *el pueblo*.

5. In Domitila Barrios de Chungara's account of the massacre and the general character of the Bolivian armed forces, she prompts us to conclude that this episode represents Sanjinés's effort to document the presence of the "Manchego (cheesy? peninsular?) regiment"—a squadron of Green Beret rangers, trained and equipped by the United States—in the Bolivian army. It is significant, of course, that at this moment Sanjinés drives a wedge between the Indian community and the army by underscoring the racism of the soldier bearing the patch (Barrios de Chungara, 99).

6. For those interested in getting a better handle on the cinematographic value and function of the zoom, I refer them to a useful essay from the early 1970s, "The Aesthetics of the Zoom Lens" by Paul Joannides. An issue I will not wrestle with in any detail, namely, the distinction between anthropological and fictional appropriations of the zoom (I'm not sure this distinction is as reliable as it may seem), is treated with some care by Joannides.

7. It is worth noting in passing that in *Let Me Speak!* Barrios de Chungara discusses her interaction with Sanjinés during the filming of *El coraje*. Significantly, she emphasizes two things: first, the fact that Sanjinés solicited support from the miners in his struggle against the production tax levied on films by the Bolivian government, and second, that she was willing to offer her support on the condition that his films not "degenerate," by which she meant that they not exhibit the formal qualities of the "new wave." It is difficult to know what precisely she is referring to here, since her text was written in the seventies, after she was traveling widely, but clearly she is focused on the very issue that is theorized with such ambivalence in Sanjinés's work: the language of the people. It is interesting that, when she comes to discuss the significance of the radio at Siglo XX, she emphasizes that it was perceived as the voice of the miners because "it spoke the language of the people" (182). In *El coraje* that language is, surprisingly, Spanish.

8. This debate has been articulately, though somewhat "Italocentrically," summarized by Teresa de Lauretis in chapter 2 of *Alice Doesn't*. One gets a clear sense of both the rigor and the divisiveness of the debate around the "linguistic paradigm" from her discussion, but the consensus-producing attack on speech (and therefore the very concept of "foreign film languages") was laid out in Christian Metz's pathbreaking study, *Film Language* (see chapter 3 in particular).

Works Cited

Academy of Motion Picture Arts and Sciences (AMPAS) archive, Margaret Herrick Library, Beverly Hills, CA.

Achebe, Chinua. 1994. "The African Writer and the African Language." In *Colonial Discourse and Post-Colonial Theory*, eds. Patrick Williams and Laura Chrisman, 428–34. New York: Columbia University Press.

Ahmad, Aijaz. 1995. "The Politics of Literary Postcoloniality." *Race and Class* 36, no. 3 (January–March): 1–20.

Amrane, Djamila. 1991. *Les femmes algériennes dans la guerre*. Paris: Plon.

Anderson, Benedict. 1991. *Imagined Communities: Reflections on the Origin and Spread of Nationalism*. Revised edition. London: Verso Books.

Appiah, Anthony Kwame. 1991. "Is the Post- in Postmodernism the Post- in Postcolonial?" *Critical Inquiry* 17 (Winter): 336–57.

Armes, Roy. 1987. *Third World Film Making and the West*. Berkeley and Los Angeles: University California Press.

Arteaga, Alfredo, ed. 1994. *An Other Tongue: Nation and Ethnicity in the Linguistic Borderlands*. Durham, NC: Duke University Press.

Badran, Margaret, and Miriam Cooke, eds. 1990. *Opening the Gates: A Century of Arab Feminist Writing*. Bloomington: Indiana University Press.

Bailblé, Claude, Michel Marie, and Marie-Claire Ropars. 1975. *Muriel: histoire d'une recherche*. Paris: Galilée.

Banfield, Ann. 1995. "*Ecriture*, Narration, and the Grammar of French." *Narrative: From Mallory to Motion Pictures*. Suffolk: Richard Clay Limited.

Barrios de Chungara, Domitila. 1978. *Let Me Speak! Testimony of Domitila, A Woman of the Bolivian Mines*. Trans. Victoria Ortiz. New York: Monthly Review Press.

Barthes, Roland. 1979. *The Eiffel Tower and Other Mythologies*. Trans. Richard Howard. New York: Hill and Wang.

———. 1994. *The Semiotic Challenge*. Trans. Richard Howard. Berkeley and Los Angeles: University of California Press.

Baudry, Jean-Louis. 1986. "Ideological Effects of the Basic Cinematographic Apparatus." In *Narrative, Apparatus, Ideology: A Reader in Film Theory*, ed. Philip Rosen, 286–95. New York: Columbia University Press.

Benveniste, Emile. 1970. "L'appareil formel de l'énonciation." *Langages* 17 (March): 12–18.

———. 1971. *Problems in General Linguistics*. Trans. Mary Meek. Miami, FL: University of Miami Press.

Bhabha, Homi. 1989. "The Commitment to Theory." In *Questions of Third Cinema*, eds. Jim Pines and Paul Willemen, 111–32. London: BFI.

———. 1994. *The Location of Culture*. New York: Routledge Press.

Bordwell, David. 1985. *Narration in the Fiction Film*. Madison: University of Wisconsin Press.

———. 1988. *Ozu and the Poetics of Cinema*. Princeton, NJ: Princeton University Press.

Bordwell, David, and Noël Carroll, eds. 1996. *Post-Theory: Reconstructing Film Studies*, Madison: University Wisconsin Press.

Bordwell, David, Janet Staiger, and Kristen Thompson. 1985. *The Classical Hollywood Cinema: Film Style and Mode of Production to 1960*. New York: Columbia University Press.

Bourdieu, Pierre, and Loïc Wacquant. 1999. "The New Global Vulgate." Trans. Loïc Wacquant. *The Baffler* 12:69–78.

Buckland, Warren. 1989. "Critique of Poor Reason." *Screen* 30, no. 4 (Winter): 80–103.

———, ed. 1995. *The Film Spectator: From Sign to Mind*. Amsterdam: Amsterdam University Press.

Carroll, Noël. 1982. "Address to the Heathen." *October* 23 (Winter): 89–163.

———. 1988. *Mystifying Movies: Fads and Fallacies in Contemporary Film Theory*. New York: Columbia University Press.

———. 1992. "Cognitivism, Contemporary Film Theory, and Method: A Response to Warren Buckland." *Journal of Dramatic Theory and Criticism* 6, no. 2 (Spring): 199–219.

Cham, Mbye, ed. 1992. *Ex-iles: Essays on Caribbean Cinema*. Trenton, NJ: African World Press.

Chanan, Michael, ed. 1983. *Twenty-Five Years of the New Latin American Cinema*. London: British Film Institute Press.

Cherchi Usai, Paolo. 2001. *The Death of Cinema: History, Cultural Memory, and the Digital Dark Ages*. London: BFI.

Cheyfitz, Eric. 1997. *The Poetics of Imperialism: Translation and Colonialization from "The Tempest" to Tarzan*. Philadelphia: University Pennsylvania Press.

Copjec, Joan. 1995. *Read My Desire: Lacan against the Historians*. Cambridge, MA: MIT Press.

De Lauretis, Teresa. 1984. *Alice Doesn't: Feminism, Semiotics, Cinema*. Bloomington: University of Indiana Press.

Derrida, Jacques. 1978. *Writing and Difference*. Trans. Alan Bass. Chicago: University Chicago Press.

———. 1982. *Margins of Philosophy*. Trans. Alan Bass. Chicago: University Chicago Press.

———. 1998. *The Monolingualism of the Other; or, The Prosthesis of Origin*. Trans. Patrick Mensah. Stanford, CA: Stanford University Press.

Diawara, Manthia. 1989. "Oral Literature and African Film: Narratology in *Wend Kuuni*." In *Questions of Third Cinema*, 199–211. London: British Film Institute.

Dickinson, Thorold. 1971. *A Discovery of Cinema*. London: Oxford University Press.

Downing, John, ed. 1987. *Film and Politics in the Third World*. New York: Autonomedia.

Dussel, Enrique. 1998. "Beyond Eurocentrism: The World System and the Limits of Modernity" In *The Cultures of Globalization*, 3–31. Durham, NC: Duke University Press.

Eagleton, Terry. 1999. "In the Gaudy Supermarket." *London Review of Books* 21, no. 10 (May 31): 3–6.

Fanon, Frantz. 1967. *A Dying Colonialism*. Trans. Hakon Chevalier. New York: Grove Press.

Fernández Retamar, Roberto. 1989. *Caliban and Other Essays*. Trans. Edward Baker. Minneapolis: University of Minnesota Press.

Foucault, Michel. 1998. "The Return of History." In *Aesthetics, Method, Epistemology*, ed. James Faubion, 419–32. New York: The New Press.

Freud, Sigmund. 2001. *The Standard Edition of the Complete Psychological Works of Sigmund Freud*. Vol. 12 and 20. Ed. and trans. James Strachey. New York: Vintage Books.

Gabriel, Teshome. 1985. "*Xala*: A Cinema of Wax and Gold." In *Jump Cut: Hollywood Politics and Counter-Cinema*, 334–43. New York: Praeger Publishers.

Gadjigo, Samba et al., eds. 1993. *Ousmane Sembene: Dialogue with Critics and Writers*. Amherst: University of Massachusetts Press.

García-Canclini, Néstor. 2001. *Consumers and Citizens: Globalization and Multicultural Conflicts*. Trans. George Yudice. Minneapolis: University of Minnesota Press.

García-Pabón, Leonardo. 2001. "*The Clandestine Nation:* Indigenism and National Subjects of Bolivia in the Films of Jorge Sanjinés." *Jump Cut* 44 (Fall). www.ejumpcut.org.

Gerima, Haile. 1977. "Interview with Paul Willemen." *Framework* 7/8: 31–37.

Gledhill, Christine, and Linda Williams, eds. 2000. *Re-inventing Film Studies*. New York: Oxford University Press.

Glissant, Edouard. 1997. *The Poetics of Relation*. Trans. Betsy Wing. Ann Arbor: University of Michigan Press.

Gomery, Douglas. "Economic Struggle and Hollywood Imperialism: Europe Converts to Sound." 1980. *Yale French Studies* 60.

Gordon, Avery, and Christopher Newfield, eds. 1996. *Mapping Multiculturalism*. Minneapolis: University of Minnesota Press.

Guattari, Félix. 1977. *La révolution moléculaire*. Paris: Editions Recherches.

———. 1984. *Molecular Revolution: Psychiatry and Politics*. Trans. Rosemary Sheed. Middlesex, UK: Penguin Books.

———. 1995. *Chaosmosis: An Ethico-Aesthetic Paradigm*. Trans. Paul Bains and Julian Pefanis. Bloomington: Indiana University Press.

———. 1996. *Soft Subversions*. Ed. Sylvère Lotringer. New York: Semiotext(e).

Hardman, Martha J., ed. 1981. *The Aymara Language in Its Social and Cultural Context*. Gainesville: University of Florida Press.

Heath, Stephen. "Le Pere Noël." *October* 26 (Fall): 66–86.

Hilger, Michael. 1986. *The American Indian in Film*. Metuchen, NJ: Scarecrow Press.

Irigaray, Luce. 1970. "Le sexe fait 'comme' signe." *Langages* 17 (March): 42–55.

———. 1983. *This Sex Which Is Not One*. Trans. Catherine Porter. Ithaca, NY: Cornell University Press.

———. 1995. "The Question of the Other." *Yale French Studies* 87, "Another Look, Another Woman": 7–19.

Jameson, Fredric. 1986. "Third World Literature in the Era Multinational Capitalism." *Social Text* 15 (Fall): 65–88.

Joannides, Paul. 1970–71. "The Aesthetics of the Zoom Lens." *Sight and Sound* 40, no. 1 (Winter): 40–42.

Khatibi, Abdelkebir. 1990. *Love in Two Languages*. Trans. Richard Howard. Minneapolis: University of Minnesota Press.

Kindem, Gorham. 1982. *The American Movie Industry: The Business of Motion Pictures*. Carbondale: Southern Illinois University Press.

Klor de Alva, Jorge. 1992. "Colonialism and Postcolonialism as (Latin) American Mirages." *Colonial Latin American Review* 1:1–2.

Kristeva, Julia. 1991. *Strangers to Ourselves*. Trans. Leon Roudiez. New York: Columbia University Press.

———. 1993. *Nations without Nationalism*. Trans. Leon Roudiez. New York: Columbia University Press.

Lacan, Jacques. 1981. *The Four Fundamental Concepts of Psychoanalysis*. Trans. Alan Sheridan. New York: W. W. Norton and Company.

Landy, Marcia. 1996. *Cinematic Uses of the Past*. Minneapolis: University of Minnesota Press.

Lazarsfeld, Paul. 1993. *On Social Research and Its Language*. Ed. Raymond Boudon. Chicago: University of Chicago Press.

Lazreg, Marnia. 1994. *The Eloquence of Silence: Algerian Women in Question*. New York: Routledge Press.

Lotman, Jurij. 1976. *Semiotics of Cinema*. Trans. Mark Suino. Ann Arbor: University Michigan Press.

Lotringer, Sylvère, ed. 1996. *Foucault Live: Collected Interviews 1961–1984*. Trans. Lysa Hochroth and John Johnston. New York: Semiotext(e).

Lukács, Georg. 1971. *Realism in Our Time: Literature and the Class Struggle*. Trans. John and Neche Mander. New York: Harper Torchbooks.

Lund, Joshua. 2001. "Barbarian Theorizing and the Limits of Latin American Exceptionalism." *Cultural Critique* 47 (Winter): 54–90.

Marin, Louis. 2001. *On Representation*. Trans. Catherine Porter. Stanford, CA: Stanford University Press.

Marx, Karl. 1974. *Political Writings I*. Trans. Various. New York: Vintage Books.

Mattelart, Armand. 1994. *Mapping World Communication: War, Progress, Culture*. Trans. Susan Emanuel and James Cohen. Minneapolis: University of Minnesota Press.

———. 1996. *The Invention of Communication*. Trans. Susan Emanuel. Minneapolis: University of Minnesota Press.

Mehrez, Samia. 1990. "The Poetics of a Tattooed Memory: Decolonialization and Bilingualism in North African Literature." *Emergences* 2 (Spring): 105–29.

Metz, Christian. 1974. *Film Language: A Semiotics of the Cinema*. Trans. Michael Taylor. New York: Oxford University Press.

———. 1975. *The Imaginary Signifier: Psychoanalysis and Cinema*. Trans. Celia Britton et al. Bloomington: Indiana University Press.

———. 1991. *L'Enonciation impersonnelle, ou le cite du film*. Paris: Méridiens Klincksieck.

Milner, Jean Claude. 1990. *For the Love of Language*. Trans. Ann Banfield. New York: St. Martin's Press.

Mowitt, John. 1992. "Algerian Nation: Fanon's Fetish." *Cultural Critique* 22 (Fall): 165–86.

Mulvey, Laura. 1993. "*Xala*, Ousmane Sembene 1974: The Carapace That Failed." *Camera Obscura* 31 (January–May): 49–70.

Nandy, Ashis. 1995. *The Savage Freud and Other Essays on Possible and Retrievable Selves*. Princeton, NJ: Princeton University Press.

Nichols, Bill, ed. 1976. *Movies and Methods I*. Berkeley and Los Angeles: University of California Press.

Njie, Codu Mbassy. 1982. *Description Syntaxique du Wolof du Gambie*. Dakar: Les Nouvelles Editions Africaines.

Okrand, Marc. 1992. *The Klingon Dictionary*. Hollywood: Star Trek Publications.

Pfaff, Françoise. 1984. *The Cinema of Ousmane Sembene: A Pioneer of African Cinema*. Westport, CT: Greenwood Press.

Pines, Jim, and Paul Willemen, eds. 1989. *Questions of Third Cinema*. London: BFI.

Potts, James. 1979. "Is There an International Film Language?" *Sight and Sound* 48, no. 2 (Spring): 74–81.

Prakash, Gyan, ed. 1995. *After Colonialism: Imperial Histories and Postcolonial Displacements*. Princeton, NJ: Princeton University Press.

Pudovkin, Vsevolod. 1976. *Film Technique and Film Acting*. Trans. Ivor Montagu. New York: Grove Press.

Pustet, Regina. 2003. *Copulas: Universals in the Categorization of the Lexicon*. New York: Oxford University Press.

Rabinow, Paul, ed. 1997. *Michel Foucault: Ethics, Subjectivity, and Truth*. Trans. Robert Hurley, et al. New York: New Press.

Readings, Bill. 1996. *The University in Ruins*. Cambridge, MA: Harvard University Press.

Ropars-Wuilleumier, Marie-Claire. 1975. "A propos du cinéma africain: la problématique culturelle de *La Noire de . . .*" *Recherche, Pédagogie et Culture* 17/18:10–15.

Rosen, Philip, ed. 1986. *Narrative, Apparatus, Ideology: A Film Theory Reader*. New York: Columbia University Press.

Rothstein, Edward. 2001. "Attacks on U.S. Challenge the Perspectives of Post-modern True Believers." *New York Times*, September 22, A17.

Rouch, Jean. 2003. "The Camera and Man." In *Ciné-Ethnograpy*, ed. and trans. Steven Feld, 29–46. Minneapolis: University of Minnesota Press.

Said, Edward. 1982. "Traveling Theory." *Raritan* 1, no. 3 (Winter): 41–67.

———. 1983. *The World, the Text, the Critic*. Cambridge, MA: Harvard University Press.

———. 1994. *Culture and Imperialism*. New York: Vintage Books.

Sands, Pierre Norman. 1973. *A Historical Study of the Academy of Motion Pictures Arts and Sciences (1927–47)*. New York: Arno Press.

Sanjinés, Javier. 1985. *Tendencias actuales en la literatura boliviana*. Minneapolis/Valencia: Institute for the Study of Ideologies and Literature.

Sanjinés, Jorge (y grupo Ukamau). 1979. *Teoría y práctica de un cine junto al pueblo*. Mexico City: Siglo XXI Editores.

Schivelbusch, Wolfgang. 1986. *The Railway Journey: The Industrialization of Time and Space in the 19th Century*. Berkeley and Los Angeles: University of California Press.

Schwarzer, Alice. 1984. *After the Second Sex: Conversations with Simone de Beauvoir*. Trans. Marianne Howath. New York: Pantheon Books.

Sembene, Ousmane. 1983. *Xala*. Trans. Clive Wake. Westport, CT: L. Hill.

———. "Conversation with Hamid Naficy." Unpublished transcript. No pagination.

Shohat, Ella, and Robert Stam. 1994. *Unthinking Eurocentrism: Multiculturalism and the Media*. New York: Routledge Press.

Spivak, Gayatri Chakravorty. 1988. "Making and Unmaking in *To the Lighthouse*." In *Other Worlds*, 30–45. New York: Routledge Press.

———. 1999. *A Critique of Postcolonial Reason: Toward a History of the Vanishing Present*. Cambridge, MA: Harvard University Press.

———. 2003. *The Death of a Discipline*. New York: Columbia University Press.

Susz, Pedro. 1991. *Filmo-videografia boliviana básica (1904–1990)*. La Paz: Cinemateca.

Thiong'o, Ngugi wa. 1986. *Decolonising the Mind: The Politics of Language in African Literature*. London: Heinemans.

Tinkcom, Matthew, and Amy Villarejo, eds. 2001. *Keyframes: Popular Cinema and Cultural Studies*. New York: Routledge Press.

Todorov, Tzvetan, ed. 1970. *Langages* 17 (March). Special issue on "Enonciation."

Trumpbour, John. 2002. *Selling Hollywood to the World: U.S. and European Struggles for Mastery of the Global Film Industry, 1920–1950*. Cambridge: Cambridge University Press.

Ukadike, N. Frank, ed. 2002. *Questioning African Cinema: Conversations with Filmmakers*. Minneapolis: University of Minnesota Press.

Virilio, Paul. 1989. *War and Cinema: The Logistics of Perception*. Trans. Patrick Camiller. London: Verso Books.

Vogel, Robert M.W. 1991. *An Oral History with Robert M. W. Vogel*. Interviewed by Barbara Hall. Beverly Hills, CA: Academy of Motion Picture Arts and Sciences.

Williams, Raymond. 1976. *Keywords: A Vocabulary of Culture and Society*. New York: Oxford University Press.

———. 1977. *Marxism and Literature*. Oxford: Oxford University Press.

Žižek, Slavoj. 1989. *The Sublime Object of Ideology*. London: Verso Books.

———. 1992. *Looking Awry*. Cambridge, MA: MIT Press.

Index

Prepared by Julietta Singh

John Mowitt is professor of cultural studies and comparative literature at the University of Minnesota. He is author of *Text: The Genealogy of an Antidisciplinary Object* and *Percussion: Drumming, Beating, Striking*, and he is a senior editor of the journal *Cultural Critique*.